Hiram Edson:
The Man and the Myth

Brian E. Strayer

Hiram Edson:
The Man and the Myth

Brian E. Strayer

OAK & ACORN
PUBLISHING
Westlake Village, California

For information contact:
Oak and Acorn Publishing
PO Box 5005
Westlake Village, CA 91359-5005

Cover design by Lauren Smith

First edition, June 2023

Photos courtesy of the Review and Herald Publishing Association and the General Conference of Seventh-day Adventists.

10 9 8 7 6 5 4 3 2 1

Dedication

To the memory of

Robert H. Allen (1923-2018)

zealous amateur historian whose private collection
of Edson materials filled many gaps in this biography

Contents

Acknowledgements

John Donne's famous statement, "No man is an island, entire of itself," certainly applies to the process of researching and writing a book. Although the cover bears my name, many individuals assisted in the search for artifacts, books, buildings, newspapers, photographs, and other sources concerning Hiram Edson and his era.

I am grateful to Merlin Burt, Denis Kaiser, and Kevin Burton, successive directors of the Center for Adventist Research (CAR) in the James White Library at Andrews University, for granting me free access as a CAR Scholar to source material in the file cabinets, bookshelves, and vault. Likewise, Jim Ford, associate director at CAR, and Judymae Richards, administrative assistant, helped me track down hard-to-find sources both at CAR and on the internet. Drawing from his own doctoral research in Millerite and early Sabbatarian Adventist history, Kevin Burton was also generous in sharing with me online newspapers, letters, and other materials relating to Hiram Edson.

When the COVID-19 pandemic of 2019-2021 temporarily closed the doors of archives, libraries, and historical societies, I was especially grateful that many years ago employees at the Office of Archives, Statistics, and Research at the General Conference of Seventh-day Adventists made copies of the *Present Truth, Advent Review and Sabbath Herald, Atlantic Union Gleaner*, and other denominational papers available online. My research would have taken far longer to complete without their efforts.

Yet despite the hundreds of sources available online and in Adventist archives and libraries, significant gaps would have remained in this biography had it not been for the untiring efforts of the late Robert Allen, chemical engineer, amateur historian, and active member of the Bay Knoll Seventh-day Adventist Church in Rochester, New York. With unflagging enthusiasm throughout his long life, Allen assembled detailed records of the Edson genealogy; collected deeds testifying to Hiram Edson's many property purchases; searched for old maps and court records; and compiled an impressive array of articles, letters, and reports relating to Adventist Heritage Ministries' development of the Edson site at old Port Gibson (near Clifton Springs), New York. In the summer of 2021, Robert's son, James Allen, handed me a box containing those artifacts, and for that I am deeply grateful.

During my several visits to the Edson property, site directors Jim and Linda Everhart gave me tours of the visitor center and took me through the recently developed Bible Prophecy Garden. Linda's creatively written and well-researched articles about Edson have added much to my understanding of his contributions to Adventism. Joining one of local historian Howard Krug's annual camp meeting tours of early Adventist sites in central New York likewise enhanced my knowledge, especially regarding Edson's role in founding the Roosevelt Seventh-day Adventist Church in New York.

As a scholar who values accuracy in facts and interpretations, I am especially grateful to such knowledgeable friends as Jim Nix, Jim and Linda Everhart, Michael Campbell, Kevin Burton, Ronald Knott, Deborah Everhart, and RosAnne Tetz for their critical reading of earlier versions of this manuscript. I found their comments and corrections immensely helpful.

In 1971, James R. Nix, a 23-year-old graduate student in the Seventh-day Adventist Theological Seminary at Andrews University, wrote a seminar paper entitled "The Life and Work of Hiram Edson" for a Problems in Church History course. In his lengthy paper, Nix brought to light several controversial issues and raised many questions that I will address in this biography. For his seminal research at such a young age, I owe him, too, a debt of gratitude. I hope that this book, the first biography of Hiram Edson ever published, will correct some of the misinformation concerning him and provide an accurate picture of the life and times of this early Adventist pioneer.

Brian E. Strayer
Professor Emeritus of History
Andrews University

Preface

During the 140 years since Hiram Edson died in 1882, no one has written a book about his life, either for adults or for children. Why? Certainly, one reason is the paucity of primary sources. Unlike many other Adventist pioneers, Edson kept no diaries, wrote no books, and sent very few articles, letters, and reports to church papers. Consequently, most of what is known concerning his life comes from sources written by others. A second reason could be that, at the time of his death, Edson was out of favor with several church leaders due to his uncooperative spirit and his unorthodox interpretations of biblical prophecies and symbols. This fact created yet a third problem: How to write an honest biography of a man whom many distrusted and one even called a crank? The denomination's first official historian, J.N. Loughborough, whose books and articles from the 1860s to the 1920s adopted an apologetic tone, briefly summarized Edson's contributions in four sentences in his books *Rise and Progress* (1892) and *The Great Second Advent Movement* (1905).

Therefore, when Arthur W. Spalding[1] assumed the mantle of researching and writing the Adventist past in the 1940s, 1950s, and 1960s, he faced strong opposition from administrators, teachers, and pastors whose ideas of the Adventist pioneers had already been set in cement by Loughborough's haloed portrayal of them. In a letter

---

[1]In the late 19th and early 20th centuries, Arthur W. Spalding spelled his surname "Spaulding," but at some unknown date prior to the publication of his book *Footprints of the Pioneers* in 1947, he changed the spelling of his surname to "Spalding." I will use this latter spelling throughout this book.

to M.W. Thurber at the Review and Herald Publishing Association, Spalding warned him that some of his interpretations concerning the church's past "may be franker writing than some will approve; but I believe we ought to be frank in a history, instead of trying to hush up the unpleasant or damaging facts. Quite the contrary."[2] Referring to his writing style as "episodic" rather than "analytical," Spalding said that he intended to take "representative episodes to portray the history rather than writing a day-by-day chronicle" as Joseph Bates, J.N. Loughborough, and others had done before him.[3]

When Arthur S. Maxwell expressed disapproval of his approach to the past, Spalding defended himself:

> If I were a partizan [partisan], which I could easily be, I could write a history of the times which would please the orthodox, who are indeed my sponsors. But I conceive my mission to be...to weigh issues, to write turhtfully [truthfully] and as disinterestedly as I can, and to present a picture which, though not altogether flattering, is a correct likeness, and may help in leading this people to reformation. How to write thus without offending powers that be, and so giving a fatal stab to the project, is the biggest problem before me. Every important statement must have documentation and, whether expressed or implied, the backing of the Spirit of Prophecy. More than that, it must be more diplomatic than the Laodicean Message, yet as uncompromising...[I]t is a task that shakes my soul.[4]

---

[2] Arthur W. Spalding to M.W. Thurber, Dec. 20, 1946, Spalding Correspondence, Collection 10, Box 1, Folder 3, Center for Adventist Research (CAR), James White Library (JWL), Andrews University (AU).
[3] Arthur W. Spalding to M.W. Thurber, March 10, 1947, Spalding Correspondence, Collection 10, Box 1, Folder 4, CAR, JWL, AU.
[4] Arthur W. Spalding to Arthur S. Maxwell, July 6, 1947, Spalding Correspondence, Collection 10, Box 1,

Although some leaders in the General Conference Missionary Volunteer Department criticized his history books as "ornate and pompous," "more sound and soporific than substance," Spalding struggled to write "at least to the intellectual level of the eighteen-year-old" rather than simply producing "a book for Juniors or children," seeking to imitate the style of the popular writer Van Wyck Brooks.[5] Others, like associate *Review* editor F.M. Wilcox, who accused him of being more of an essayist than a historian, considered his colorful description of the pioneers as "more horseflesh than angels" to be "rather crude."[6]

Spalding admitted that he was caught between the Charybdis of Loughborough, whose memory "I can not trust...[because of] his testimony which is opposed to other records that I think more authentic," and the Scylla of Mahlon E. Olsen's *Origin and Progress*, which "leaned over backward to get the kiss of the brethren" but which reflects "a congenital inability to be warm and human."[7] Rather than adopting the "detached, disinterested attitude" of a professional historian that "never espouses the cause it portrays," Spalding resolved to write a "warm, human document" that was "unbiased" and "fair" yet demonstrated his "passionate" belief in the Adventist message. What one "loses in equipoise," he added, "he gains in momentum."[8] Spalding recognized that in applying these methods to pioneers like Hiram Edson, however, he faced a conundrum:

Folder 4, CAR, JWL, AU.

[5]Arthur W. Spalding to M.W. Thurber, Nov. 25, 1947, Spalding Correspondence, Collection 10, Box 1, Folder 4, CAR, JWL, AU.

[6]F.M. Wilcox to Arthur W. Spalding, Oct. 7, 1947, Spalding Correspondence, Collection 10, Box 1, Folder 4, CAR, JWL, AU.

[7]Arthur W. Spalding to C.L. Taylor, March 4, 1948, Spalding Correspondence, Collection 10, Box 2, Folder 1, CAR, JWL, AU.

[8]Arthur W. Spalding to C.L. Taylor, March 4, 1948, Spalding Correspondence, Collection 10, Box 2, Folder 1, CAR, JWL, AU.

Should a writer of church history wholly ignore the faults and failings of the actors in it, and present a smooth, unwrinkled account of the journey across the plains, with no Injuns [sic] and no broken axles?—everybody perfect, everybody sweet and true, everybody with an unblemished record in vision and application of Christian education? Some think it is treason to the church to say anything of its faults and failures.[9]

In light of the fact that many Adventist scholars today would place Spalding in the same apologetic camp as Loughborough, the above correspondence reveals that he was acutely aware of some of the problems he faced in seeking to write an honest, balanced history of the church. While modern critics may judge him harshly for not getting it exactly right, Spalding at least recognized the challenges he faced and attempted to steer a middle course between factual objectivity and partisan apologetics in his efforts to rehabilitate the tarnished reputation of Hiram Edson. (See Chapter 12.)

The author of this biography faces the same challenge, recognizing that many Adventists have grown up with certain embedded preconceptions concerning Edson: That he was a simple farmer; that he had a vision in the cornfield; that he was the first to write about the heavenly sanctuary; that all the "S" doctrines (second coming, sanctuary, Sabbath, Spirit of Prophecy, state of the dead) came together at his Port Gibson home; and that he died a highly revered pioneer. Yet when the facts don't fit the myth, what should a historian do? Like Ronald Wells, who declared in his book *History Through the Eyes of Faith* (1989) that he had written "an honest Western Christian history

---

[9]Arthur W. Spalding to Dr. (Leon) L. and Mrs. Agnes Caviness, April 9, 1948, Spalding Correspondence, Collection 10, Box 2, Folder 1, CAR, JWL, AU.

book,"[10] it is hoped that readers will find this biography of Hiram Edson to be an honest Adventist history book.

Yet in order to fulfill that promise, it is necessary to examine the life of this charismatic, Victorian, Millerite, Sabbatarian Adventist farmer from upstate New York in all its complexity. Just as a jigsaw puzzle is never complete until all of its pieces are in their proper place, so it is not possible to understand who the *real* Hiram Edson was until we see him in his historical, geographical, cultural, political, intellectual, and religious settings. This bigger picture is also important because it shaped the type of man, preacher, writer, and church leader he became, especially in the 1840s and 1850s, which represent the peak of his influence within the burgeoning Adventist movement.

Consequently, Chapter 1, "Edson's World," describes the 19th century as he saw it: an era torn by wars, revolutions, and revolts across Europe, South America, and even in the United States, yet also an age that witnessed the end of slavery and serfdom in most of the world. In the 1830s and 1840s, his region of upstate New York, called the "Burned-over District," witnessed radical social, educational, intellectual, philosophical, and religious reforms, including women's suffrage, free public education, Transcendentalism, pacifism, Mormonism, Spiritualism, and Millerism, to mention only a handful. Edson also benefited from new inventions such as the steel plow and the mechanical reaper. He frequently rode stagecoaches, packet boats on the Erie Canal, and slow-moving trains to spread the third angel's message across New York and Pennsylvania. The chapter also examines life in Edson's local environment, especially Port Gibson, Canandaigua, and Rochester.

---

[10]Ronald A. Wells, *History Through the Eyes of Faith* (San Francisco: HarperCollins Publishers, 1989), p. 2.

Although many have stereotyped Edson as a simple farmer (he raised sheep), in reality, his genealogy outshone those of most other Adventist pioneer families. As Chapter 2 ("Pilgrim Roots") shows, three of his ancestors sailed to America aboard the *Mayflower* and also signed the Mayflower Compact in 1620. Five of his great uncles fought in the American Revolution, and one died at Valley Forge. Hiram's father, Luther Edson, fought in the War of 1812 and built a barn in the 1840s that stands on the Edson property today. Hiram also experienced tragic losses: In 1839 his first wife, Effa, died at 28, and in 1842 he and his second wife, Esther, lost their daughter, Viah Ophelia, at only 13 months.

While it is true that all the state and federal censuses describe Edson as a farmer, he was far more than that in the eyes of his contemporaries, who either loved or hated him. Chapter 3, "Charismatic Farmer," reveals that while some Adventist pioneers like the Whites and the Beldens admired Hiram so highly that they named sons after him, some of his neighbors despised his new religion and resorted to verbal and physical abuse to intimidate him. To understand Edson's claim to receiving "presentments" between 1843 and 1848, this chapter briefly looks at his religious milieu (the Shakers, Quakers, Mormons, Spiritualists, and Millerites) who also practiced emotional spiritual exercises and believed in supernatural phenomena such as speaking in tongues and faith healings, all of which Edson experienced many times during his life.

Like tens of thousands of other Millerite Adventists, Hiram and Esther also endured the Great Disappointment when October 22, 1844, passed and Christ did not come. What was that experience really like? In order to better understand Edson's famous line, "We wept, and wept, till the day dawn,"[11] Chapter 4, "Disappointed Millerite," takes a look at the mental, emotional, psychological, and even physiological reactions expressed by William Miller, Joseph Bates, Washington Morse, James White, Henry Emmons, and Hiram Edson himself. In the depths of their depression, some (including Hiram) set new dates for Christ's second coming; others spiritualized His return on October 22; while about 200 others joined the Shakers. What actually happened to Hiram Edson and his companion, O.R.L. Crosier, in the cornfield early on Wednesday morning, October 23, 1844? Adventist writers have offered widely divergent interpretations of that event. Chapter 4 cites Edson's own brief statements as written in a manuscript he penned, and then shares the views of dozens of writers who fall into four broad camps: Edson received a vision, a flash of light, an impression or insight, or he had no divine illumination at all that day.

Chapter 5, "Friends and Foes," begins with biographical sketches of Hiram's two closest companions—Franklin Hahn and Owen Crosier—and then shares a brief historical overview of those who studied and preached about the heavenly sanctuary before October 22, 1844. It then reveals the circumstances surrounding the publication of Crosier's articles on the sanctuary in *The Day-Dawn* (1845) and *Day-Star* Extra (1846) newspapers before examining the seven key points Crosier made in those articles and the subsequent reactions he received from his contemporaries.

Two of the key Sabbath and Sanctuary Conferences convened in Hiram and Esther's home in Port Gibson in 1846 and 1848. Therefore, Chapter 6, "Active Layman," takes a look at Edson's role as organizer and participant in several of these conferences that hammered

---

[11]Hiram Edson, undated manuscript VT00272, CAR, JWL, AU.

out "present truth" and brought unity to the movement. It also examines the autobiographical elements in one of Edson's favorite hymns, "Here Is No Rest," and then describes certain unique phenomena connected with Samuel Rhodes's rescue from a hermit's existence in the Adirondacks in 1849.

Edson's roles in establishing and supporting the early publishing work and tent evangelism in New York during the 1850s, the family's frequent moves around the state, and his unique ministry of partnering with nine pioneer preachers are the focus of Chapter 7, "Ministerial Partners." Likewise, his enthusiastic support for "Gospel Order" in the 1850s can be seen in his efforts to organize local churches and, during the 1860s and 1870s, his participation in sessions of the New York-Pennsylvania Conference.

Without a doubt, the most difficult chapter to write (and perhaps to read) is Chapter 8, "Speculative Theologian," which analyzes Edson's articles and pamphlets written between 1845 and 1867. Full of numerology, arcane symbols, types and antitypes, and even an odd prophetic timeline he promoted (the 2520 days), these articles are tough slogging even for theologians, most of whom have simply ignored them. Taken together, they deal with such topics as the seven churches and many beasts in Revelation, the shut door, numerous prophetic timelines, God's covenants and laws, and Hiram's frequent attacks on the Roman Catholic Church and particularly the papacy.

Although Edson gets the credit for introducing the subject of the heavenly sanctuary to Sabbatarian Adventists, in actuality, he wrote almost nothing on that subject after 1844. Consequently, Chapter 9, "Sanctuary Expositors," takes a look at the six men who actually did all the work of hammering out the details of this teaching in their 44 articles in the *Advent Review and Sabbath Herald* between 1850 and

1860: Owen Crosier[12] (six articles), James White (six articles), J.N. Andrews (nine articles), Uriah Smith (20 articles), Charles Sperry (one article), and Elon Everts (two articles).

The narrative of the Edson family's lives resumes in Chapter 10, "Sunset Years," which describes events in the 1860s. After the family moved to Palermo, New York, in 1860, Hiram's health deteriorated so rapidly, with frequent colds and typhoid fever, that he was sent to Dr. Jackson's water cure in Dansville in 1864. Nonetheless, upon his release, he once again perambulated the state, establishing new churches (such as the Roosevelt Seventh-day Adventist Church that stands today) and attending the New York-Pennsylvania Conference sessions (where he was granted a ministerial license in 1866 and ministerial credentials in 1870).

Despite battling tuberculosis and catarrh in the 1870s, Edson soldiered on. As Chapter 11, "Dark Days," reveals, between 1870 and his death in 1882, Hiram continued to attend Conference sessions, baptize converts, fund church institutions, and share one of his favorite hymns, "Calvary." Yet after 1874 his ministerial credentials were not renewed, and this chapter examines some possible reasons why, as well as why he died beneath a cloud of doubt and distrust in 1882.

Finally, Chapter 12, "Edson's Legacy," focuses on those individuals and groups who have been primarily responsible for rehabilitating the reputation of Edson today, especially the writings of Arthur W. Spalding and the roles played by volunteers in Adventist Historic Properties and Adventist Heritage Ministries. Today on Hiram and Esther Edson's former sheep farm, one can see Luther Edson's barn, a visitor center, and a Bible Prophecy Trail and Garden with 12 sta-

---

[12]From his birth in 1820 until the late 1840s, Owen spelled his surname as "Crosier," but at some unknown date in the 1850s, he changed the spelling of his last name to "Crozier." I will use the former spelling throughout this book.

tions. One can also watch the DVD "Meet Hiram Edson," attend annual Sabbath and Sanctuary Festivals, and join Adventist Heritage Tours of upstate New York and New England. Doubtless, as Spalding wrote in 1948, Hiram Edson "would be astonished at the celebrity he has become among us in recent years."[13]

---

[13]Arthur W. Spalding to C.L. Taylor, June 20, 1948, Spalding Correspondence, Collection 10, Box 2, Folder 1, CAR, JWL, AU.

Chapter 1

Edson's World

From a 21st-century vantage point, the 19th century, lacking world wars, a Holocaust, terrorism, and global warming, appears on the surface to be a peaceful era. But that is not how Hiram Edson and the Adventist pioneers experienced it. As he scanned the world news in the Canandaigua *Ontario Messenger*, the *Ontario Repository and Freeman*, and issues of the *Advent Review and Sabbath Herald*, Edson saw a world in turmoil that was fulfilling Bible prophecy almost daily. As *Review* editors and writers often declared, prophecy was history in advance, while history was prophecy fulfilled.[1]

Everywhere he looked, Edson saw wars and rumors of wars. By 1806, the year of his birth, the French had been fighting a European coalition for 14 years; their bloody battles did not end until Napoleon Bonaparte was exiled to St. Helena in 1815. In three *Review* articles, Edson would have much to say about Napoleon I and his nephew, Louis Napoleon III.[2] During Edson's lifetime, Britain also seized Hong

---

[1]The *Ontario Messenger* was published in Canandaigua, New York, between 1810 and 1856. The *Ontario Repository and Freeman*, also printed in Canandaigua, appeared between 1836 and 1839, and then, after shortening its name to the *Ontario Repository*, continued from 1840 to 1862. The *Advent Review and Sabbath Herald* (hereafter cited as *Review*), successor to the *Present Truth* (1849), was printed by secular printers in Auburn and Saratoga Springs, New York, and Paris, Maine, between 1850 and 1852 until the Sabbatarian Adventists established their first press at Rochester, New York, from 1852 to 1855.
[2]Hiram Edson, "An Appeal to the Laodicean Church," *Review* Extra, Sept. 1850, pp. 8-9; "The Times of the Gentiles and the Deliverance and Restoration of the Remnant of Israel from the Seven Times, or 2520

Kong and fought China in the Opium War (1839-1842).[3] Britain, France, and Turkey opposed Russia in the Crimean War (1853-1856), France defeated Austria in the Piedmont War (1859), while the Germans crushed Austria in the Austro-Prussian War (1864).[4] Flexing its military muscles, France invaded Mexico in 1861 and Cambodia in 1863,[5] only to be defeated by Germany in the Franco-Prussian War (1870-1871).[6] Toward the end of Edson's life, the Russians fought the Turks for dominance in the Balkans (1878) while the British occupied Egypt in 1882, the year he died.[7]

In addition to the above conflicts, revolts and revolutions convulsed Europe. During Edson's youth in the 1820s, the Spanish, Greek, and South American peoples declared their independence from autocratic, often foreign, rulers.[8] Bloody revolts in the 1830s occurred in Greece, Belgium, France, and Poland,[9] followed by equally violent (but unsuccessful) uprisings in Spain, France, Italy, Germany, Hungary, and Poland in 1848.[10] In the second half of the century, the Sepoy Mutiny in India (1857-1858), the Polish revolution against Russia (1863-1864),[11] the Balkan revolts against Turkish domination (1875),[12] and the Russian pogroms against the Jews[13] convinced some

---

Years of Assyrian or Pagan and Papal Captivity Considered," *Review*, Jan. 24, 1856, p. 131 and Feb. 14, 1856, p. 154.

[3] Margaret L. Coit, *The Life History of the United States*, vol. 4: *The Sweep Westward, 1829-1849*, ed. Henry F. Graff (New York: Time-Life Books, 1975), p. 153.

[4] T. Harry Williams, *The Life History of the United States*, vol. 5: *The Union Sundered, 1849-1865*, ed. Henry F. Graff (New York: Time-Life Books, 1975), pp. 152-153.

[5] Williams, *The Union Sundered*, p. 153.

[6] T. Harry Williams, *The Life History of the United States*, vol. 6: *The Union Restored, 1861-1876*, ed. Henry F. Graff (New York: Time-Life Books), p. 169.

[7] Bernard A. Weisberger, *The Life History of the United States*, vol. 7: *The Age of Steel and Steam, 1877-1890*, ed. Henry F. Graff (New York: Time-Life Books, 1975), p. 169.

[8] Margaret L. Coit, *The Life History of the United States*, vol. 3: *The Growing Years, 1789-1829*, ed. Henry F. Graff (New York: Time-Life Books, 1975), p. 169 and Coit, *The Sweep Westward*, p. 152.

[9] Coit, *The Sweep Westward*, p. 152.

[10] Coit, *The Sweep Westward*, p. 153.

[11] Williams, *The Union Sundered*, pp. 152-153.

[12] Williams, *The Union Restored*, p. 169.

[13] Weisberger, *Steel and Steam*, p. 152.

people that these violent political eruptions were fulfillments of Bible prophecy and harbingers of Christ's soon coming. Edson referenced some of these events in his pamphlets. (See Chapter 8.)[14]

Around the world, the 19th century also ushered in significant changes. In 1807, Parliament abolished slavery in the British Isles and, in 1834, throughout the British Empire.[15] France did the same in 1848, while the Austro-Hungarian Empire[16] and the Russian Empire brought an end to centuries of serfdom in 1848 and 1861, respectively.[17] Doubtless Edson, an abolitionist, rejoiced at these developments. In 1845-1846, a potato blight in Ireland brought sudden demographic changes, including widespread famine, the deaths of over a million Irish, and the emigration of another million, many of whom came to New York to build the canals and railroads on which Edson and other Adventist pioneers traveled.[18]

Edson's America

Although relatively isolated from the above conflicts, the United States was not immune to war and strife. In the wake of the Revolutionary War (in which several of Edson's ancestors participated), the United States entered into an undeclared war with France (1798-1800) and the bloody War of 1812 against Britain (1812-1815),[19] during which British ships were sighted on Lake Ontario near Edson's home.[20] In the Mediterranean Sea, pirates from Algiers boarded Amer-

---

[14]See, for example, Hiram Edson's pamphlets *An Exposition of Scripture Prophecy: Showing the Final Return of the Jews in 1856* (Canandaigua, NY: n.p., 1849), pp. 10-11, and *The Time of the End: Its Beginning, Progressive Events, and Final Termination* (Auburn, NY: Henry Oliphant, 1849), pp. 4-6, 11-12.
[15]Coit, *The Sweep Westward*, p. 152.
[16]Coit, *The Sweep Westward*, p. 153.
[17]Williams, *The Union Sundered*, p. 153.
[18]Coit, *The Sweep Westward*, p. 153.
[19]Coit, *The Growing Years*, pp. 97-119, 168-169.
[20]Charles F. Milliken, *A History of Ontario County, New York and Its People*, vol. 1 (New York: Lewis Historical Publishing Company, 1911), p. 70.

ican ships.[21] Soldiers also fought against the Creeks (1813-1814),[22] Black Hawks (1832), Seminoles (1835-1842),[23] Sioux (1862, 1875),[24] Nez Perce (1877), Utes (1879), and Mexican border raiders (1880).[25] Even more bloody, the Mexican-American War (1846-1848)[26] and the Civil War (1861-1865)[27] pitted American citizens against their neighbors to the south and against one another, but to Edson's relief, the latter brought an end to slavery.

Rapid American expansion during Edson's lifetime engendered further conflicts. Between his birth in 1806 and his death in 1882, 19 states joined the Union and the United States acquired 17 new territories, most of which eventually became states.[28] But the cost of following the policy of Manifest Destiny[29] remained high: as mentioned above, there were conflicts with Native Americans who were forcibly removed; war with Mexico; violence in the gold fields of California, Colorado, Nevada, Montana, and Alaska;[30] and the deaths of 265 cavalrymen at the Battle of the Little Bighorn in Montana in 1876.[31]

Given the hotly debated issue of slavery during the Antebellum Era (1815-1860), American politics constituted yet another battlefield, one in which many Adventists (including the Bates, Byingtons, Whites, Smiths, and Edsons) participated. Although Congress outlawed the slave trade in 1808, the debate over extending slav-

---

[21]Coit, *The Growing Years*, pp. 60, 62-63, 168.
[22]Coit, *The Growing Years*, pp. 105-106, 169.
[23]Coit, *The Sweep Westward*, pp. 43, 153.
[24]Williams, *The Union Sundered*, p. 153 and *The Union Restored*, pp. 145-147, 169.
[25]Weisberger, *Steel and Steam*, pp. 52, 152.
[26]Coit, *The Sweep Westward*, p. 153.
[27]Williams, *The Union Sundered*, pp. 131-153.
[28]For chronological lists of these territories and states, see *Life History of the United States*, vol. 3, pp. 168-169; vol. 4, pp. 152-153; vol. 5, pp. 152-153; and vol. 6, pp. 168-169.
[29]In the 19th century, the doctrine of Manifest Destiny postulated the continued territorial expansion of the United States into the Trans-Mississippi West, the Pacific islands, and the Caribbean Sea as part of America's God-ordained destiny.
[30]Williams, *The Union Sundered*, pp. 54, 152-153.
[31]Williams, *The Union Sundered*, pp. 146-147, 169.

ery to the West precipitated verbal and physical conflicts between southern Democrats and northern Liberty, Free Soil,[32] and Republican party members. Americans debated the ramifications of the Missouri Compromise of 1820[33] and the Compromise of 1850 with its Fugitive Slave Act[34] (against which Ellen White urged civil disobedience[35]), the Kansas-Nebraska Act of 1854, the secession of 11 states forming the Confederacy, the Emancipation Proclamation of 1863, and the Thirteenth Amendment abolishing slavery in 1865.[36] Many citizens viewed with alarm the enforcement of Black codes and the rise of the Ku Klux Klan across the South after 1866, but strongly approved of the Fourteenth Amendment (1868) granting African Americans citizenship and the Fifteenth Amendment (1870) giving them the vote.[37]

During the 1820s, some 213 individuals had been held in bondage in Ontario County, New York. But in 1827, the state abolished slavery.[38] During the height of the Millerite movement of the 1840s, Ontario County was a stronghold of Free-Soil proponents, and in the 1850s, it became a Republican center. Hiram and Esther Edson paid 50 cents a year for a subscription to *The Gospel Standard,* an openly abolitionist Millerite newspaper edited by Silas Howley and David Plumb, which supported the Liberty Party between 1844 and 1848.[39] After William Morgan, who had revealed Masonic secrets, was abducted by Masons from the Canandaigua jail in 1826 and al-

---

[32]Between 1844 and 1848, members of the Liberty Party wished to abolish slavery immediately, while between 1848 and 1854, members of the Free-Soil Party opposed the extension of slavery into the territories and new states of the Trans-Mississippi West.

[33]Coit, *The Growing Years,* pp. 122-124, 169.

[34]Williams, *The Union Sundered,* pp. 36-38, 47-54, 152.

[35]Ellen White, *Testimonies for the Church,* vol. 1 (Mountain View, CA: Pacific Press Publishing Association, 1948), pp. 201-202.

[36]Williams, *The Union Sundered,* pp. 55-57, 67-68, 116-118, 152-153.

[37]Williams, *The Union Restored,* pp. 15, 68, 74, 169.

[38]Milliken, *Ontario County,* vol. 1, pp. 73, 85.

[39]"Receipts," *The Gospel Standard,* Aug. 1, 1844, p. 19.

legedly drowned in the Niagara River, local citizens formed the Anti-Masonic Party,[40] whose members (including the abolitionist Byington and Hilliard families of St. Lawrence County, New York) refused to vote for any candidate who belonged to a Masonic Lodge. Edson, like many early Adventist pioneers, was strongly influenced by the Free-Soil, Republican, and Anti-Masonic currents swirling about him during his youth and early manhood.[41]

It is also worth mentioning that Edson lived during one of the coldest eras in America's climatic history. Called by scientists "The Little Ice Age," this period, which lasted from 1300 to 1850, experienced such harsh winters across Europe and America that some rivers froze solid.[42] In 1800, several southern states, including Florida and Louisiana, reported deep snow.[43] The year 1810 was appallingly cold while the year 1816, when Edson turned 10, was known as "the year without a summer" and "Eighteen Hundred and Froze to Death."[44] The 1820s and 1830s were rife with droughts, floods, epidemics as well as coups, assassinations, revolts, and revolutions.[45] Throughout history, such harsh conditions have inspired the growth of apocalyptic ideas and the rise of potent revivals, religious movements, and new churches.[46] In New York's case, these revivals and religious movements included the Shakers, Mormons, Spiritualists, and Sabbatarian Adventists.

---

[40]Between 1826 and 1843, the Anti-Masonic Party opposed secret societies, Catholics, and immigrants from southern and eastern Europe (Italians, Germans, Slavs, etc.), many of whom were Catholics.

[41]Milliken, *Ontario County*, vol. 1, pp. 75-78.

[42]Philip Jenkins, *Climate, Catastrophe, and Faith: How Changes in Climate Drive Religious Upheaval* (New York: Oxford University Press, 2021), pp. 61, 90-91, 141.

[43]Jenkins, *Climate, Catastrophe, and Faith*, p. 162.

[44]Jenkins, *Climate, Catastrophe, and Faith*, pp. 159, 164. In New England in 1810 the temperature dropped 60 degrees on what was called "Cold Friday."

[45]Jenkins, *Climate, Catastrophe, and Faith*, pp. 166-168.

[46]Jenkins, *Climate, Catastrophe, and Faith*, pp. 159-168.

Edson's New York

Upstate New York between Buffalo and Albany has come to be known as "the Burned-over District" because it was the center of many political, social, intellectual, philosophical, and religious reforms during the 1830s and 1840s.[47] Edson's Port Gibson farm in Ontario County was located only a few miles east of Rochester in Wayne County, a hub of numerous progressive movements. Leading suffragists such as Lucretia Mott, Elizabeth Cady Stanton, Susan B. Anthony, and Margaret Fuller lectured there, as did Lydia Maria Child, the editor of the *National Anti-Slavery Standard* in New York City and the leading female author of the 1840s.[48] Many of the founders of the American Peace Society (John and Lewis Tappan, Francis Parkman, Oliver Wendell Holmes, Elias Boudinot, and William Ladd) also visited the city.[49] So did the leading temperance advocates of the day, including Dr. James Caleb Jackson, whose "Our Home on the Hillside" hydrotherapy sanitarium in Dansville would treat many ailing Adventists, Edson among them, in the 1860s.[50] Advocates for Victorian dress reform, including Amelia Bloomer (who created a short skirt with Turkish "bloomers") and Ellen White (whose later "Reform Dress" in 1867 featured trousers and a longer skirt) also lived in Rochester.[51]

Spokesmen for numerous utopian societies could also be heard recruiting members for their isolated communities. In New York, there were the Amana societies near Buffalo[52] and the Skaneateles

---

[47]Whitney R. Cross, *The Burned-over District: The Social and Intellectual History of Enthusiastic Religion in Western New York, 1800-1850* (New York: Cornell University Press, 1950).

[48]For more information on these significant individuals, see Jerome L. Clark, *1844* (Nashville, TN: Southern Publishing Association, 1968), vol. 2, pp. 79, 273; vol. 3, pp. 67-69, 78.

[49]Clark, *1844*, vol. 3, pp. 88-89.

[50]Clark, *1844*, vol. 2, p. 254.

[51]Clark, *1844*, vol. 2, pp. 273-274.

[52]Clark, *1844*, vol. 2, pp. 162-169. Members of the Amana societies, who were discouraged from marrying, shared all material goods in common, refused to take oaths, practiced foot washing and the Lord's Supper, but opposed musical instruments, theatrical entertainments, and worldly recreation.

Community on the lake of the same name.[53] Over in Massachusetts were the Hopedale Community in Milford,[54] Fruitlands near Harvard,[55] and the Transcendentalist center at Brook Farm.[56] To the south was the Ephrata group in eastern Pennsylvania;[57] farther west, the Rappites in New Harmony, Indiana[58] and the Zoarites in Ohio;[59] besides numerous Fourierist Phalanxes in New York, New Jersey, and Wisconsin.[60] Since all of these groups were thriving in the 1840s, Edson must have been aware of some of them. Nevertheless, as he expected to join the Advent band in heaven in 1844, these earthly utopias held no appeal for him.[61]

Yet he did benefit from many of the improvements here on earth during the 19th century. As a farmer, he probably found John Deere's

---

[53]Clark, *1844*, vol. 2, pp. 175-176. Members of the Skaneateles Community did not believe in any special revelations from God to humanity or support organized religion of any kind. They opposed organized governments, armies, paying taxes, testifying in court, and property ownership (but held all material goods in common), but endorsed marriage, education at home, and vegetarianism.

[54]Clark, *1844*, vol. 2, pp. 170-172. Most residents of Hopedale were Universalists who fostered social justice causes (temperance, anti-slavery, peace, women's rights). They developed their own constitution, laws, regulations, police, savings institution, fire insurance organizations, and favored property ownership and marriage.

[55]Clark, *1844*, vol. 2, pp. 176-178. For seven months in 1843-1844, the residents of Fruitlands, near Harvard College, practiced Transcendentalism, strict vegetarianism (no animal products), anti-slavery, communal living, bartering (no money allowed), and drank only water.

[56]Clark, *1844*, vol. 2, pp.190-196. Residents at Brook Farm shared all material goods in common and advocated Transcendentalism, vegetarianism, combining study and manual labor.

[57]Clark, *1844*, vol. 2, pp. 172-175. One of the few utopian societies based on religion, Ephrata was established as a haven for German Dunkers who practiced baptism by immersion, denounced war, refused to testify in court, and renounced the use of flesh foods, but emphasized preaching, education, music, charitable works, and hard physical labor in a variety of mills and workshops.

[58]Clark, *1844*, vol. 2, pp. 141-158. The Rappites advocated celibacy, vegetarianism, uniform dress, fraternal love, and hard labor in mills and factories, and they followed strict daily schedules for worshiping, eating, and laboring.

[59]Clark, *1844*, vol. 2, pp. 158-160. The Zoarites, like the Rappites, came from southern Germany seeking religious freedom. They opposed the state as "Babylon," paying taxes, serving in the army, and sending their children to public schools. While they believed firmly in the Bible, Christ as Savior, and the Trinity, they had no preachers, no church organization, no liturgy, and no baptismal rites, but treated women equal with men and, like the Quakers, addressed one another as "thee" and "thou."

[60]Clark, *1844*, vol. 2, pp. 178-190. Followers of Charles Fourier of France, the Fourierists established tightly regimented communities called "phalanxes" wherein everyone was assigned tasks based on their abilities. Music, uniforms, emblems, and endless rules were designed to make the participants into skilled, efficient, educated, and cooperative individuals.

[61]Clark, *1844*, vol. 2, pp. 141-196.

steel plow of 1837 superior to its predecessors, Thomas Jefferson's 1793 wooden moldboard plow and the heavy 1797 iron plow.[62] After 1834, Cyrus McCormick's horse-drawn mechanical reaper enabled Edson to harvest his wheat, barley, and oats more quickly.[63] The completion of the 363-mile Erie Canal in 1825, which passed within a mile of Edson's Port Gibson farm, and the appearance of steamboats on the Great Lakes after 1818, made it easier for him to market his wool in Albany, Buffalo, and even distant Chicago.[64] After 1842, when railroads spanned the distance between Albany and Buffalo, Edson and his Millerite colleagues used them to spread the message of Christ's soon return.[65] A decade later, New York's Adventist ministers greatly benefited from the consolidation of three railway lines under the aegis of the New York Central Railroad.[66] While canals and railroads boosted trade and transportation, Samuel Finley Breese Morse's telegraph (1844) and Alexander Graham Bell's telephone (1876) facilitated communication.[67] Finally, Thomas Edison's invention of the incandescent light bulb in 1879 and the construction of the first hydroelectric plant on the Niagara River in 1882 provided a source of reliable light by which the Adventist pioneers could read their Bibles and the *Review* after sunset.[68]

Philosophical currents

While Hiram Edson readily adopted technological improvements, he was more critical of several philosophical and intellectual currents in his contemporary setting. For a Bible-believing Adven-

---

[62]Coit, *The Growing Years*, pp. 66, 168 and *The Sweep Westward*, p. 152.
[63]Coit, *The Sweep Westward*, pp. 139, 152.
[64]Coit, *The Growing Years*, pp. 147, 158-159, 169.
[65]Coit, *The Sweep Westward*, p. 153.
[66]Williams, *The Union Sundered*, pp. 9-10, 38, 152.
[67]Clark, *1844*, vol. 3, pp. 192-194.
[68]Weisberger, *Steel and Steam*, pp. 34, 38, 40-41, 152.

tist, the Transcendentalists, including Bronson Alcott, Ralph Waldo Emerson, Margaret Fuller, and Henry David Thoreau, placed too much emphasis on self-reliance, free thought, and the divinity of nature.[69] The theory of evolution, as propounded in Charles Darwin's *Origin of Species* (written in 1844, published in 1859), undermined the biblical account of Creation and the 6,000-year age of the earth that most Victorian Christians accepted.[70] Likewise, phrenology, the pseudoscience of determining one's character by reading the bumps on one's head, was advocated by many leading figures in the 1840s and practiced at Dr. Jackson's water cure, but it did not appeal to most Adventists.[71] Neither did mesmerism, in which electric currents were passed through some participants' bodies while others entered hypnotic trances. Both forms of mesmerism were popularized by John Greenleaf Whittier and Samuel Morse.[72] Although Sabbatarian Adventists saw the papacy as the beast of Revelation 13, they also refused to participate in the nativism[73] that swept America in the 1830s and 1840s, with its virulent anti-Catholic, anti-papal, and anti-immigrant prejudices that inspired mobs to burn Roman Catholic convents and churches, to attack Irish and German Catholics, and to write anti-Catholic screeds such as Maria Monk's *Awful Disclosures* (1836), a highly emotional but largely fictional account of convent life in Montreal.[74]

---

[69]Clark, *1844*, vol. 1, pp. 373. The 19th-century Transcendentalists, which also included such famous individuals as the preacher Henry Ward Beecher, the newspaper editor Horace Greeley, and the poets Walt Whitman and Edgar Allen Poe, searched for ultimate reality through spiritual intuition.
[70]Clark, *1844*, vol. 1, pp. 171-173.
[71]Clark, *1844*, vol. 1, pp. 374-380. Popular advocates of phrenology in America included the founder of public and normal schools Horace Mann, the inventor Samuel Gridley Howe, and the famous atheist Robert Dale Owen.
[72]Clark, *1844*, vol. 1, pp. 352-358.
[73]Nativism is the practice or policy of favoring native-born American citizens over immigrants.
[74]For a detailed study of nativism in America, see Clark, *1844*, vol. 1, pp. 203-278.

Religious movements

From the 1820s to the 1840s, the hills in upstate New York were alive with the sounds of the supernatural. In Palmyra, four miles northwest of Edson's farm, the boy Joseph Smith allegedly began receiving visits from the angel Moroni in the 1820s. According to Smith, in 1827, Moroni gave him the golden plates from which Smith translated the *Book of Mormon*. In 1830, Smith had the book published in Palmyra and founded the Church of Jesus Christ of Latter-Day Saints.[75] In 1844, when Smith and his brother were lynched by a mob in the Carthage, Illinois, jail, Brigham Young assumed the leadership of the fledgling Mormon movement.[76]

Unlike early Adventists, Mormons worshiped on Sunday, practiced polygamy, prayed for the dead, and based their beliefs on extra-biblical sources (such as the *Book of Mormon* and *Doctrine and Covenants*). Nevertheless, the public sometimes confused Adventists with Mormons due to their conservative lifestyles.[77] The term "lying Mormons" was applied to Merritt Cornell and Moses Hull in Iowa,[78] to J.N. Loughborough and Daniel Bourdeau in California,[79] and to James and Ellen (Harmon) White in the Midwest.[80] In 1835, when Ellen Harmon was eight, her second cousin, Agnes Coolbrith, married a Mormon, Don Carlos Smith. When he died, she wed his brother, the prophet Joseph Smith, in 1842.[81] This made Ellen understand-

---

[75]Clark, *1844*, vol. 1, pp. 90-94, 103-104.

[76]Coit, *The Sweep Westward*, p. 153.

[77]Roger Dudley and Edwin Hernandez, *Citizens of Two Worlds: Religion and Politics among American Seventh-day Adventists* (Berrien Springs, MI: Andrews University Press, 1992), p. 9.

[78]Doug R. Johnson, *Adventism on the Northwestern Frontier* (Berrien Springs, MI: Oronoko Books, 1996), pp. 2-3.

[79]Brian E. Strayer, *J.N. Loughborough: The Last of the Adventist Pioneers* (Hagerstown, MD: Review and Herald Pub. Assn., 2014), p. 177.

[80]Arthur L. White, *Ellen G. White: The Early Years, 1827-1862* (Hagerstown, MD: Review and Herald Pub. Assn., 1985), pp. 415-416.

[81]Gary Land, "Biographies," in Terrie Dopp Aamodt, Gary Land, and Ronald L. Numbers, eds., *Ellen Harmon White: American Prophet* (Oxford: Oxford University Press, 2014), p. 323.

ably sensitive to charges of having been a Mormon leader at Nauvoo, Illinois,[82] and being responsible for "breaking up churches and causing divisions."[83]

Also, northwest of Edson's farm, in the tiny village of Hydesville, Margaret and Kate Fox began hearing strange knocking sounds in 1848 that they attributed to a supernatural being they named "Splitfoot."[84] Creating an alphabetically based code, they asked this spirit questions and listened for its rapping responses. Before long, they were conducting public demonstrations in Rochester and elsewhere, using a special draped table with a mechanical knocker underneath (in case the spirits didn't respond promptly).[85] Although they later declared it was all a hoax, their claims to be able to communicate with the spirits of the dead led to the modern spiritualist movement, whose chief American proponent, Andrew Jackson Davis, provided its vocabulary, suggested its theology, and brought unity through his periodical, *The Univercoelum*.[86]

The Shakers, whose tiny celibate groups dotted the rural landscapes of New England and New York from the 1820s to the 1850s, welcomed the news of the Fox sisters' alleged communication with the spirit world. They had for several years practiced spirit communication with individuals once mortal and received "visitations from beyond the grave."[87] Believing, however, that these spirits had departed in 1847, they interpreted the Hydesville phenomena as evidence

---

[82]Ellen G. White, *Spiritual Gifts*, vol. 2 (Battle Creek, MI: Published by James White, 1860), p. iv.
[83]Ellen G. White, *Evangelism* (Washington, D.C.: Review and Herald Pub. Assn., 1946), p. 410.
[84]Clark, *1844*, vol. 1, p. 352. Clark did not include the term "Splitfoot" in volume 1, but he did mention it in a lecture on spiritualism I attended as one of four students in his Antebellum America course at Southern Missionary College in 1971.
[85]Merlin D. Burt, *Adventist Pioneer Places: New York and New England* (Hagerstown, MD: Review and Herald Pub. Assn., 2011), p. 119. The draped table used by the Fox sisters in their public séances is on display in the upstairs local history museum of the Central Library of Rochester and Monroe County in Rochester, New York.
[86]Clark, *1844*, vol. 1, p. 361.
[87]Clark, *1844*, vol. 1, pp. 345-352.

that they had once more returned to bring humans goodwill.[88]

The Shakers also believed in a spiritual rather than physical second coming of Christ. This was attractive to disappointed Adventists after October 22, 1844, when some 200 former Millerites joined the Shaker movement.[89]

Considering the context of this 1840s era in the Burned-over District—where Joseph Smith claimed to dialogue with the angel Moroni, the Fox sisters rapped questions to Splitfoot, and the Shakers allegedly communicated with the spirits of the dead—helps us to understand the reactions Hiram Edson received when he reported his experience in the cornfield on October 23, 1844. While Adventists accepted his new insights as truth from God, Edson's neighbors proved more skeptical, and sometimes hostile, as discussed in Chapters 4 and 5.

Stagecoach travel

Before the construction of 19th-century canals, railroads, and paved roads eased travel, the pace of daily life was considerably slower. For example, men and women working as "drovers" herded geese, turkeys, goats, sheep, cattle, hogs, and horses from Ohio to Albany, New York City, and New England over rutted turnpikes, corduroy roads,[90] and dirt paths. Decades before the great cattle drives from Texas to Oklahoma, the autumn cattle drives across upstate New York were big business; such journeys took 10 weeks or more, with friendly farmers along the route renting their pastures and ponds to

---

[88]Clark, *1844*, vol. 1, p. 352.
[89]George Knight, *William Miller and the Rise of Adventism* (Nampa, ID: Pacific Press Pub. Assn., 2010), p. 222. Perhaps the most famous among them was Elizabeth Temple, whose popular "Renovating Remedy" (a cure for cholera consisting of bloodroot, spicy cubeb, snake root, brandy, and laudanum) made her fabulously wealthy. Some Sabbatarian Adventists, including James and Ellen White, tried it. See Ron Graybill, "Mrs. Temple: A Millennial Utopian," *Spectrum* 47, no. 4 (2019), pp. 73-77. Ellen White's secretary described Temple's remedy as "the bitterest stuff imaginable."
[90]Corduroy roads were constructed by placing split logs flat-sides down with gravel and dirt filling the cracks.

the herds.[91] In one 10-week period, 5,620 hogs passed through the state on what are today Routes 5 and 20.[92] These same roads were often black with hundreds of turkeys, their feathers clipped and their feet tarred to keep them from escaping, following a man who spread corn on the road to keep them moving seven to 10 miles a day.[93]

These slow-moving animals jostled with troops of tinkers, peddlers, and people on foot, as well as those riding in stagecoaches, the supreme mode of public conveyance in the state between 1790 and the 1840s. Weighing in at 2,400 pounds, a large coach could carry nine passengers, their baggage (limited to 14 pounds apiece), and the mail on a bumpy ride over mud holes, deep sloughs, stinking swamps, swift streams, and bone-rattling corduroy roads.[94] Passengers, wedged tightly together, smelled cigar and cigarette smoke and hot tar lubricant. They heard the shouting driver crack his bullwhip and blow his tin horn. Some felt nauseated at the swaying of the coach on its leather straps. Everyone swallowed dust and ate bad food at the wayside inns, where they slept two to a bed, often with dirty linen, bed bugs, and snoring bedmates.[95] With only flaps to cover the coach windows, passengers felt the heat, cold, rain, and wind during their jarring journey. The 360-mile trip from Albany to Buffalo took seven days, averaging four miles per hour; passengers paid five or six cents a mile.[96] From his home in Port Gibson, Edson could take coaches to nearby Rochester and Canandaigua—or to Buffalo, if he had the stomach for it.[97]

---

[91] Richard F. Palmer, The "Old Line Mail": Stagecoach Days in Upstate New York (Lamont, NY: North Country Books, 1977), pp. 58-59.
[92] Palmer, "Old Line Mail," p. 59.
[93] Palmer, "Old Line Mail," pp. 60-61.
[94] Palmer, "Old Line Mail," pp. 16, 43-45.
[95] Palmer, "Old Line Mail," pp. ix-x, 3, 16, 161.
[96] Palmer, "Old Line Mail," pp. xi, 3, 45.
[97] Palmer, "Old Line Mail," p. 9.

Erie Canal travel

Even before the completion of the "Great Western Canal"[98] in 1825, stagecoach lines began radiating across the countryside from canal "ports" like Weedsport, Port Byron, Centerport, Port Gibson, and Lockport, as well as from major towns and cities like Utica, Syracuse, Rochester, and Buffalo, making it relatively easy for Millerites and Sabbatarian Adventists to spread their apocalyptic message.[99] Canal travel, at two or three miles per hour, was far more pleasant due to better food, more comfortable beds, less cost, no dust, and a much smoother ride.[100]

When traveling on the canal between Albany and Buffalo, passengers floated over 18 aqueducts and through 83 locks,[101] passing heavily laden barges (carrying 25 to 100 tons of freight), line boats (carrying freight and passengers), and faster packet boats (for passengers only). Passengers could sit on deck and watch the forests, swamps, and farms go by, or go below to eat and sleep (women at the front, men in the rear).[102] During his frequent canal trips, Edson may have watched the Irish and Welsh workmen widening and deepening it using the new inventions that this biggest American engineering project of the century had produced: hydraulic (waterproof) cement, one-man tree-fellers, stump-pullers, and rounded wheelbarrows.[103] The canal enabled farmers like Edson to get their grain, hogs, cattle,

---

[98]Gerard Koeppel, *Bond of Union: Building the Erie Canal and the American Empire* (Philadelphia: Da Capo Press, 2009), p. 317. Before its eastern and western sections were joined to the middle section in 1825, the Erie Canal was popularly known by those who lived on the East Coast as the "Great Western Canal."

[99]Palmer, *"Old Line Mail,"* p. 77.

[100]Burt, *Adventist Pioneer Places*, pp. 116-117.

[101]Burt, *Adventist Pioneer Places*, p. 116.

[102]Burt, *Adventist Pioneer Places*, p. 116. Famous individuals who traveled on the canal included the Englishman John Howison, the Frenchman Lafayette, and the American writers Nathaniel Hawthorne and Herman Melville. None of them enjoyed the accommodations. See Koeppel, *Bond of Union*, pp. 265-266, 391-394.

[103]Koeppel, *Bond of Union*, pp. 9, 217, 238, 247, 254.

and sheep to market far easier and cheaper than taking them over-land. It had cost him $10 a ton to haul wheat flour from Port Gibson to Rochester before 1825, but shipping it on the canal cost only a dollar a ton.[104] While the canal was originally only four feet deep and 40 feet wide, by 1862 it had been enlarged to 70 feet wide at the surface and seven feet deep.[105] Relays of horses or mules every 12 miles could take a packet boat from Rochester to Albany in five days at three miles per hour traveling day and night.[106]

Railroad travel

Whereas stagecoaches operated primarily during the day all year round, the Erie Canal boats ran day and night—but only from April to November, because the canal was drained during the winter to prevent ice from damaging the locks. From November to March, farmers and merchants were under a distinct disadvantage in shipping their goods to market.[107] The solution for their dilemma proved to be the railroads.

In 1838, about the time Edson moved to Port Gibson, the first railroad in the state covered 13 miles from Syracuse to Auburn.[108] Its two passenger cars (resembling stagecoaches on wheels that held 48 people) were pulled by horses over wooden rails at a cost of one dollar per person.[109] By 1842, when the tracks paralleling the canal stretched from Albany to Buffalo, the stagecoach lines ended their service. Whereas a stagecoach trip from Rochester to Albany had taken seven *days*, the same journey by rail took only seven *hours*.[110] In

---

[104]Koeppel, *Bond of Union*, p. 307.
[105]Koeppel, *Bond of Union*, pp. 389-390.
[106]Milliken, *Ontario County*, vol. 1, p. 72.
[107]Koeppel, *Bond of Union*, p. 262.
[108]Palmer, *"Old Line Mail,"* pp. 129-130.
[109]Palmer, *"Old Line Mail,"* p. 130.
[110]Palmer, *"Old Line Mail,"* p. 137.

a curious holdover from coach days, the first railway engineers still blew tin horns to announce the train's arrival in towns.[111]

Ontario County

When Luther Edson's family purchased property in Port Gibson in 1839, they entered the oldest county in the central New York region. Established shortly after the American Revolution, on January 27, 1789, Ontario County was barely 50 years old.[112] The first settlers chose Canandaigua as the county seat. The nearby lake, full of trout, bass, pickerel, and whitefish, bore the same name. Canandaigua Academy (1796-1890s) educated local boys, while the Ontario Female Academy (1825-1870s) trained girls.[113] In 1804, the first turnpike road connected the log cabins of Canandaigua with Geneva; in 1815, at the end of the War of 1812, the hamlet was incorporated as a village, and a year later, it acquired its first fire company.[114] In 1823, when Edson was 17, the first steamboat, the *Lady of the Lake*, provided transportation across the lake; another steamboat followed in 1845.[115] With the completion of the Canandaigua to Rochester Railroad in 1840,[116] the Edsons of Port Gibson and the Loofboroughs (who took the name "Loughborough" after 1850[117]) of Victor easily traveled to the big city—yet slowly enough so that little Johnny Loofborough counted the farmers' fence posts during trips with his

---

[111]Palmer, *"Old Line Mail,"* p. 143.

[112]Harry R. Melone, *History of Central New York: Embracing Cayuga, Seneca, Wayne, Ontario, Tompkins, Cortland, Schuyler, Yates, Chemung, Steuben, and Tioga Counties* (Indianapolis, IN: Historical Publishing Company, 1932), vol. 1, p. 427.

[113]George S. Conover, ed., and Lewis C. Aldrich, comp., *History of Ontario County, New York with Illustrations and Family Sketches of Some of the Prominent Men and Families* (Syracuse, NY: D. Mason and Company, 1893), pp. 203, 209-210, 219, 226-228.

[114]Conover and Aldrich, *History of Ontario County*, pp. 203, 219, 222.

[115]Conover and Aldrich, *History of Ontario County*, p. 269.

[116]Milliken, *Ontario County*, vol. 1, p. 240.

[117]When he married Mary J. Walker in 1851, John Norton Loofborough changed his name to "J.N. Loughborough," and most of his relatives quickly did the same. See Strayer, *Loughborough*, p. 60.

grandpa, Nathan Loofborough. Beside Canandaigua Lake, wild huckleberries, a cash crop for many local citizens, grew in abundance.[118]

The citizens of Canandaigua were so law-abiding that they did not build the first jail until 1813.[119] Perhaps the fact that they established so many churches—Methodist, Congregational, Protestant Episcopal, Methodist Episcopal, Baptist, Roman Catholic, Presbyterian, and Wesleyan Methodist—provides some explanation.[120] Likewise, social and professional societies abounded. With Edson's interest in farming, he might have joined the local Agriculture Society; given his yen for history, he probably visited the Wood Library seeking sources to support his prophetic interpretations. As a poor farmer, however, he would not have been welcome at the Red Jacket Club attended by the city's business elite.[121] As an abolitionist, he no doubt read weekly issues of the *Ontario Freeman* or the more radical *Ontario County Times*, the organ of the Free-Soil wing of the Whig Party, which in the 1850s became the only Republican Party newspaper in town—and nearly all Sabbatarian Adventists were Republicans.[122]

Fifteen miles northeast of Canandaigua and barely four miles from Joseph Smith's home in Palmyra stood the village of Port Gibson,[123] named for the millionaire Henry B. Gibson, owner of the Ontario Bank, president of the Rochester and Auburn Railroad, and a major investor in the Erie Canal.[124] At its peak in the 1830s and 1840s, Port Gibson, the only village in Ontario County that bordered the canal,[125] was the main shipping point for wheat, oats, barley, and corn through-

[118]Milliken, *Ontario County*, vol. 1, p. 265.
[119]Melone, *History of Central New York,* vol. 1, p. 430.
[120]Conover and Aldrich, *History of Ontario County*, pp. 238-240.
[121]Conover and Aldrich, *History of Ontario County,* pp. 249-251.
[122]Conover and Aldrich, *History of Ontario County*, pp. 249-251.
[123]*In the Footsteps of the Pioneers* (Washington, DC: Ellen G. White Estate, 1981), pp. 16-19.
[124]Milliken, *Ontario County*, vol. 1, p. 282.
[125]Conover and Aldrich, *History of Ontario County*, p. 348.

out the Northeast by way of the Great Lakes and the St. Lawrence River and farther south via the Finger Lakes.[126] At various times during the 19th century, Port Gibson contained a malt house (for beer), a lumber planing mill, a fruit drying facility, several merchants' warehouses, a small hotel, three stores, several smaller shops, a public school, and a Methodist Episcopal Church with nearly 130 congregants,[127] including several members of Luther Edson's family.[128]

Wayne County

Thirty miles west of Port Gibson lay the burgeoning city of Rochester in Wayne County, which had been formed in 1821. The fastest growing community in the United States in the 1820s,[129] by 1835 Rochester had 14,000 citizens, including large contingents of Irish, Scottish, English, German, Italian, Polish, Russian, Romanian, and Jewish people.[130] It was a transportation hub where three railroads intersected near the Erie Canal.[131] During the 1840s, when the Edson family traded there, it was a thriving center with 137 factories, many of them producing window sash locks (including the new Arnold's Patent Sash Locks that John Loofborough sold).[132] Its 24 flour mills produced 500,000 barrels of flour every year, giving the city its nickname, "The Flour City of America."[133] Textile manufacturing was a leading industry, employing some 1,000 seamstresses (one of whom was Mary Walker, future wife of J.N. Lough-

---

[126]*In the Footsteps of the Pioneers* (1981), p. 19.
[127]Conover and Aldrich, *History of Ontario County*, pp. 348-349. See also the entry "Port Gibson" on the website https://www.visitfingerlakes.com, accessed June 16, 2021.
[128]Lou Ann Wurst, Jason Reimers, and Nicole Burque, *Archaeological-Historical Investigations: The Hiram Edson Farm Site in Upstate New York* (Syracuse, NY: Department of Anthropology, Syracuse University, Aug. 27, 1996), p. 26; document in the author's possession.
[129]Strayer, *Loughborough*, p. 38.
[130]Howard C. Hosmer, *Monroe County, 1821-1971* (Rochester, NY: Rochester Museum and Science Center, 1971), pp. 22-23, 59.
[131]Hosmer, *Monroe County*, p. 38.
[132]Strayer, *Loughborough*, p. 38.
[133]Strayer, *Loughborough*, p. 38.

borough), and scores of tailors labored in its 30 clothing shops.[134]

As a microcosm of New York's Burned-over District, Rochester attracted reform groups like moths to a flame. Thurlow Weed, one of the founders of the Whig Party in 1834, edited the *Anti-Masonic Inquirer* there, a newspaper whose harsh rhetoric against Masons, Catholics, and immigrants fomented nativist riots across America as Protestant mobs attacked Irish, Italian, and German Catholics.[135] The city also boasted five of the six Fourierist colonies in the state, where followers of the French utopian socialist Charles Fourier lived in communities called phalanxes and shared all work equally irrespective of gender.[136] In 1839, the year the Edsons moved to Port Gibson, William Ladd's American Peace Society and the American Anti-Slavery Party established headquarters in Rochester.[137] The abolitionist Frederick Douglass started his newspaper, *The North Star*, there in 1847 and made Rochester a hub on the Underground Railroad, funneling escaping slaves to Canada.[138] In addition, citizens formed the Society for the Promotion of Temperance and other groups to enforce Sunday observance, encourage Bible study, promote moral reform, and advance women's rights.[139] The fiery orator Susan B. Anthony often lectured on women's suffrage to enthusiastic crowds in the city.[140] Likewise, from 1852 to 1855, thanks in part to Edson's sacrificial generosity, Rochester became the locus of the Sabbatarian Adventists' publishing enterprise under the leadership of James White, one of four men by that name in the city.[141]

---

[134]Strayer, *Loughborough*, p. 38.
[135]Strayer, *Loughborough*, p. 39.
[136]Strayer, *Loughborough*, p. 39.
[137]Strayer, *Loughborough*, p. 39.
[138]Strayer, *Loughborough*, p. 39.
[139]Strayer, *Loughborough*, p. 39.
[140]Strayer, *Loughborough*, p. 39.
[141]The Rochester city directories for 1853 to 1855 list four men by the name of James White: a carriage maker on 49 Adam Street, two day laborers at 13 Monroe Street and Grape Street, and the printer James Springer White at 109-111 Monroe Street, the headquarters of the Review and Herald press.

Chapter 2

Pilgrim Roots

Although Hiram Edson faithfully recorded the names of his children and grandchildren in the flyleaf of his 1838 Bible,[1] there is no indication that he was interested in his genealogy. Six decades after his death in 1882, his granddaughter, Viah May Cross, told Adventist historian LeRoy Froom that her family was descended from Elijah Edson, a Puritan clergyman who had immigrated from England to Boston around 1670.[2] Further research into the family's genealogy by Ron Shoemaker has revealed that this assertion was inaccurate. While Hiram Edson was *related* to Elijah Edson, he was not directly *descended* from him. Instead, his ancestry can be traced back half a century earlier to a group of Separatists that left England, believing that its state-supported church was corrupt beyond reform.[3] On November 11, 1620, after a grueling 10-week voyage from England, a 180-ton, four-deck Dutch cargo ship named the *Mayflower*, with 30 crew members and 102 cramped passen-

---

[1]In 1983, Walter Saxby, Hiram Edson's great-grandson, donated Edson's 1838 Bible to Jim Nix, director of the Department of Archives and Special Collections at the Loma Linda University Library, where it can be seen today. See "Edson Bible Donated to Loma Linda," *Review*, Nov. 10, 1983, p. 22.
[2]Viah May Cross to L.E. Froom, Aug. 23, 1944, manuscript VT000274, CAR, JWL, AU.
[3]Ron Shoemaker, "The Hand of God on Hiram Edson's Ancestors" (April 2010), pp. 1-2; document in the author's possession.

gers, landed at Cape Cod, Massachusetts.[4] During the bitter winter months, they established a democratic society known as the Plymouth Colony, based upon the Mayflower Compact that 41 males had signed aboard the ship.[5] Three of those signers—John Alden, Peter Browne, and William Mullen—were direct ancestors of Hiram Edson. Consequently, based on this bloodline, Edson would have qualified to be a member of the very exclusive General Society of Mayflower Descendants. Unfortunately for him, however, the Society would not be founded until 1897, nearly 15 years after his death.[6]

Revolutionary roots

As this tight-knit group of Pilgrims struggled to survive that first winter of 1620-1621, many of its young people were united in marriage. Mayflower Compact signer John Alden wed Priscilla Mullins, the sister of William Mullins, also a signer. Their son Joseph married Mary Simmons,[7] and following the biblical admonition to "be fruitful and multiply" (Genesis 1:22, KJV), they had five children. Their son, Joseph Alden, Jr., wed Hannah Dunham.[8] Joseph and Hannah's daughter Mary married Timothy Edson. This union proved fruitful as well, producing six children.[9] One son, Abijah, wed Susanna Snow, and together they reared seven children.[10] When Susanna died, in 1761 Abijah married Hannah Ruggles, who was 37 years his senior.[11]

---

[4]Thomas A. Bailey, *The American Pageant: A History of the Republic*, 3rd ed. (Boston: D.C. Heath, 1966), p. 23.

[5]Bailey, *American Pageant*, p. 24.

[6]Shoemaker, "Edson's Ancestors," p. 2. The General Society of Mayflower Descendants was founded in 1897 at Plymouth, Massachusetts. For further information, see their website at https://www.themayflowersociety.org.

[7]Shoemaker, "Edson's Ancestors," p. 1.

[8]Shoemaker, "Edson's Ancestors," p. 2.

[9]Shoemaker, "Edson's Ancestors," p. 2.

[10]Shoemaker, "Edson's Ancestors," p. 2.

[11]Shoemaker, "Edson's Ancestors," p. 2.

Abijah and Susanna's son James wed Lovina Hancock.[12] Their son Luther married Susan Taylor, and they had four children: Hiram, Jackson, Belinda, and Luther, Jr.[13]

Hiram Edson's great-grandfather, Abijah Edson, watched five of his sons march off to fight in the American Revolution.[14] One of them, Joseph, served under General George Washington and died during the bitter winter of 1777 at Valley Forge.[15] Another, 16-year-old potter James of Springfield, Massachusetts, (Hiram's grandfather), was a private in Captain Charles Colton's Company from 1776 to 1779 and then served in Colonel Greaton's Massachusetts Regiment for several months.[16] At the end of his term, he reenlisted in December 1779 and served in the artillery units of Captain Bolton, Captain Howes, and Major Ayers from that year until his honorable discharge in 1782.[17] James also fought against British General John Burgoyne at the Battle of Saratoga (1777) in New York's Hudson River valley and was present when Burgoyne was captured. This pivotal victory persuaded King Louis XVI of France to support the patriotic cause by sending money, men, ammunition, and ships to America.[18] In 1818, when James was 58, the United States government paid him a pension of eight dollars a month, in addition to back pay totaling $133.03, because it recognized that as an old man suffering from "Aswatick [asthmatic?] Complaint," he was living in "Reduced Circumstances and absolutely stands in need of the assistance of his Country for support, and that he has no other evidence now in his power of his said services."[19]

12Shoemaker, "Edson's Ancestors," p. 2.
13Shoemaker, "Edson's Ancestors," p. 2.
14Shoemaker, "Edson's Ancestors," p. 4.
15Shoemaker, "Edson's Ancestors," p. 4.
16Shoemaker, "Edson's Ancestors," p. 4.
17Shoemaker, "Edson's Ancestors," pp. 4-5.
18Shoemaker, "Edson's Ancestors," p. 4.
19James Edson's Revolutionary War Pension Claim #S.45369, Onondaga County Public Library, Syracuse, New York, cited by Shoemaker, "Edson's Ancestors," pp. 5-6.

The patriotic military service of Hiram Edson's grandfather, James Edson, as well as that of his great-uncles' service during the American Revolution, was no doubt a source of pride in the Edson family. Their distinguished contribution to the independence of the United States would have qualified Hiram for membership in the exclusive National Society of the Sons of the American Revolution (NSSAR). But once again, chronology was not kind to him: The NSSAR was founded in 1889, seven years after his death.[20]

Luther Edson's family

Sometime after 1790, Hiram's grandparents, James and Lovina Edson, moved from Massachusetts to upstate New York and acquired land in Ontario County that was once occupied by the Iroquois until they were defeated and exiled to Canada after the Sullivan-Clinton campaign in the American Revolution.[21] In 1786, the Commonwealth of Massachusetts received this upstate territory in exchange for relinquishing land between the Hudson River and the Berkshire Hills to New York. Massachusetts then sold these newly acquired properties to Oliver Phelps and Nathaniel Gorham, two land speculators, who then subdivided them into plots, which they sold to Revolutionary War veterans and their families beginning in 1790. The United States Census of 1810 shows James and Lovina Edson living in Farmington (later renamed Manchester) in Ontario County.[22]

When their son, Luther, was 32, America went to war against Great Britain yet again during the War of 1812 to end the British navy's practice of impressing American sailors on the high seas and

---

[20]The National Society of the Sons of the American Revolution was founded on April 30, 1889, and has its headquarters in Louisville, Kentucky. See their website at https://www.sar.org.
[21]Jessie Ravage, "Hiram Edson Site Report," July 1, 2005, p. 7, in "Hiram Edson Farm Master Plan" (n.d.); document in the author's possession.
[22]U.S. Census of 1810, cited by Ravage, "Hiram Edson Site Report," p. 7.

forcing them to serve aboard His Majesty's (George III) ships; setting up blockades along the East Coast; and refusing to abandon western frontier forts.[23] Luther Edson joined the United States Militia as a private during the War of 1812, and like his contemporary, the 20-year-old Joseph Bates, he was captured by the British and held as a prisoner of war for several months until a prisoner exchange could be arranged. On June 16, 1813, Luther was one of 73 officers and 229 privates traded for an equal number of British soldiers detained by the Americans.[24]

Shortly after his release, Luther purchased a farm on Lot 51 in the Town of Manchester. In 1825, he sold a portion of his land to Azel Throop, a family friend who later executed Luther's will. Ten years later, Esbon Blackmer purchased six acres from Luther. When Luther died on October 21, 1837, he left his remaining property to his wife, Susan, and after her death, the land was to be divided between their sons Luther Jr. and Jackson; their daughter Belinda was to receive $100 while Hiram would receive $250.[25] Luther's will indicates that he was a prosperous farmer. In addition to owning a farm wagon, a lumber wagon, a lumber sleigh, a cutter, a pair of horses, and an ox yoke, he had a fanning mill, a threshing machine, a patent plough, and a patent drag (harrow)—all worth about $64.50 (about $2,002.08 today[26]). Moreover, in one year, the farm produced six and a half tons of hay, 100 bushels of oats, 26 bushels of wheat, and 36 bushels of potatoes, besides many bushels of turnips, corn, and apples, most of which were stored in his three-bay, 30- by 43-foot barn made of

---

[23]Bailey, *American Pageant*, pp. 204-205.
[24]Shoemaker, "Edson's Ancestors," pp. 7-8, contains a list of 73 officers and 229 privates of the United States Militia exchanged on June 16, 1813, with Luther Edson's name among the privates.
[25]Wurst, et al., *Archaeological-Historical Investigation*, p. 26.
[26]The "Inflation Calculator" at https://www.officialdata.org>1837 indicates that an 1837 dollar would be worth about $31.04 in 2022.

hand-hewn lumber that had been pegged (rather than nailed) together.[27] Their house had curtains at the windows, carpeted floors, tables, chairs, a chest of drawers, brass candlesticks, a grandfather clock, and fireplaces in nearly every downstairs room.[28]

According to the 1830 Federal Census, Hiram already owned property in Attica over in Genesee County.[29] Then on March 14, 1832, he purchased 56 acres and 57 rods of land from Jacob and Mary Cost on Lot 58 for $788.98, close to his father's farm in Manchester, where he built a house and a large barn.[30] The 1840 Federal Census shows Hiram, his second wife, Esther, and three children living on this farm. But on September 26, 1844, Hiram sold sections of his land to his brother Jackson and his sister Belinda for one dollar. Since he fully expected to see Christ come in the clouds of glory in less than four weeks, he had no need for earthly property.[31]

Hiram Edson's family

Hiram Edson was born in Jefferson County, New York, on December 30, 1806.[32] Like Luther, he became a farmer; however, through no fault of his own, he was not nearly as well-to-do as his father. His 56 acres were covered by drumlins (low hills) left behind by retreating glaciers during the Wisconsin Era. They contained marsh and swamp-

---

[27]For these details in Luther Edson's will, see Ravage, "Hiram Edson Site Report," pp. 7-8.
[28]Ravage, "Hiram Edson Site Report," p. 8.
[29]Federal Census of 1830, cited by Ravage, "Hiram Edson Site Report," p. 3.
[30]Indenture (Deed) for March 14, 1832; document in the author's possession.
[31]Lou Ann Wurst, et al., *Archaeological-Historical Investigation*, p. 26, and Arthur W. Spalding, *Footprints of the Pioneers* (Washington, DC: Review and Herald Pub. Assn, 1947), p. 77. While Spalding claims that Hiram Edson bought this land in 1835, Shoemaker, a more meticulous researcher, proves that the sale took place in 1832. Furthermore, while Spalding lists the sale price as $750, the actual deed shows that Edson paid $788.98. Moreover, much of Spalding's evidence cited in *Footprints* (published in 1947) appears to be based on oral interviews and letters of inquiry decades after the fact rather than archival research. See, for example, Arthur W. Spalding to Mrs. W.F. Garlock of Port Gibson, New York, Nov. 10, 1947, and Mrs. W.F. Garlock to A.W. Spalding, Nov. 21, 1947, in A.W. Spalding Correspondence, Collection 10, Box 1, Folder 4, CAR, JWL, AU.
[32]Shoemaker, "Edson's Ancestors," p. 2.

land, gravel, sandy loam, and organic soil from decayed wood peat, which proved too wet for spring planting without artificial drainage. Consequently, due to the high water table, most of his property was unsuitable for agriculture. Hiram therefore chose to raise sheep instead. A few acres sported Arkport fine sandy loam that was suitable for growing vegetables.[33]

Hiram did not farm alone, however. Four days before his 24th birthday, he married 20-year-old Effa Chrisler on December 2, 1830, in a Methodist ceremony.[34] Together they reared three children: George W. (born October 17, 1831), Susan Frances (born March 10, 1833), and Belinda Adelaide (born March 14, 1835). Tragically, however, Effa died of unknown causes on May 21, 1839, at the age of 28.[35] As so often happened during the 19th century when a husband or wife with very young children lost a spouse, Hiram remarried within a matter of months because his children, ages eight, six, and four, needed a mother. On October 10, 1839, he wed the 23-year-old Esther Mariah Persons in another Methodist ceremony, with the Reverend Ralph Bennet officiating. To this union were born three children: Viah Ophelia (born June 5, 1841), who died at nearly 13 months on June 26, 1842; a second daughter they also named Viah Ophelia (born June 2, 1843); and Lucy Jane (born July 30, 1856), who was born after the family had moved to Oswego County, New York.[36]

Before he died in 1882, Hiram Edson was able to enjoy visits from his many grandchildren. On September 19, 1855, Susan Frances Edson married Chester R. Wells, and they had four children: Bertie,

---

[33]Lou Ann Wurst, "Public Archaeology Facility Report: Archaeological Investigations of the Hiram Edson Farm Site" (Binghamton, NY: State University of New York, Nov. 15, 1994), p. 13.

[34]Shoemaker, "Edson's Ancestors," p. 2.

[35]"Edson's Marriages," typed family genealogy, manuscript DF3006, No. 11, CAR, JWL, AU.

[36]"Edson's Marriages." While few parents who lose a child in death today would assign the deceased's name to the next child of the same gender, this practice was fairly common in previous centuries when child mortality rates often hovered between 25 and 50 percent in some parts of America and the world.

Frankie, Carrie, and George. Two years later, Belinda Adelaide Edson wed William W. Cobb on February 3, 1857; together they reared two boys, Douglas and Willie. After William died, Belinda married George W. Bennett on May 2, 1871, and they had a daughter, Effie. Five years earlier, on July 17, 1866, Viah Ophelia Edson had wed Washington J. Cross, and together they reared three children: Edson W., Viah M., and Gracie E. Cross. Likewise, after Lucy Jane Edson wed Charles E. Pickard on January 15, 1880, they had two children: Bertha M. and Harlow Edson Pickard.[37]

To accommodate his growing family at mealtimes, Hiram made a large, red drop-leaf table crafted from wild cherry trees he cut on his Port Byron farm. After sawing the lumber into boards and curing it, he nailed the boards together and polished them to a high sheen. At this table, James and Ellen White, O.R.L. Crosier, Joseph Bates, and other pioneers ate their meals while lodging at the Edson home. Two of Edson's granddaughters, Viah and Grace Cross, recalled sitting on Ellen White's lap in the kitchen while she regaled them with stories of her childhood.[38] On October 23, 1844, Edson, Crosier, and Hahn breakfasted at this table before praying for understanding as to why Christ had not come one day before. (See Chapter 5.) Years later, Edson's daughter, Viah Cross, inherited the table. She bequeathed it to her daughter, Grace Cross Crews, who took it with her to Houston, Texas.[39] If cherry wood could speak, what stories that table might tell about a certain charismatic farmer who experienced "presentments" on

---

[37]James R. Nix, "The Life and Work of Hiram Edson" (term paper for CH600-Problems in Church History, Seventh-day Adventist Theological Seminary, Andrews University, 1971), pp. 118-119.

[38]Everett Allen Calhoun, "Hiram Edson" (May 12, 1980), p. 1; handwritten manuscript in the author's possession.

[39]Calhoun, "Hiram Edson," p. 2. Edson's cherry table currently (2023) stands in the visitor center at the Hiram Edson Farm Site.

his Port Gibson farm and scribbled them down in the kitchen as he sat at that table. Chapter 3 describes some of Edson's unique experiences.

Chapter 3

Charismatic Farmer

Like most of his Ontario County neighbors and many of his
Adventist friends, Hiram Edson was a farmer. Like them, he
raised corn and perhaps other grain crops, cultivated a veg-
etable garden, kept one or two milk cows, raised sheep, and stored
tons of hay and grain in his barn. In some respects, he reflected the
milieu of the Burned-over District, with its emphasis on radical reforms, perfectionism, and emotional religion. Yet in other ways, Edson was unique, even among his Millerite and Sabbatarian Adventist
peers. Before discussing his experiences as recorded in his undated,
handwritten autobiographical manuscript, it will be instructive to
discover what Edson's contemporaries thought of him and to examine how his experience fit the religious climate of the 1840s.

Edson in the eyes of his friends

James and Ellen White and Stephen and Sarah Belden, née Harmon (Ellen's sister) all thought highly of Edson. Although Sabbath-
keeping Adventists did not follow the practice of choosing godpar-
ents for their children, in 1849 the Whites named their second son

James Edson White to show their love for their friend.[1] Likewise, when Stephen and Sarah Belden had a son in 1858, they named him Franklin Edson Belden, thus testifying to their esteem for Hiram.[2]

Throughout her 87 years of life, Ellen White wrote much about Edson. In a passage that referenced Joseph Bates, Stephen Pierce, and Hiram Edson, among others, she called these men "keen, noble, and true," who "searched for the truth as for hidden treasure," who "studied and prayed earnestly," often "late at night, and sometimes through the entire night," until "all the principal points of our faith were made clear to our mind, in harmony with the word of God."[3] She described Edson's insights regarding the sanctuary in heaven as "a line of truth extending...[to] the city of God," one of the "pillars of our faith," and one of the "fundamental principles that are based upon unquestionable authority."[4] After receiving a vision on August 24, 1850, she described Edson's peripatetic ministry: "I then saw Brother Edson, that he must gird on the whole armor and stand in readiness to go, for a journey was before him, and that souls needed help."[5]

Whenever Edson was present during one of her visions, he studiously copied down her utterances as she spoke them. White sometimes used Edson's notes to refresh her memory and write out her interpretation of those visions, often generating five or 10 testimonies (letters of counsel) to the individuals involved.[6] During 1850

[1]Gerald Wheeler, *James White: Innovator and Overcomer* (Hagerstown, MD: Review and Herald Pub. Assn., 2003), p. 66.

[2]Denis Fortin and Jerry Moon, eds., *The Ellen G. White Encyclopedia*, s.v. "Belden, Franklin Edson," pp. 308-311.

[3]Ellen G. White, *Special Testimony*, Series B, no. 2, pp. 56-57, cited by T. Housel Jemison, *A Prophet Among You* (Mountain View, CA: Pacific Press Pub. Assn., 1955), p. 209.

[4]Ellen G. White, *Selected Messages Book 1* (Washington, DC: Review and Herald Pub. Assn, 1958), pp. 206-208.

[5]Ellen G. White, Vision, Aug. 24, 1850, Record Book 1, p. 112, cited by Arthur L. White, *Ellen G. White: Messenger to the Remnant* (Washington, D.C.: Review and Herald Pub. Assn., 1969), p. 47. For further details concerning the context of White's counsel to Edson, see Chapter 7, "Ministerial Partners."

[6]Graeme Sharrock, "Testimonies," in Terrie Dopp Aamodt, Gary Land, and Ronald L. Numbers, eds.,

alone, Edson took notes on three visions Ellen received in Vermont, Massachusetts, and New York, proofread his notes, and offered her his records of these visions.[7] Probably in 1859, believing that Edson was hesitant to fulfill his proper role, White sent him the following testimony:

> I saw that bro Edson has not taken his place in the church, he has kept back for fear of getting out of his place. I saw that bro E. has good judgment in matters of the church, it needs cool, collected, patient, persevering men to judge in matters of the church, a hurried spirit must not decide in matters of the church. bro E. must take his place. Dear bro E I saw you must comfort the church, the Lord loves the church and you must try to help them up.[8]

In 1903, more than two decades after Edson's death, Ellen White, reminiscing about events in the 1840s, once again praised Edson as "keen, noble, and true." Edson had "fasted and prayed" with the Whites, Joseph Bates, Stephen Pierce, and others as they searched for biblical understanding. As a result, "great power came upon us.... The leading points of our faith as we hold them today were firmly established. Point after point was clearly defined, and all the brethren came into harmony."[9] Apparently not everyone was in harmony,

Ellen Harmon White, American Prophet (NY: Oxford University Press, 2014), p. 59.

[7]Fernand Fisel, "Three Early Visions of E.G. White Copied by Hiram Edson: An Evaluation," pp. 1-2, typed manuscript no. 011528, CAR, JWL, AU. The Sutton, Vermont, vision is found in Ellen White's *Early Writings*, (Washington, D.C.: Review and Herald Pub. Assn., 1945 [1882]), pp. 52-54, 57-58, and 61-62; the Dorchester, Massachusetts, vision is found in *Early Writings*, pp. 74-76; and the Oswego, New York, vision is found in *Early Writings*, pp. 59-60, 73.

[8]Ellen G. White, "Pennsylvania Vision for the Church in Central New York" (c. 1859), CAR, JWL, AU. As Jim Nix, in "Edson," p. 75, indicates, there is no specific date on this letter.

[9]Ellen G. White, "Establishing the Foundation of Our Faith," manuscript 135, Nov. 4, 1903, *Manuscript Releases*, vol. 3, p. 412.

however, for she added, "There were those who came in with strange doctrines, but we were never afraid to meet them."[10]

Elder A.E. Place was one of Edson's converts who began his public ministry in 1882. He later served as president of the New York Conference from 1895 to 1898. Place often visited with Edson toward the end of his life when Edson lived in Oswego. In 1890, recalling how Edson never left his house without prayer, Place called him "the mightiest man in prayer I have ever heard pray."[11] When the aged man visited the Place home and prayed for the family, Place declared that "it seemed that the angels were in the home all around him, and I was always thrilled and trembled greatly. And many times I prayed that I might pray as Elder Edson prayed."[12] Moreover, when Edson sang one of his (Edson's) favorite hymns, "Come, O My Soul to Calvary" in his "deep, sweet voice," it never failed to bring tears to Place's eyes.[13]

In 1924, J.N. Loughborough, whom Edson had trained as a young preacher in the 1850s, referenced Edson, Joseph Bates, and John Byington as "a trio of venerable pioneers, benign, vigorous leaders and counselors."[14] Decades later, William Spicer said that Edson was not only a good farmer, but also "a man of good Christian experience."[15]

Arthur W. Spalding, a member of the second Adventist generation who grew up hearing stories of the pioneers, described Edson as "stanch and true."[16] Among the many Adventist pioneers in the Northeast, Edson was the "foremost exponent" of the Advent mes-

[10]White, manuscript 135 (1903), p. 413.
[11]A.E. Place (1890), quoted in Robert N. Randall, "The Rome, N.Y. [SDA] Church, 1875-1890," p. 29, manuscript 007372 (1975), CAR, JWL, AU.
[12]A.E. Place, quoted in Randall, "Rome, N.Y. Church," p. 29.
[13]A.E. Place, quoted in Randall, "Rome, N.Y. Church," p. 29.
[14]J.N. Loughborough, *Review Anniversary Issue* 101, no. 38 (1924), p. 63.
[15]William A. Spicer, *Pioneer Days of the Advent Movement with Notes on Pioneer Workers and Early Experiences* (Washington, D.C.: Review and Herald Pub. Assn., 1941), pp. 218-219. Spicer based his views of Edson on earlier conversations he had with Phineas Z. Kinne, New York Conference president from 1871 to 1874, who had known Edson personally.
[16]A.W. Spalding, "The House of Refuge," *Review*, March 9, 1950, p. 11.

sage in New York State.[17] In addition, Spalding called him "one of the deep-thinking students who developed the Seventh-day Adventist faith." Moreover, he was "a self-sacrificing servant of God, who placed his possessions on the altar, and made possible the early enterprises of the work." Finally, Edson "labored in the evangelistic field with earnestness and ardor, and imparted his spirit to many a younger man."[18]

These many positive testimonies from those who knew Hiram personally indicate that they believed Edson was a zealous, pious, deep-thinking Christian man. In short, like many other Adventist pioneers, Edson fit the spiritual milieu of the times. What was that milieu?

The spiritual milieu of the 1840s

As discussed in greater detail in Chapter 1, during the Antebellum Era from the 1820s to the 1850s, the Burned-over District of upstate New York proved to be fertile soil for a number of religious movements, including Quakers, Shakers, Mormons, and Spiritualists. While these groups differed greatly in their doctrines and practices, they had in common leaders who claimed to communicate with the supernatural realm either directly, by talking with extraterrestrial beings, or indirectly, through receiving visions or spirit infilling. The Quakers, for example, trembled like a leaf, leaped for joy, shouted, and sang joyful songs when they felt themselves seized by the spirit. Mother Ann Lee, the Shaker leader who sometimes sweated blood through her pores, allegedly received revelations from God the Father and God the Mother. Claiming to be the reincarnation of Jesus Christ

---

[17]A.W. Spalding, *Captains of the Host* (Washington, D.C.: Review and Herald Pub. Assn., 1949), p. 175.
[18]A.W. Spalding, *Origin and History of Seventh-day Adventists* (Washington, D.C.: Review and Herald Pub. Assn., 1962), vol. 3, p. 216.

on earth, she taught her followers how to receive spirit guidance from individuals once mortal.[19] Likewise, Jemima Wilkinson asserted that Christ's Spirit occupied her body and would continue to do so for a thousand years.[20] At the age of 14, Joseph Smith began having visions in which a celestial being named Moroni led him to a nearby hill where he found some golden plates, a breastplate, the Urim and Thummim mentioned in the Old Testament, and two crystals set like spectacles in a silver bow. From these plates, Smith translated the Book of Mormon for his followers to read.[21] In like manner, the Fox sisters of Hydesville claimed to receive supernatural messages that they wrote down and shared with others.[22]

Many of these religious groups also faced skepticism and outright hostility from nonbelievers. In the Massachusetts Bay Colony, the Puritans had whipped, branded, fined, and even executed Quakers who broke their bans and returned from exile. Shakers were likewise scorned and not infrequently attacked for their belief in a female deity, their practice of celibacy, and their strange trance-like dances. On Seneca Lake, local prejudice toward Jemima Wilkinson finally persuaded her to substitute Sunday worship for that of the seventh-day Sabbath, which she believed to be biblical.[23] Likewise, public skepticism of the Fox sisters' claim that they could communicate with the spirits of the dead compelled them later in life to confess that it had all been a hoax created to amuse themselves and others.[24] In the case of the Mormons,

---

[19]For more details on Mother Ann Lee and the Shakers, see Richard W. Schwarz and Floyd Greenleaf, *Light Bearers: A History of the Seventh-day Adventist Church* (Nampa, ID: Pacific Press Pub. Assn., 2000), p. 15, and Clark, *1844*, vol. 1, pp. 331-352.

[20]For more details on Jemima Wilkinson, see Schwarz and Greenleaf, *Light Bearers*, pp. 14-15, and Clark, *1844*, vol. 1, p. 88.

[21]For more details on Joseph Smith and the Mormons, see Schwarz and Greenleaf, *Light Bearers*, pp. 15-16, and Clark, *1844*, vol. 1, pp. 84-181.

[22]For more details on the Fox sisters and Spiritualism, see Schwarz and Greenleaf, *Light Bearers*, pp. 16-17, and Clark, *1844*, vol. 1, pp. 359-374.

[23]Schwarz and Greenleaf, *Light Bearers*, pp. 15-16.

[24]Clark, *1844*, vol. 1, p. 352.

public hostility hounded them wherever they settled—in Kirtland, Ohio; Zion City, Missouri; and Nauvoo, Illinois. That hostility turned deadly on June 27, 1844, when Joseph Smith and his brother Hyrum were murdered by a lynch mob in Carthage, Illinois.[25]

Although differing from the foregoing religious groups in some respects, many Millerites and post-1844 Sabbatarian Adventists believed that God communicated with human beings through supernatural manifestations such as visions and dreams. In 1842 William Foy, an African American Baptist studying for the Episcopal ministry in Boston, received three visions, two of which he related to large crowds.[26] Two years later, following the Great Disappointment of October 22, 1844, Hazen Foss of Poland, Maine, likewise received a vision, but, fearing public opposition, he refused to relate it.[27] In nearby Portland, Maine, Ellen Harmon, who was acquainted with both Foy and Foss, had her first vision in December of 1844.[28] At least four other women in and around Portland also professed to have received visions in the 1840s: Dorinda Baker, Emily Clemons, Mary Hamlin, and Phoebe Knapp. Moreover, across the United States, some 55 American men and women claimed to have the prophetic gift, while an additional 200 individuals professed to be seers of future events.[29] It is evident, therefore, that the American spiritual landscape was replete with supernatural manifestations, especially in the 1830s and 1840s. Keeping this larger context in mind makes it easier to understand Edson's experiences in upstate New York between 1839 and 1848.

---

[25]Schwarz and Greenleaf, *Light Bearers*, p. 16, and Clark, *1844*, vol. 1, pp. 159-172.
[26]Clark, *1844*, vol. 1, pp. 62.
[27]Schwarz and Greenleaf, *Light Bearers*, p. 62.
[28]Schwarz and Greenleaf, *Light Bearers*, pp. 62-63.
[29]Michael Campbell, "Dreams and Visions in American Religious History," in Alberto Timm and Dwain Esmond, eds., *The Gift of Prophecy in Scripture and History* (Silver Spring, MD: Review and Herald Pub. Assn., 2015), pp. 232, 240.

Hiram Edson's experiences

Sometime around 1839, Edson was chosen as a steward in the Port Gibson Methodist Episcopal Church about two and a half miles from his house. As such, he was responsible for the judicious use of the funds, literature, and other materials donated by his congregation. He was also widely respected as an earnest, soul-winning layman. Then in 1843, during a three-week series of Millerite revival meetings, possibly led by Thomas F. Barry in Rochester, he accepted the second advent message.[30] When the Methodist Episcopal denomination opposed the preaching of Christ's imminent advent and began expelling members who accepted it, Hiram and Esther began holding private meetings in their home. Occasionally at these spirited gatherings, revivals occurred; at one meeting, 13 attendees experienced conversion.[31]

Although Edson's autobiographical manuscript mentions no dates, internal evidence indicates that most if not all of his supernatural encounters probably occurred in 1843 or 1844 at the height of the Millerite movement. Yet Edson never claimed to have received a vision or dream. According to his granddaughter, Viah May Cross, Hiram referred to these experiences as "presentments." In contrast to the term *presentiment*, which implies a foreboding or feeling that something unfortunate or evil is about to happen, he chose to use the term *presentment*, implying that these supernatural experiences presented to his mind new understandings, often through visual images

---

[30]Nix, "Edson," pp. 4-6.

[31]LeRoy Edwin Froom, *The Prophetic Faith of Our Fathers*, vol. 4 (Hagerstown, MD: Review and Herald Pub. Assn., 1982 [1954]), pp. 889-890. William Miller, Joshua V. Himes, Charles Fitch, and Thomas Barry held several weeks of revivals in Rochester in the fall and winter of 1843. The entire Loofborough family attended these meetings, and it is likely that Hiram Edson and some of his Methodist Episcopal friends from Port Gibson did as well. For further details, see Strayer, *Loughborough*, pp. 45-50 and Nix, "Edson," pp. 5-7.

of events he anticipated would soon come to pass.[32] What happened during these presentments?

One day as Hiram Edson, alone in his barn, knelt to pray near the horse stalls, "a personage" whom he believed to be Jesus stood above him. Edson tried to rise, but fell to his knees once again. While prostrate on the floor, he witnessed a scene flash before his eyes. He saw a minister delivering a bland discourse, then calling for those who wanted special prayer to stand and the entire congregation leaped to their feet. When this scene faded, Edson rose to his feet and walked to the house. Shortly thereafter, while his family attended meetings at their church, he believed that this presentment was fulfilled when, after the preacher's boring sermon and call for special prayer, a three-week revival followed the prayer service, and members began holding prayer and song services in their homes as their neighbors sat on nearby hillsides listening to them sing.[33]

On another occasion, similar to Joseph Smith's alleged experience with the angel Moroni, Edson said he saw "a shadowy form in human shape." He then heard what he took to be an angel's voice telling him to go talk with his neighbor about his eternal salvation, which he did.[34]

Another time, while relaxing by his fireplace, Edson heard an audible voice telling him to go and heal a deathly ill Methodist friend. When he refused to go, thinking that this presentment came from the devil, the floor suddenly seemed to drop from under him and he saw

[32]Viah Cross, "Hiram Edson's Experience," p. 1, affidavit as related to P.Z. Kinne (no original date), typed manuscript, Nov. 11, 2002, CAR, JWL, AU. F.W. Bartle also stated that Edson called these experiences "presentments" in a letter to W.A. Spicer, Sept. 4, 1935, CAR, JWL, AU.

[33]Cross, "Hiram Edson's Experience," p. 1.

[34]Hiram Edson, handwritten autobiographical manuscript (undated), VT000272, CAR, JWL, AU; also available in typed format in George Knight, comp. and ed., *1844 and the Rise of Sabbatarian Adventism: Reproductions of Original Historical Documents* (Hagerstown, MD: Review and Herald Pub. Assn., 1994), pp. 123-126.

himself falling toward hell. Crying out for God to save him, he heard the voice once again saying, "Go heal thy sick neighbor." Making his way to the man's home late that night, Edson entered and found his way to the man by the light of a candle. Stumbling up the stairway to the sick man's bedroom, he placed his hands upon the man's head and cried, "Brother, the Lord Jesus make you whole." Immediately, the man opened his eyes, threw back the covers, and jumped out of bed, leaping around the room and praising God. As the rest of the family rushed upstairs to ascertain the cause of the commotion, Edson prayed for them, and some of them experienced conversion.

The next day, as this healed man was outside chopping wood, his physician rode by on his horse and expressed amazement at the man's miraculous recovery: "I expected to find you dead!" The man replied, "I am a well man. The Lord has healed me." Furthermore, a great revival occurred in the church because of this healing.[35] Eighty were converted at one meeting and between 300 and 400 individuals experienced conversion within a few years' time.[36]

According to Edson's own account, he observed "many incidents" of healing in response to the prayers of believers. For example, while attending a Sabbath Conference in David Arnold's barn at Volney, New York, in August of 1848, Edson and several other men prayed for Ellen White's recovery from illness, and she revived. "I also learned an additional lesson," he declared, "namely, that God was ready and willing to hear and answer prayer for the sick, and to stretch forth his hand to heal and raise them up, and restore them to health. Since that time, I have shared in, and witnessed many incidents of like character."[37]

---

[35]Cross, "Hiram Edson's Experience," pp. 2-3.
[36]C. Mervyn Maxwell, *Tell It to the World: The Story of Seventh-day Adventists* (Mountain View, CA: Pacific Press Pub. Assn., 1976), p. 48.
[37]Hiram Edson, handwritten autobiographical manuscript, VT000272, CAR, JWL, AU; also available in Knight, *1844 and the Rise of Sabbatarian Adventism*, p. 123.

Indeed, faith healings, as they were often called, were a common occurrence in the Millerite and early Sabbatarian Adventist movement. J.N. Loughborough's uncle, Alfred Norton, racked with fever and chills, experienced instant healing after two Advent Christian ministers prayed for him. Harvey Cottrell, another Advent Christian suffering from malaria, also experienced instant restoration to full health after Sabbatarian Adventists placed their hands upon him and prayed for him. The *Review* compositor, Oswald Stowell, who was dying of pleurisy, gained immediate healing after James and Ellen White prayed for him. Those who experienced faith healings included Frances Howland, William Hyde, Clarissa Bonfoey, Anna White, and Lumen Masten, among others. According to Loughborough, among the Advent band in Rochester during 1852, nearly every case of illness brought before the Lord in prayer resulted in healing.[38]

As zealous Christians, Hiram and Esther felt a burden to bring their neighbors to Christ. This is one explanation for their eagerness to host evening prayer, praise, and song services in their home. On one such occasion, a wagonload of people traveled five miles to join the Edsons. While they sang together, the Holy Spirit came down with such power that many were convicted of their sins and requested prayers as, on their knees, they pleaded with God for pardon. Some among them were "so deeply convicted" that they fell prostrate on the floor, "slain by the power of God" and uttering "agonizing cries and pleading for mercy."[39] While one couple with a child, upset by such emotional manifestations, left and walked home, they returned the

---

[38]For further details on these faith healings, see Strayer, *Loughborough*, pp. 68-69; J.N. Loughborough, quoted in Ellen G. White Estate, *A Critique of the Book Prophetess of Health* (Washington, D.C.: Ellen G. White Estate, 1976), p. 43; and Richard E. Kuykendall, *The Dreamer and the Two Men She Loved* (n.p.: Trafford Publishing, 2021), p. 8.

[39]Hiram Edson, handwritten autobiographical manuscript, CAR, JWL, AU; also available in typed format in Ronald L. Numbers and Jonathan M. Butler, eds., *The Disappointed: Millerism and Millenarianism in the Nineteenth Century* (Bloomington, IN: Indiana University Press, 1987), pp. 214-215.

following evening and experienced conversion.[40]

Speaking in tongues

Not all of Edson's presentments, however, were delivered in plain English. Occasionally, as happened on the Day of Pentecost (recorded in Acts 2), he and others experienced glossolalia or speaking in unknown tongues. In 1849 when he, the Whites, the Beldens, and a certain Brother Ralph were kneeling in prayer in the Harris home in Centerport, New York, seeking divine guidance regarding Samuel Rhode's future, Ralph asked God to pour out His Spirit upon them. Immediately, Ralph began speaking in an unknown language. He interpreted what he had uttered as directions from God for Edson and himself to go to the Adirondacks, find Rhodes, and appeal to him to return to active ministry. When the two men found Rhodes, Ralph once again broke into glossolalia and assured his downcast friend that God extended hope, mercy, and forgiveness for him and that he should return with them. Rhodes did so, and within weeks, his preaching led to the conversion of some 40 souls.[41]

Likewise, James White, writing to an unknown correspondent, related an experience that happened to Ezra L.H. Chamberlain, a painter and former Millerite living in Middletown, Connecticut. While those gathered in a meeting debated regarding the proper time to observe the Sabbath, Chamberlain, "filled with power," began speaking

---

[40]Hiram Edson, handwritten autobiographical manuscript, CAR, JWL, AU; also available in typed format in Kinne, "Experience," pp. 3-4.

[41]D.E. Robinson, "The Gift of Tongues in Early Adventist History" (n.d.), pp. 1-4, manuscript 032461, CAR, JWL, AU. Samuel W. Rhodes (1813-1883) had been an active Millerite preacher. But after the Great Disappointment, he became deeply depressed and sought isolation from society by retreating to the Adirondack Mountains to fish and hunt. Largely due to Edson's influence, he converted to Sabbatarian Adventism and began preaching. In 1850 he designed a *Pictorial Illustration of the Visions of Daniel and John,* which Ellen White endorsed as an important teaching tool for Adventist evangelists. See P. Gerard Damsteegt, *Foundations of the Seventh-day Adventist Message and Mission* (Grand Rapids, MI: William B. Eerdmans Publishing Company, 1977), p. 193.

in an unknown tongue, which another person interpreted as "Bring me the chalk!" Drawing a large clock face on the wooden floor, he told the group that God desired them to observe His Sabbath from six o'clock Friday evening to six o'clock Saturday evening, just as Joseph Bates recommended. James White concluded his letter by saying, "I should have more faith in his [Bates'] opinion than any other man's."[42]

Facing violent reactions

So how did the citizens of Ontario and Wayne counties react when the word got out that Edson was experiencing presentments and that some Millerites and Sabbatarian Adventists had been instantly healed by prayer while others were speaking in unknown tongues? As might be expected, reactions were mixed: Most people simply ignored these phenomena, several saw them as divinely inspired and experienced conversion as a result, while a handful reacted violently. During one of Hiram and Esther's many cottage meetings in 1844, a gang of 40 men, intent on tarring and feathering every Millerite leader they could lay their hands on, stormed into the house. Grabbing one Adventist man, they dragged him toward the door. When another believer tried to intervene, one member of the mob snatched a griddle iron from the wood stove and hit him hard above the eye, cutting a bloody gash in his forehead and knocking him nearly unconscious to the ground. Edson stepped between the two men and shouted, "I won't give up my faith [even] if you cut me into inch pieces and feed my flesh to the foxes of the desert and the fowels [*sic*] of the air." Surprisingly, Hiram's biblical allusions to Isaiah 13:21 and 1 Samuel 17:44 calmed the angry mob, and one by one, they backed up

---

[42]James White to "My Dear Brother," July 2, 1848, typed manuscript, CAR, JWL, AU. See also Fortin and Moon, eds., *Ellen G. White Encyclopedia*, s.v. "Chamberlain, Ezra L.H.," pp. 340-341.

toward the door and left the premises.[43] However, the Edsons alleg-edly received death threats from hostile neighbors in 1847 who had probably read (and believed) Joseph Marsh's slanderous charges of Hiram's brutal whipping of his son the year before. Following Ellen White's advice, the Edsons moved out of the area and temporarily rented a farm near Centerport.[44]

Physical violence morphed into verbal invective when, in the February 24, 1847, issue of the Advent Christian newspaper *The Voice of Truth and Glad Tidings*, the editor, Joseph Marsh, sought revenge against Edson and Crosier, alleging that they had accused him of "get-ting rich in this world's goods" rather than sacrificing for the Advent cause. In his editorial, Marsh accused Edson of taking his 15-year-old son George out into the woods, removing his coat, tying his hands, and whipping him with six beech whips "so unmercifully that by the cries of murder of the son, the neighbors were called to his relief." Furthermore, Marsh stated that for this offence, Edson had been ar-rested by the sheriff, tried before a jury, found guilty, and fined $15 for "his barbarity."[45] Despite the title of his newspaper, *The Voice of Truth*, no evidence has ever been found to support Marsh's allega-tions that Edson was arrested, tried, and fined for beating George.[46]

One suspects, however, that given the prevalence of whipping disobedient children, students, sailors, and others throughout the 19th century (and well into the 1920s at some Adventist boarding

---

[43]Viah Ophelia Cross to O.A. Olsen, Sept. 14, 1913, manuscript VT000274, CAR, JWL, AU. This inci-dent, however, occurred when Viah was about a year old, so one must assume others told her about it years later.

[44]These slanderous charges are found in Joseph Marsh, *The Voice of Truth and Glad Tidings*, Feb. 24, 1847, p. 1.

[45]Joseph Marsh, "Greatly Mistaken," *The Voice of Truth and Glad Tidings*, Feb. 24, 1847, p. 1.

[46]In response to Robert Allen's 1997 inquiry into this matter, Pauline Mitzewich, the Deputy Town Clerk of Manchester, New York, informed him that after searching the docket books and one justice book covering the 1840s, "we cannot find anything on your request for information regarding Hiram Edson and the child abuse case against him." See Pauline Mitzewich to Robert Allen, Nov. 17, 1997; letter in the author's possession.

schools), it was not Edson's alleged beating of his son that upset Marsh.[47] Instead, he charged Edson with "receiving a revelation from God" to punish George. Furthermore, he accused him of teaching "the wild delusions of the doctrine of the shut door and its kindred absurdities." In short, Marsh was using his newspaper to mock Edson's claim to receiving divinely inspired presentments, including his October 23, 1844, insights regarding the heavenly sanctuary with its open and shut doors. (See Chapter 4.) Therefore, while on the one hand, Marsh's accusation that Edson had been arrested and fined for severely beating his son appears to be pure gossip, on the other hand, Marsh's statement that Edson followed a divine order in doing so probably reflects widespread knowledge and, no doubt, strong disapproval of Edson's claim to receive celestial revelations.[48]

Understanding the hostile atmosphere that Hiram and Esther faced in Port Gibson places in a broader perspective a strongly worded testimony that Ellen White sent them in 1850:

I saw that Brother and Sister Edson would have to move soon from the place where they now live, for there was enmity enough in the hearts of the wicked there to take their lives, for they hated them for the truths they believed and have advocated for it condemned them, and a number of times the

---

[47]As a boy, John Andrews and his friend, a certain Mr. Davis, were threatened with a whipping by an angry anti-Millerite mob. In 1843, James White and two of his Adventist friends were horsewhipped by some rowdies in Maine. Throughout the 19th century, British and American sailors who defied their captains' orders were tied to the mast and beaten with the cat o' nine tails. In the late 1890s, the author's grandfather, Charles Willis White, was taken to the barn by his Adventist father and horsewhipped so severely that the scars on his back were still visible in the 1960s. At Union Springs Academy in upstate New York, whippings for delinquent boys were a routine punishment in the 1920s. For further details about these incidents, see Norma J. Collins, *Heartwarming Stories of Adventist Pioneers*, Book 1 (Hagerstown, MD: Review and Herald Pub. Assn., 2005), p. 150; Kuykendall, *Dreamer*, p. 9; and Brian E. Strayer, *Where the Pine Trees Softly Whisper: The History of Union Springs Academy* (Union Springs, NY: Union Springs Academy Alumni Association, 1993), pp. 338-341.
[48]See Fernand Fisel, "Edson's Cornfield 'Vision': Frisson or Figment?" *Adventist Currents* (July 1983), p. 27.

wicked had it in their hearts to take the lives of Brother and Sister Edson; but God had defeated the wicked and guarded their lives.[49]

Although Ellen White occasionally employed hyperbolic prose to emphasize the points she was making, given the evidence at hand, it appears that the wisest course for the Edsons under the circumstances was to leave Port Gibson. Heeding her advice, they sold their farm and moved farther east, first to Oswego in 1850, and then to Port Byron on the Erie Canal in 1852. Before this move, however, the family faced the greatest crisis of their newfound faith on October 23, 1844.

---

[49]Ellen G. White, manuscript no. 7, Aug. 24, 1850, *Manuscript Releases*, vol. 6, p. 251.

Chapter 4

Disappointed Millerite

Williiam Miller never set a specific date for Christ's second coming. Instead, he estimated that, according to his calculations, the Second Advent would occur sometime between the spring of 1843 and the spring of 1844. Consequently, when this period passed uneventfully, his followers experienced their first and second disappointments. Then at the Exeter, New Hampshire, camp meeting in mid-August 1844, Samuel Sheffield Snow suggested that, based upon the Karaite Jewish calculation for the Day of Atonement in 1844, Christ's coming would occur on October 22. This so-called "seventh-month movement"[1] spread like wildfire. Within weeks, William Miller, Joshua V. Himes, Charles Fitch, Josiah Litch, and most of the other Millerite preachers, writers, and agents had accepted it. So did between 50,000 and 100,000 people across the United States.[2] With Christ's return only two months away, believers everywhere began greeting one another with the exclamation, "The Lord is coming!"[3]

As Tuesday, October 22, neared, many shopkeepers and mer-

[1]Named after the tenth day of the seventh month, *Tishri*, in the Karaite Jewish Calendar, which Snow believed corresponded with Oct. 22, 1844, in the Gregorian Calendar.
[2]For a brief summary of the Millerite movement, see Schwarz and Greenleaf, *Light Bearers,* pp. 29-49. For a more extensive treatment, see George Knight, *Millennial Fever and the End of the World* (Boise, ID: Pacific Press Pub. Assn., 1993).
[3]Mary B. Smith to A.W. Spalding, n.d., Arthur W. Spalding Correspondence, Collection 10, Box 1, Folder 1a, CAR, JWL, AU.

chants gave away their merchandise and closed their doors, while some farmers left their crops in the field unharvested. Workers resigned from their jobs, debtors paid their debts, sinners confessed their sins.[4] Attendance books for urban and country schools reveal that hundreds of students skipped classes on Tuesday and Wednesday, expecting never to return to their blue-back spelling books and their McGuffey Readers. Believers gathered in small groups in homes, churches, and halls to sing, pray, and encourage one another.[5] In New York City, Lydia Maria Child, at the time America's most famous female writer, passed shops in the Bowery advertising "MUSLIN FOR ASCENSION ROBES!" After receiving letters from Millerites urging her to "make haste to escape from the wrath that is impending over all unbelievers," she wrote, "I feel sincerely grateful to these kind, well-meaning persons for their anxiety to save me." Moreover, she expressed regret that so many sincere Adventists "have attracted the attention of a portion of our population, who delight to molest them, though it is more from mirth than malice. All sincere convictions should be treated respectfully. Neither ridicule nor violence can overcome delusions of this sort."[6] In Port Gibson, Edson invited his neighbors to attend a final meeting on October 22, telling them, "I never expect to see you again, for the Lord is to come to-day."[7]

Reactions to the Great Disappointment

The Lord did not return to earth on that day, however, leaving thousands of disheartened Adventists to endure yet a third disap-

---

[4]Schwarz and Greenleaf, *Light Bearers*, p. 49.
[5]Wurst, et al., *Archaeological-Historical Investigations*, p. 31.
[6]Lydia Maria Child, Letter XXVI, October 21, 1844, in *Letters from New York* (New York: C.S. Francis, 1846), pp. 235-240.
[7]Hiram Edson, quoted by J.N. Loughborough to R.M. Kelley, Dec. 13, 1910, WDF3006, manuscript 8, CAR, JWL, AU.

pointment, often called the Great Disappointment. Their words reveal not only that they were sorry they had been mistaken about the date, but they also show the depths of their emotional, psychological, and even physiological reactions at not seeing their Savior in the clouds of glory. For example, on October 24, 1844, Josiah Litch wrote to William Miller: "It is a cloudy and dark day here—the sheep [Advent believers] are scattered—and the Lord has not come yet."[8]

For some disappointed saints, the failure of Christ to appear brought humiliation from their friends and neighbors. Luther Boutelle, a Millerite lecturer, stated:

The 22nd of October passed, making unspeakably sad the faithful and longing ones.... Everyone felt lonely with hardly a desire to speak to anyone. Still in the cold world! No deliverance—the Lord [had] not come! No words can express the feelings of disappointment of a true Adventist then. Those only who experienced it can enter into the subject as it was. It was a humiliating thing, and we all felt it alike.[9]

Millerite circulation agent Joseph Bates agreed that

the effect of this disappointment can be realized only by those who experienced it.... Hope sunk and courage died within them.... With these taunts [of unbelievers shouting, "I thought you were going up yesterday!"] thrown at me, if the earth could have opened and swallowed me up, it would have

---

[8]Josiah Litch to William Miller, Oct. 24, 1844, quoted in Knight, *Millennial Fever*, p. 218.
[9]Luther Boutelle, *Life and Religious Experience*, pp. 67-68, quoted in Francis D. Nichol, *The Midnight Cry* (Takoma Park, MD: Review and Herald Pub. Assn., 1945), pp. 248-249.

been sweetness compared to the distress I felt.[10]

Many of the disappointed Millerites who later became Sabbatarian Adventists experienced not only humiliation and sadness but also deep depression and grief. More than half a century later, Washington Morse recalled:

> But that day came and passed, and the darkness of another night closed in upon the world. But with the darkness came a pang of disappointment to the Advent believers that can find a parallel only in the sorrow of the disciples after the crucifixion of their Lord.... When Elder Himes visited Waterbury, Vt., a short time after the passing of the time, and stated that the brethren should prepare for another cold winter, my feelings were almost uncontrollable. I left the place of meeting and wept like a child.[11]

James White expressed his grief in words that mirrored Morse's. When Himes visited Portland, Maine, "and stated that the brethren should prepare for another cold winter, my feelings were almost uncontrollable. I left the place of meeting and wept like a child."[12]

In addition to the mental, emotional, and psychological shock of the Great Disappointment, a few believers suffered physiologically. Writing in *The Day-Star* a year later, Henry Emmons related his experience:

---

[10]Joseph Bates, quoted in Gary Land, ed., *Adventism in America* (Grand Rapids, MI: William B. Eerdmans, 1986), p. 30; bracketed material mine.

[11]Washington Morse, Letter to *Review*, May 7, 1901, p. 291.

[12]James White, *Life Incidents, in Connection with the Great Advent Movement, as Illustrated by the Three Angels of Revelation XIV* (Battle Creek, MI: Steam Press of the Seventh-day Adventist Pub. Assn., 1868), p. 182.

I waited all Tuesday [October 22] and dear Jesus did not come;—I waited all forenoon of Wednesday, and was [as] well in body as ever I was, but after 12 o'clock I began to feel faint, and before dark I needed some one to help me up to my [bed] chamber, as my natural strength was leaving me very fast, and I lay prostrate for two days without any pain—sick with disappointment.[13]

Hiram Edson's reaction

As the sun rose over the Edson farm on October 23, Hiram and Esther, perhaps still grieving the premature death of their first baby two years earlier, faced a crisis of faith. Had they believed a lie?[14] In a handwritten document, Edson described the doubt and grief he felt in 1844:

Our fondest hopes and expectations were blasted, and such a spirit of weeping came over us as I never experienced before. It seemed that the loss of all earthly friends could have been no comparison. We wept, and wept, till the day dawn.—I mused in my own heart, saying, My advent experience has been the richest and brightest of all my christian [sic] experience. If this had proved a failure, what was the rest of my christian [sic] experience worth? Has the Bible proved a failure? Is there no God—no heaven—no golden home city—no paradise? Is all this but a cunningly devised fable? Is there no reality to our fondest hopes and expectations of these things? And thus we had something to grieve and weep over, if all

---

[13]Henry Emmons, *Day-Star*, Oct. 25, 1845, p. 6; bracketed material mine.
[14]Burt, *Adventist Pioneer Places*, p. 132.

our fond hopes were lost. And as I said, we wept till the day dawn.[15]

Subsequently, he saw this heartrending experience as a direct fulfillment of the prophecy of Revelation 10:8-10 in which an angel handed the apostle John a little book, instructing him to eat it. After doing so, John found the book sweet in his mouth but bitter in his belly. In like manner, the seventh-month movement had engendered sweet expectations of Christ's imminent return, but His failure to do so on October 22 had brought bitterness to those waiting for Him.[16]

Subsequent results

Following the Great Disappointment, some individuals manipulated Bible prophecies and set new dates for the second coming of Christ. One scholar estimates that there were at least 20 attempts to set dates advanced for the Second Advent.[17] Other groups, known as "spiritualizers," suggested that Christ actually had come on October 22, but in the form of an invisible spirit who now dwelt in the soul of each believer.[18] As mentioned in Chapter 1, following the Great Disappointment, some 200 Millerite Adventists joined Shaker celibate communities across New England, the Mid-Atlantic, and the Midwest. The Shakers, too, believed in an invisible, spiritualized advent, and this probably brought some comfort to those who had wept at not witnessing Christ's literal return to earth. However, across upstate New York, some newspaper editors between 1850 and 1900 contin-

---

[15]Edson, handwritten autobiographical manuscript, available in typewritten form in Knight, *William Miller*, p. 185.

[16]Damsteegt, *Foundations*, p. 105.

[17]Jon Paulien, *What the Bible Says About the End-Time* (Hagerstown, MD: Review and Herald Pub. Assn., 1994), p. 20.

[18]Brian C. Wilson, *Dr. John Harvey Kellogg and the Religion of Biologic Living* (Bloomington and Indianapolis: Indiana University Press, 2014), pp. 22-23.

ued to label Sabbatarian Adventists as "Millerites," thus stigmatizing future Seventh-day Adventists for the mistakes of their 1844 Advent predecessors.[19]

But most Millerites—and certainly all those who eventually became Sabbatarian Adventists—firmly rejected this spiritualized view because of its tendency toward antinomian behavior, convincing some that they were inherently sinless and did not need to obey God's law.[20] Edson also rejected the spiritualizers' view of Christ's secret coming. Yet as he, Esther, and several close friends ate breakfast together on the morning of October 23, they did not have a clue as to why Jesus had not appeared in the clouds of glory as they had expected Him to the day before. Edson found that clue in a cornfield.

Cornfield Cleopas

Luke 24 tells the story of two of Christ's disciples, Cleopas and his unnamed friend, who were returning to their home in Emmaus following the crucifixion of Jesus when the risen Christ appeared beside them, although they did not recognize Him. After listening to them express their disappointment at His death and subsequent disappearance from the tomb, Christ revealed to them all that the law and the prophets had predicted about His death and resurrection. During supper at the men's home that evening, as Jesus was dividing the bread among them, they saw the nail scars in His hands and knew who He was, but He disappeared. Forgetting their supper, they returned to Jerusalem to share the good news of a resurrected Savior with the other disciples. As they ran, one of them said to the other, "When he talked with us along the road and explained the Scriptures

---

[19]Wurst, et al., *Archaeological-Historical Investigations*, p. 33.
[20]Wilson, *Dr. John Harvey Kellogg*, p. 23.

to us, didn't it warm our hearts?" (Luke 24:32, CEV). Suddenly, they experienced a paradigm shift in their understanding of the Old Testament prophecies concerning Christ that they had read many times before.

Drawing a modern parallel to that experience, one author emphasized that, just as Cleopas and his friend expected Christ to come as a king and conqueror of the Romans and not as a crucified Savior on a cross of shame, so Edson and his Millerite friends expected Him to come in glory to cleanse the earth by fire on October 22, 1844. And just as He opened those two disciples' eyes to the true meaning of the Old Testament Scriptures relating to His mission on earth, His death at Calvary, and His resurrection, so He opened Edson's and Crosier's eyes to the Scriptures regarding His ministry in the Most Holy Place of the heavenly sanctuary beginning on October 22, 1844. In both cases, sincere seekers after truth received new light that led to a major shift in their understanding.[21]

Yet while Cleopas and his companion trod a well-worn road to share this new paradigm, Edson and Crosier cut through a cornfield to encourage their disappointed friends on October 23, 1844.[22] Why? Most writers have assumed that, in light of the verbal and physical abuse many Millerites had endured, the two men ducked across the field to avoid facing hostile neighbors. While this explanation might apply to the 24-year-old Crosier, it does not fit the profile of 38-year-old Edson, who, as the previous chapters have shown, exhibited boldness and courage rather than cowardice and fear in the face of physical threats. Edson may have felt embarrassed at not knowing how to ex-

---

[21]Clark Allan Floyd, "Who Was Cleopas?" *Our Firm Foundation*, Sept. 2013, pp. 4-6.
[22]Although Hiram Edson, like the Gospel writer Luke, never mentioned the name of his cornfield companion, the consensus among Adventist historians and scholars from J.N. Loughborough in 1892 to the present has been that it was probably his close friend and houseguest Owen R.L. Crosier.

plain to his neighbors why he had not ascended to heaven the previous day, but it is unlikely that he was afraid of them. One explanation would be simple geometry: Since country roads stretched for miles with few intersections, taking a shortcut through a field saved time. Another explanation would be meteorological: If it had rained recently, the dirt roads would have been quagmires deeply rutted with mud, whereas the cornfields, often planted with squash and pumpkins (as Native Americans had taught the early settlers), would have absorbed much of that rainfall and thus provided firmer ground for walking. In the 19th century, people sometimes cut across fields when heavy rainstorms and blizzards made the dirt roads impassable.[23]

Edson's autobiographical manuscript

While reading Edson's handwritten manuscript is obviously of the utmost importance in understanding his view of what happened on October 23, this document has raised some questions among church historians. It is generally acknowledged that Edson wrote it, but since it is not dated, scholars are unsure as to when it was actually written: in 1844, in the mid-1850s, during the 1860s, or late in his life? Obviously, a document written in 1844 would be more reliable than one penned years later when Edson's memory had faded.

Originally more than 200 pages long, the document included autobiographical material as well as prophetic speculation concerning the future of England.[24] When Edson took it to the press in Battle Creek, requesting that it be published, the reading committee (including James White, J.N. Loughborough, Uriah Smith, and J.N. Andrews) agreed to print the autobiographical section but refused to

---

[23]For accounts of the bad roads that Adventist pioneers faced even in the second half of the 19th century, see *Review*, Feb. 12, 1862, p. 85; May 15, 1879, p. 159; April 18, 1882, p. 253; and Feb. 26, 1884, p. 140.
[24]Herbert M. Kelley to L.E. Froom, July 1, 1936, manuscript VT000273, no. 4, CAR, JWL, AU.

publish the theological parts, viewing them as "a little too visionary [speculative]." Edson told Andrews, "But I have got some light [from God]." Andrews allegedly replied, "Then let me spoil your light." Edson told them either to publish it all or publish nothing. The Review published none of it.[25]

Subsequently, Edson gave the manuscript to Abby Lindsay, who edited it nine times, allegedly keeping a portion of it (about 33 pages), which she later shared with Arthur W. Spalding in June 1907.[26] Three years later he quoted extensively from it in an article in the *Youth's Instructor*.[27] The rest of the manuscript was entrusted to John E. Place for safekeeping.[28] After Edson's death, Place presumably returned it to Edson's daughter, Viah Ophelia Cross, who took it with her when she moved to Florida.[29] Sometime later, Cross gave it to her daughter, Viah May Cross, of Pensacola, Florida.[30] Cross loaned the manuscript to Herbert M. Kelley in 1921 and again in 1936, and Kelley subsequently mailed it to LeRoy Froom, who placed it in the Advent Source Collection at the General Conference in Takoma Park, Maryland.[31] The manuscript was lost for nearly two decades until Mary Jane Mitchell, head librarian for the Adventist Theological Seminary in Takoma Park, rediscovered it in the 1950s.[32] Over the ensuing decades, largely due to neglect, the extant manuscript shrank

---

[25]J.N. Loughborough to A.W. Spalding, Aug. 2, 1921, A.W. Spalding Correspondence, Collection 10, Box 1, Folder 2, CAR, JWL, AU; bracketed material mine.

[26]Kelley to Froom, July 1, 1936, manuscript VT000273, no. 4, CAR, JWL, AU.

[27]Arthur W. Spalding, "Light on the Sanctuary: Adapted from the Manuscript of Hiram Edson," *Youth's Instructor*, March 8, 1910, pp. 4-6.

[28]Kelley to Froom, July 1, 1936, manuscript VT000273, no. 4, CAR, JWL, AU.

[29]Spicer, *Pioneer Days*, p. 66.

[30]Affidavit signed by Viah Cross, Sept. 30, 1936, in Pensacola, Florida, manuscript VT000273, CAR, JWL, AU.

[31]Kelley to Froom, July 1, 1936, manuscript VT000273, CAR, JWL, AU. There is some disagreement over whether Kelley mailed the Edson manuscript to Froom first in 1921 and later in 1936. Don F. Neufeld, speaking of his article "The Disappointment According to Hiram Edson" in the *Review*, Oct. 22, 1970 (pp. 2-4), states on p. 30 that this exchange occurred in 1933.

[32]L.E. Froom to Jim Nix, Nov. 3, 1971, in Nix, "Edson," Appendix E, p. 159.

even further to only a dozen pages. But thanks to references to it in the writings of Froom, Spalding, Spicer, and others, it soon became more widely known among Adventist scholars.[33]

As related in this manuscript, on the morning of October 22, a few believers met in the Edson home to prepare for the Lord's imminent return. When midnight came and Christ did not come, they wept together until dawn. The men then retired to the granary in the barn to kneel in prayer, asking God for light regarding their disappointment. Following this prayer session, most of the attendees went home, but Edson and Crosier decided to walk together to "encourage some of our brethren." In Edson's own words:

> We started, and while passing through a large field I was stopped midway of the field. Heaven seemed open to my view, and I saw distinctly, and clearly, that instead of our High Priest coming out of the Most Holy of the heavenly sanctuary to come to this earth on the tenth day of the seventh month, at the end of the 2300 days, that he, for the first time entered on that day the second apartment of that sanctuary; and that he had a work to perform in the Most Holy before coming to this earth. That he came to the marriage at that time; in other words, to the Ancient of days, to receive a kingdom, dominion, and glory; and we must wait for his return from the wedding; and my mind was directed to the tenth ch[apter] of Rev[elation] where I could see the vision had spoken and did not lie.[34]

[33]See, for example, A.W. Spalding to D.E. Robinson, Dec. 6, 1934, Spalding Correspondence, Collection 10, Box 1, Folder 2, CAR, JWL, AU; L.E. Froom to A.W. Spalding, Aug. 22, 1949; A.W. Spalding to L.E. Froom, Aug. 25, 1949, Spalding Correspondence, Collection 10, Box 2, Folder 2, CAR, JWL, AU; W.A. Spicer, *Certainties of the Advent Movement* (Washington, D.C.: Review and Herald Pub. Assn., 1929), pp. 169-170.

[34]Hiram Edson, "Description of Hiram Edson's Experience in the Cornfield on October 23, 1844 Plus Some Other Experiences in His Life Around the Same Time," undated manuscript VT000272, CAR,

No doubt absorbed in his own thoughts, Crosier had continued walking across the field until he realized that his friend had stopped. Turning around, he inquired why Edson had paused in the middle of the field. Edson informed Crosier that the Lord was answering their morning prayers and that the sanctuary was not this earth, but was located in heaven.[35]

What exactly Edson "saw distinctly and clearly" in the cornfield has divided church historians, scholars, skeptics, and popular writers for nearly two centuries. Was it a revelation—a visible or audible intervention by God as in a vision? Was it inspiration—the Holy Spirit's special urging of a messenger to speak or write with "fire in his bones"? Could it have been illumination—the Holy Spirit enlightening his mind with a great idea to share with his Adventist friends?[36] Or did nothing of any significance occur in the cornfield?[37] Thus, there are four distinct views of Edson's cornfield experience.

Edson received a vision

In a manuscript prepared for the *Youth's Instructor* in 1910, Spalding asserted that Owen Crosier and Franklin Hahn had accompanied Edson across the field "to comfort some of the brethren." As Spalding

---

JWL, AU; bracketed material mine.

[35]Claiming that Edson had related to him the events of Oct. 22-23, 1844, as they were traveling together in 1852, Loughborough tells a much different story: That on Oct. 22, believers met in the Port Gibson schoolhouse, not in the Edson home; that they sang and prayed all night there, not returning to Edson's farm until the next morning; and that while crossing the cornfield, they prayed three times by the corn shocks, after which Hiram received "light" about the heavenly sanctuary. As several historians have pointed out, however, Loughborough's accounts of Adventist history prior to his conversion in 1852 are frequently unreliable. See J.N. Loughborough to A.W. Spalding, Aug. 2, 1921, Spalding Correspondence, Collection 10, Box 1, Folder 2, CAR, JWL, AU; A.W. Spalding to L.E. Froom, Aug. 25, 1949, Spalding Correspondence, Collection 10, Box 2, Folder 2, CAR, JWL, AU; Nix, "Edson," p. 151; and Strayer, *Loughborough*, pp. 326-330, 341, 391-395, 405.

[36]These three differing viewpoints are ably discussed in Alden Thompson, *Inspiration: Hard Questions, Honest Answers*, 2nd ed. (Gonzalez, FL: Energion Publications, 2016), p. 62.

[37]This is the view advanced by such critics as Donald Barnhouse and Fernand Fisel, discussed as a fourth group.

dramatized the scene, suddenly Edson "felt as it were a hand upon him, stopping him where he was," and "a glory shone around him, and looking as in a vision he saw that Jesus, our High Priest, had entered that day into the most holy place of the sanctuary in heaven, and there he would stay until he had finished the work of cleansing it." Furthermore, Edson heard "a voice" declaring, "'The sanctuary to be cleansed is in heaven.'" Finally, he allegedly told Crosier, "We must prophesy again before many people and nations and tongues." Although the article's title claimed that the information conveyed had been "adapted from the manuscript of Hiram Edson," Spalding obviously added several elements that Edson's account omitted. His assertion that Edson foresaw a worldwide mission work in 1844 also contradicts the shut-door views that he and most other Adventists espoused at the time.[38]

It is possible that Spalding's account was based on information provided him by Edson's daughter, Viah Cross. Although she did not publish her view of her father's cornfield experience until 1920, her words are so similar to Spalding's a decade earlier as to suggest a direct connection. After declaring that Edson and "others" were crossing the field, she wrote: "Suddenly father saw a bright light shining around him and heard these words, as if spoken by an audible voice: 'The temple of God was opened in heaven, and there was seen in his temple the ark of his testimony.'"[39]

For the next century, many other writers followed the lead of Spalding and Cross in declaring that Edson had actually seen a vision in the cornfield. In 1935, F.M. Bartle, who had once copied Edson's manuscript in his own handwriting, informed retired General

---

[38]Spalding, "Light on the Sanctuary."
[39]Viah O. Cross, "Recollections of the Message," *Review*, April 1, 1920, pp. 22-23.

Conference President William A. Spicer that "Elder Hiram Edson had visions before Sr. [Ellen G.] White did"—in fact, he said, Edson's October 23 vision had come two months prior to White's vision in December 1844.[40]

In 1947, Spalding wrote that "looking up, [Edson] saw, as in a vision, the sanctuary in heaven."[41] Two years later in a letter to Froom, he referred to Edson's experience as "the revelation" and "the vision."[42] When Spalding's *Captains of the Host* was published in 1949, Crosier had become Edson's only visible cornfield companion, although the author asserted that on that morning of October 23, Christ walked "with these two disciples on their Port Gibson way."[43] A year later, possibly mirroring Cross's words, Spalding described a hand stopping Edson in his tracks, a vision of the High Priest entering the Most Holy Place, and a voice saying, "The sanctuary to be cleansed is in heaven."[44]

Froom obviously agreed with Spalding, asserting in 1948 that Edson had "a veritable vision from heaven."[45] When the General Conference Department of Education issued the textbook *The Story of Our Church* in 1956, thousands of Adventist youth around the world learned that Edson had received "his vision" in a cornfield.[46] Those who purchased Jerome Clark's three-volume set *1844* received the same message.[47]

---

[40]F.M. Bartle to W.A. Spicer, Sept. 4, 1935, in Nix, "Edson," Appendix H, pp. 201-203.

[41]Spalding, *Footprints*, p. 75.

[42]A.W. Spalding to L.E. Froom, Aug. 25, 1949, Spalding Correspondence, Collection 10, Box 2, Folder 2, CAR, JWL, AU.

[43] Spalding, *Captains*, pp. 94, 97.

[44]Spalding, "A Western Ally," *Review*, Jan. 19, 1950, p. 11. It is possible, even probable, that Spalding had Viah Cross's earlier manuscript about her father's experience at hand when he wrote his article, and this might explain their similarity in wording.

[45]LeRoy E. Froom, "How the Full Light on the Sanctuary Came to Us," *Review*, Sept. 9, 1948, p. 8.

[46]General Conference Department of Education, *The Story of Our Church* (Mountain View, CA: Pacific Press Pub. Assn., 1956), p. 177.

[47]Clark, *1844*, vol. 1, p. 67.

By the 1970s and 1980s, this visionary view had become so prevalent that even non-Adventist scholars whose works were published by secular presses adopted it. In *The Rise of Adventism* (1974), Edwin Gaustad suggested that Edson had received "a new vision of the atypical sanctuary" highlighting "a new phase of Christ's ministry in heaven that placed earth under judgment."[48] Although highly critical of Ellen White's visions in his book *Prophetess of Health* (1976), Ronald Numbers described Edson's experience as "a vision of heaven."[49] So did Oxford University historian Malcolm Bull and London journalist Keith Lockhart in their pathbreaking volume *Seeking a Sanctuary* (1989).[50]

Meanwhile, some Adventist writers returned to the earlier, more dramatic renditions of Edson's cornfield experience as shared by Cross and Spalding. Writing about the Adventist pioneers to inspire junior readers in 1979, James Joiner related that "a hand seemed to fall on [Edson's] broad shoulder...and heaven appeared to open above him. He seemed to see Jesus Christ...as the great High Priest.... Then, as if struck by lightning, the farmer understood."[51] Two years later, the 1981 edition of *In the Footsteps of the Pioneers* used the word "revelation" rather than "vision."[52] In 1993, George Knight placed the word "vision" in quotation marks as though recognizing that, while this was the traditional Adventist view, it might not have matched the reality of Edson's experience.[53] Seven years later, however, Knight em-

---

[48]Edwin Scott Gaustad, ed., *The Rise of Adventism: A Commentary on the Social and Religious Ferment of Mid-Nineteenth Century America* (New York: Harper and Row, 1974), p. 178.
[49]Ronald L. Numbers, *Prophetess of Health: A Study of Ellen G. White* (New York: Harper and Row, 1976), p. 13.
[50]Malcolm Bull and Keith Lockhart, *Seeking a Sanctuary: Seventh-day Adventism and the American Dream* (New York: Harper and Row, 1989), p. 75.
[51]James Joiner, "These Were the Courageous: Hiram Edson," *Guide*, Oct. 24, 1979, p. 20.
[52]*In the Footsteps of the Pioneers* (Washington, D.C.: Ellen G. White Estate, 1981), p. 21.
[53]George R. Knight, *Anticipating the Advent: A Brief History of Seventh-day Adventists* (Boise, ID: Pacific Press Pub. Assn., 1993), p. 22.

phasized that while Edson had been one of the "minor actors in the Advent drama" compared with Miller, Litch, Fitch, Himes, and other Millerite leaders prior to October 22, 1844, what happened to him on October 23 gave him more prominence in the eyes of Sabbath-keeping Adventists.[54]

At least one of the church's official periodicals published abroad employed the words "vision—scene of wonderment" in connection with Edson's experience.[55] So did writers in a few unofficial publications and even critical secular sources. For example, Glen Greenwalt, writing in the journal *Spectrum* in 1994, asserted: "I believe that Edson's experience was truly visionary. For Edson saw what many prophets have seen in their hour of deepest trial—namely, a vision that Jesus had not abandoned them, but was even then working on their behalf in the courts of heaven." Comparing Edson's vision with those of Daniel, Stephen, Paul, and John, Greenwalt concluded that what happened in 1844 resembled God's Word in every age as He seeks ways to dwell with His people.[56] Likewise, Laura Vance, in her highly critical book *Seventh-day Adventism in Crisis* (1999), expressed a belief that Edson "saw in vision" the heavenly sanctuary to be cleansed, and that from this vision "contemporary Adventist eschatology has grown."[57]

References to Edson having a vision or a divine revelation have increased in the 21st century, especially in Adventist publications aimed at young people and new Adventists. For example, in 2001, the *Youth Ministry Accent* stated that Edson had received "a sudden

---

[54]George R. Knight, *A Search for Identity: The Development of Seventh-day Adventist Beliefs* (Hagerstown, MD: Review and Herald Pub. Assn., 2000), pp. 62-64.
[55]"Hiram Edson," *Southern Asia Tidings*, Oct. 1994, p. 11.
[56]Glen Greenwalt, "The Sanctuary: God in Our Midst," *Spectrum* 24, no. 2 (Oct. 1994), pp. 42-49.
[57]Laura L. Vance, *Seventh-day Adventism in Crisis: Gender and Sectarian Change in an Emerging Religion* (Urbana and Chicago: University of Illinois Press, 1999), pp. 26-27.

revelation," which turned the Adventists' disappointment into joy when they discovered "a God of Justice and Mercy" who loved them and kept His promises (in the prophecies of Daniel, Revelation, and Hebrews) to them.[58] Taking a page from Cross and Spalding, Norma Collins, in a storybook for children, informed them that Edson "felt as if a hand were laid on his shoulder, stopping him in his tracks.... He saw what seemed to be a vision" of Jesus as High Priest, entering the Most Holy Place in the heavenly sanctuary to begin His work of judgment.[59]

Recent audiovisual media also emphasize the idea of Edson having a vision on October 23, 1844. In their 2006 CD, "Hiram Edson, God's Man," William Fagal and Lewis and Richard Walton refer to his "vision."[60] The non-Adventist actor hired to play the role of Edson in the 2012 DVD "Meet Hiram Edson" also followed a script that stated, "I saw into heaven" as in a vision.[61] Likewise, in his 2014 biography of John Harvey Kellogg, the non-Adventist historian Brian Wilson referred to Edson as a "visionary" and to his "visionary experience" in the cornfield.[62] Don Barton, in an article published in *Spectrum* calling the investigative judgment teaching "Adventism's life raft," also stated that Edson had received "a vision in a cornfield."[63]

Edson received a flash of light

Several writers, however, sought alternate explanations for Edson's cornfield experience. Most of these had something to do either

---

[58]"Inspired by Our Theology," *Youth Ministry Accent*, April-June 2001, pp. 43-44.

[59]Collins, *Heartwarming Stories*, Book 1, p. 35.

[60]William Fagal, Lewis Walton, and Richard Walton, "What Hath God Wrought? Hiram Edson, God's Man" (Harrisburg, PA: American Cassette Ministries, 2006).

[61]"Meet Hiram Edson" DVD (Silver Spring, MD: Adventist Heritage Ministry, 2012).

[62]Wilson, *Kellogg*, pp. 7, 22.

[63]Don Barton, "The Investigative Judgment: Adventism's Life Raft," *Spectrum* 41, no. 3 (Summer 2013), p. 17.

with visible light or flashes of insight. As early as 1941, retired General Conference President William A. Spicer referred to "this light that came into Hiram Edson's soul.... The light was like a message from heaven to his heart and mind."[64] Writing three decades later in *Movement of Destiny* (1971), Froom agreed, calling Edson's experience "a flash of divine light."[65] Somewhat more dramatically, New York Conference pastor Henry Uhl in 1974 asserted that Edson had been "struck by a flash of truth like a lightning bolt with the sanctuary doctrine."[66] More restrained in his rhetoric, Merlin Burt, in his travel guidebook *Adventist Pioneer Places* (2011), wrote that Hiram had received "an experience of enlightenment," "a particularly direct flash of insight," and "an insight that encouraged his faith."[67] Exercising considerably more creative license, Rachel Cabose told *Guide* readers in 2018: "Suddenly a bright light shone around Hiram. He seemed to be looking right into heaven!" Then he "heard a voice quote Revelation 11:19 [about the open door to the Most Holy Place and the ark being revealed]."[68]

Edson received an impression

Other writers, however, have been reluctant to describe Edson's experience either as a vision or as a flash of visible light. One obvious reason for their reticence is the fact that Edson never described what he saw as a vision. Another explanation would be the strong sentiment against visions and dreams among many Millerites and early Sabbatarian Adventists in the 1840s and 1850s. To counter this,

---

[64]Spicer, *Pioneer Days*, p. 221.
[65]LeRoy Edwin Froom, *Movement of Destiny* (Washington, D.C.: Review and Herald Pub. Assn., 1971), p. 78 (see footnote).
[66]Henry Uhl, "Church and State—a Dual Celebration," *Atlantic Union Gleaner*, Aug. 27, 1974, p. 3.
[67]Burt, *Adventist Pioneer Places*, pp. 130, 133.
[68]Rachel Whitaker Cabose, "Light in a Cornfield," *Guide*, Oct. 13, 2018, p. 18.

Sabbatarian Adventists placed more emphasis on the biblical basis of their beliefs rather than their visionary origin. Moreover, as mentioned above, Edson's handwritten manuscript contained speculative interpretations of Bible prophecies that not only clashed with the views of his contemporaries, they also tainted the rest of his autobiographical account in the eyes of some. (See chapter 6.)[69]

Even Loughborough avoided using visionary language in his 1892 textbook *Rise and Progress.* Instead, based on what Edson had told him in 1852, Loughborough declared that "the Spirit of God came upon him in such a powerful manner that he was almost smitten to the earth, and with it came an impression" that the sanctuary to be cleansed was in heaven.[70] Loughborough repeated the word "impression" in his 1905 updated history *The Great Second Advent Movement*[71] and in a *Review* article in 1921 in which he quoted Edson as saying that this impression came "almost as distinct as though spoken in an audible voice."[72]

Writers in the 1930s followed Loughborough's lead. W.C. White suggested that "the mind of Hiram Edson was impressed, as strongly as though by an audible voice, with the words, 'The sanctuary to be cleansed is in heaven.'"[73] Church historian Emma Howell surmised that the "conviction flashed into his [Edson's] mind" that the sanctuary was in heaven and Jesus had entered the Most Holy Place on October 22, 1844, to begin the final phase of His priestly ministry.[74]

---

[69]Ross E. Winkle, "Disappearing Act: Hiram Edson's Cornfield Experience," *Spectrum* 33, no. 1 (Winter 2005), p. 49.

[70]J.N. Loughborough, *Rise and Progress of the Seventh-day Adventists* (Battle Creek, MI: General Conference Association, 1892), p. 114.

[71]J.N. Loughborough, *The Great Second Advent Movement: Its Rise and Progress* (Washington, D.C.: Southern Pub. Assn., 1905), p. 193.

[72]Hiram Edson, quoted in J.N. Loughborough, "The Second Advent Movement—No. 8," *Review*, Sept. 15, 1921, p. 5.

[73]William C. White, "Sketches and Memories of James and Ellen G. White, V: Laying a Sure Foundation," *Review*, March 28, 1935, p. 8.

[74]Emma E. Howell, *The Great Advent Movement* (Washington, D.C.: Review and Herald Pub. Assn.,

Twelve years later, she repeated this claim.[75]

Although Froom called Edson's experience a vision in 1948, in *Prophetic Faith of Our Fathers* (1954), he stated: "Suddenly there burst upon his mind the thought that there were *two* phases to Christ's ministry in the heaven of heavens, just as in the earthly sanctuary of old."[76] Two decades later, *Review* editor Don Neufeld[77] and historian Robert Gale[78] preferred using the word "conviction" to describe Edson's experience, while Arthur Patrick[79] and C. Mervyn Maxwell[80] chose words like "insight" and "impression" instead.

During the 1980s, writers employed similar expressions. *Review* editor Don Neufeld continued to believe that "a firm conviction," and not "a vision," had come over Edson so that "he had no doubt that God had illuminated his mind." Yet it required months of Bible study "to confirm the conviction."[81] Likewise, the Advent Christian historian, Clyde Hewitt, stated that "after a lengthy prayer session" with his friends, Edson became convinced that the sanctuary was in heaven. This belief, Hewitt averred, was based on "logical" arguments and "scriptural analogy" of texts in Daniel and Hebrews.[82]

A decade after Hewitt's book, Maxwell, in *Magnificent Disappointment*, declared that Edson "was struck with dynamic new thoughts" and "suddenly realized" that Jesus had gone into the

---

1935), p. 29.

[75]Emma (Howell) Cooper, *The Great Advent Movement* (Takoma Park, Washington, D.C.: Review and Herald Pub. Assn., 1947), p. 29.

[76]Froom, *Prophetic Faith of Our Fathers*, vol. 4, p. 881; emphasis in the original.

[77]Don F. Neufeld, "Anniversary of an Important Event in Sacred History," *Review*, Oct. 22, 1970, p. 2.

[78]Robert Gale, *The Urgent Voice: The Story of William Miller* (Washington, D.C.: Review and Herald Pub. Assn., 1975), p. 128.

[79]Arthur N. Patrick, "Charles Fitch, Hiram Edson, and the Raison d'être of the Seventh-day Adventist Church" (paper presented in partial fulfillment of the courses CH570, CH597, CH600 at the Seventh-day Adventist Theological Seminary, Andrews University, 1971), p. 104.

[80]Maxwell, *Tell It to the World*, p. 50.

[81]Donald Neufeld, "Aftermath of Autumn Disappointment," Review, Jan. 10, 1980, pp. 15-16; Neufeld, "Edson's October 23 Experience," *Review*, Jan. 17, 1980, p. 18.

[82]Clyde E. Hewitt, *Midnight and Morning* (Charlotte, NC: Venture Books, 1983), pp. 182-183.

Most Holy Place on October 22. In addition, Maxwell emphasized that "the doctrine of the pre-advent investigative judgment was not invented by Seventh-day Adventists. In fact, many of its features were printed and in circulation before the great disappointment of October 22, 1844."[83] But in a posthumously published article for *Adventist World* (2006), Maxwell emphasized what Sabbatarian Adventists had added to the Millerite understanding of Christ's work in the heavenly sanctuary, concluding that God had given Edson a deeper understanding of Christ's ministry in the heavenly sanctuary, which was "brand-new in the history of theology.... In a very special sense the Seventh-day Adventist Church was born at that moment, in that field, as that farmer contemplated Christ."[84] This matter is discussed further in Chapter 9.

As the 21st century began, the words of choice for Edson's cornfield experience seemed to be "insight" and conviction." George Knight,[85] Howard Krug,[86] Derek Bowe,[87] *Guide*,[88] Michael Campbell, and Jud Lake[89] all explained Hiram's new understanding on October 23 as a spiritual insight. Much in the same vein, Ann Fisher[90] declared that "an overwhelming conviction" had come over Edson, while Gary Land[91] believed that "it most likely was a vivid thought or realization," and Lewis Walton[92] declared: "Suddenly Edson's mind

[83]C. Mervyn Maxwell, *Magnificent Disappointment: What Really Happened in 1844...and Its Meaning for Today* (Nampa, ID: Pacific Press Pub. Assn., 2000), pp. 79-80.

[84]C. Mervyn Maxwell, "Cornfield Cleopas," *Adventist World NAD Edition*, Oct. 2006, p. 35.

[85]Knight, *Search for Identity*, p. 63.

[86]Howard Krug, "October Morn," *Review*, Oct. 24, 2002, p. 12.

[87]Derek Cyril Bowe, "Night of No Return," *Guide*, May 8, 2004, p. 12.

[88]"The Great Appointment," *Guide*, Oct. 15, 2016, p. 26.

[89]Michael W. Campbell and Jud S. Lake, eds., *The Pocket Ellen G. White Dictionary* (Nampa, ID: Pacific Press Pub. Assn., 2018), p. 183.

[90]Ann Fisher, "Nothing to Fear," *Lake Union Herald*, April 2005, p. 11.

[91]Gary Land, ed., *Historical Dictionary of the Seventh-day Adventists* (Lanham, MD: The Scarecrow Press, Inc., 2005), p. 85.

[92]Lewis R. Walton, "History Preserved," *Adventist World*, July 2007, p. 27.

was drawn to the books of Daniel and Revelation, and a picture began to emerge of Jesus' ministry in heaven."

Edson received no Divine illumination

In the fourth group are those who argue that nothing of any spiritual or prophetic significance happened in that Port Gibson cornfield. These claim that Edson did not have a vision; he did not see a flash of light; he did not receive any divine insight, conviction, or understanding on that day. In 1946, Donald Barnhouse, editor of *Revelation Magazine*, called Edson's experience "stale, flat and unprofitable... nothing more than a human, face-saving idea," which was "untenable and speculative of a highly imaginative order." In short, Edson, using biblical proof-texting, had himself created the explanation of Christ entering the Most Holy Place in the heavenly sanctuary on October 22 to cover the Adventists' embarrassment at being wrong concerning His imminent return to earth on that day.[93]

Four decades later, Fernand Fisel also expressed skepticism concerning Edson's "vision" and his fragmentary manuscript, which he believed was probably written years after the fact. "It is evident," he wrote in *Adventist Currents*, "that the 'Vision in the cornfield' is not in evidence in contemporary sources and affected no one at that time." Suggesting that Edson's memory "failed him in relating exactly what happened" years later, Fisel averred that "he may have read into that experience ideas that were to arise much later." These "retrospective elaborations" included an atonement lasting longer than one day (Crosier suggested a year in March 1845, while Hale and Turner projected an ongoing atonement in *The Hope of Israel* newspaper in

---

[93] Donald Barnhouse, *Revelation* magazine, Sept. 1946, cited by Raymond Whitley, "Ellen White, a Cornfield and Hiram Edson," *North Pacific Union Gleaner*, Jan. 5, 1981, p. 6. In 1950, Barnhouse renamed the magazine *Eternity*.

April 1845). Further, these "elaborations" included an awareness of a worldwide mission "to prophesy again before nations and kings and peoples" as stated in Revelation 10:8-10 (which clashed with Sabbatarian Adventists' shut-door views from 1844 to 1851 and was only recognized by the Albany Conference of April 1845). Moreover, these views disagreed with the widespread Millerite belief that Christ's atonement in the Most Holy Place had begun when He ascended to heaven in 31 A.D. Furthermore, the concept of "the wedding of the Lamb" mentioned in Edson's manuscript did not surface until January 1845 in articles penned by Joseph Turner and Apollos Hale in the *Advent Herald* and *Advent Mirror*. Finally, the implied connection Edson made between the sanctuary message and the seventh-day Sabbath in the Decalogue contained in the ark of the covenant belied the fact that Edson did not keep the Sabbath until 1846. Consequently, Fisel declared, both Edson's cornfield vision and his fragmentary manuscript should be relegated "to the level of apocryphal literature to which, without doubt, it belongs."[94]

Although this broad spectrum of views concerning Edson's cornfield experience demonstrates no clear pattern or trend over the past century and a half, the astute reader will have noticed one noteworthy fact. For nearly half a century, between 1844 and the publication of Loughborough's *Rise and Progress* in 1892, not a single Millerite, Advent Christian, Sabbatarian Adventist, or skeptic ever mentioned Edson's cornfield experience, his manuscript, or his presentments. Even more curious, neither his close friends Crosier or Hahn, nor even Edson himself, ever referred to them in any of their extant letters, articles, reports, or private diaries. Not until the 1940s would

---

[94]Fernand Fisel, "Edson's Cornfield 'Vision': Frisson or Figment? *Adventist Currents* 1, no. 1 (July 1983), pp. 25-27. See also his revised and much expanded manuscript version of this article entitled "Edson's Cornfield 'Vision': Frisson or Fiction?" manuscript 028258, CAR, JWL, AU.

A.W. Spalding highlight the role Edson had played during the 1840s in his books *Footprints of the Pioneers* (1947) and *Captains of the Host* (1949), and not until his four-volume *Origin and History of Seventh-day Adventists* appeared (1961-1962) did many scholars and Adventists in general learn about Hiram's fragmentary manuscript. Why Edson's contributions were overlooked for so long is discussed in greater detail in Chapters 10 and 11.

Chapter 5

Friends and Foes

When Hiram Edson reached the far end of that cornfield on October 23, 1844, he had a rudimentary understanding of three topics. First, the sanctuary was not on the earth but in heaven. Second, like the Israelite tabernacle, the heavenly sanctuary contained two rooms, the Holy Place and the Most Holy Place. Third, that Jesus, in the role of High Priest, had entered the Most Holy Place to cleanse it on October 22. Edson did not, however, understand the nature of that cleansing or how long it would take. He did not grasp the meaning of the investigative judgment. And he did not know exactly when Christ would return to this earth, although he, Crosier, and Hahn believed He could come as soon as April 1845. Because his cornfield experience raised more questions than they could answer, Edson, Crosier, and Hahn spent the rest of 1844 and much of 1845 studying every Bible text that mentioned the words "sanctuary," "tabernacle," and "temple," both on earth and in heaven. Before examining the results of their study, it will be helpful to learn a little more about Hahn and Crosier themselves.

Franklin B. Hahn

Although the physician Franklin B. Hahn (1809-1866) had the

title of "doctor," it is unknown where he earned his medical degree. He and his wife lived about three miles outside Canandaigua, and their property bordered Canandaigua Lake.[1] For several years, Hahn served as president of the Canandaigua Village Corporation and secretary of the Ontario County Medical Society.[2] In late 1843, he rented a hall so that his Millerite friend, O.R.L. Crosier, could hold meetings there. After attending these services, Franklin and his wife were converted to the Advent cause.[3] From August 20 to 28, 1844, they hosted a Millerite camp meeting under a shady grove of trees on their property. The preachers included Thomas F. Barry, Joseph Marsh, and Elon Galusha, son of the governor of Vermont.[4] It is entirely possible that Crosier, who often boarded with the Edsons, introduced Edson to Hahn at those meetings. At the close of the camp meeting, Franklin and his wife were baptized by immersion in the lake.[5] Two years later, when the Hahns attended a conference at the Edson home and heard Joseph Bates present the seventh-day Sabbath, they accepted it as Bible truth.[6]

Owen Russell Loomis Crosier

Owen Russell Loomis Crosier (1820-1912), more commonly known as O.R.L. Crosier, grew up in the Canandaigua area. His parents, Archibald and Nancy Crosier, née Loomis, had moved west from Albany in 1818 to settle first in Geneva and then in Chapinville, three miles northeast of Canandaigua. There, Archibald earned fame as the cooper who could not only make more barrels in a day than anyone

---

[1]Nix, "Edson," p. 14.
[2]Froom, *Prophetic Faith*, vol. 4, pp. 891-892.
[3] Spalding, "Light on the Sanctuary," p. 5.
[4]See *The Midnight Cry*, Aug. 8, 1844, p. 32, and *The Advent Herald and Signs of the Times Reporter*, Oct. 2, 1844, p. 67.
[5]Nix, "Edson," pp. 14-15.
[6]Spalding, "Light on the Sanctuary," p. 6.

else, but also at the end of the day, he still had sufficient energy to jump into and out of every barrel he had finished. Two years after Crosier was born on February 2, 1820, the family moved yet again to Hopewell, where his mother died in 1822. Two weeks later, his father drowned in Canandaigua Lake. While his sister, Nancy, went to live with their Loomis grandparents, Owen and his brother Archibald Jr. were put out for adoption to various families over the next two decades.[7]

Since he was an orphan, living at the public's expense, Crosier was indentured to farmer Stephen Thatcher, who owned 140 acres of land on the Geneva-Canandaigua Road. Crosier slept upstairs in an unheated room with the hired man. He split firewood for the family and, using flint and steel, started fires in their hearths every morning. Like an unpaid servant, he also fetched apples, cider, tobacco, and pipes for visiting adults. When Crosier turned 13, Thatcher apprenticed him to Abram Furman to learn the blacksmith trade. In addition to attending school during the winter months and doing occasional work for neighboring farmers, Crosier enjoyed fishing, swimming, and ice skating with Stephen Thatcher's daughter.[8] Converted at 16, he began carrying a New Testament in his coat pocket; he read from it daily and committed many Bible texts to memory. Coached by a certain Dr. Dayton, a local physician, he also mastered grammar, history, and geography, becoming an exceptional student and polished writer,[9] although his writing was noteworthy more for the cogency of his reasoning than the charm of his style.[10]

In 1840, now 20 years old, Owen attended the Wesleyan Semi-

---

[7] O.R.L. Crozier, *The Daily Messenger*, Nov. 22, 1923, p. 17.
[8] Crozier, *Daily Messenger*, pp. 17, 22.
[9] Froom, *Prophetic Faith*, vol. 4, p. 891.
[10] Spalding, *Captains*, pp. 91-92.

nary at Lima, New York. He then began teaching elementary school, first at Gorham and later at Rochester, East Avon, and Lima, New York. To further his education, he took classes at the academy in Geneseo. While there, he attended lectures given by Henry Hill and a Mr. Johnson; both were Methodist exhorters who preached sermons that Christ's coming would be in 1844. As a Methodist Sunday school superintendent, Crosier began studying the prophecies of Daniel and Revelation to see whether their message was true. Although the Wesleyan Methodist Church granted him licenses to exhort and preach, Crosier voluntarily withdrew from that church in 1843 and was baptized into the Baptist Church by immersion in the Erie Canal at Seneca Falls by the Reverend E.R. Pinney.[11]

Unable to afford a house of his own, Crosier took turns boarding with the Hahns and the Edsons. Frequently, Hahn secured schoolhouses and public halls where Crosier preached the message of Christ's soon return. Crosier frequently led Bible studies in the Hahn's parlor as well. In August 1844, he attended the camp meeting held on the Hahn estate only two months prior to the expected return of Jesus on October 22. As mentioned in Chapter 4, Crosier accompanied Edson across the cornfield on the morning after the Great Disappointment and studied the Bible with him in earnest for months thereafter.[12]

At the 1846 conference held in the Edson home, Crosier, like the Hahns, accepted the seventh-day Sabbath after hearing Bates' Bible study on it. In December 1846, he published an article in *The Day-Dawn* advocating Sabbath observance, and, for about two years, he kept it.[13] By 1848, however, Crosier had returned to worshiping on

---

[11]Crozier, *Daily Messenger*, p. 22.
[12]Crozier, *Daily Messenger*, p. 22.
[13]Nix, "Edson," p. 35.

Sunday and became "a most vigorous opponent" of the seventh-day Sabbath.[14] To his mind, "the past dispensation was all law, and the present dispensation [was] all Gospel, and the ten commandments were abolished at the cross."[15] Decades later, William Spicer cited Crosier's adoption of the Age-to-Come teachings[16] in the late 1840s as the "leaven of error [which] helped to lead the younger man away from the Sabbath and sanctuary truths."[17] Nevertheless, Crosier continued doing Christian missionary work in New York, Canada, Michigan, Ohio, and Indiana. This led him to reconnect with some of his western relatives, a few of whom were Seventh-day Adventists, while others remained Methodists. From 1847 to 1853, Crosier assisted Joseph Marsh in publishing *The Harbinger* in Rochester, New York, where he also furthered his education at the University of Rochester. In 1853, at the age of 32, he married Polly Alger and they moved to Grand Rapids, Michigan, a locale that brought him once again into connection with Seventh-day Adventists.[18]

Historical overview of the sanctuary

Although many lay Seventh-day Adventists have the impression that Edson introduced the sanctuary message to the world, theologians and historians know that the study of the sanctuary had deep roots in the Christian past. In the 16th century, John Calvin highlighted Christ's two-fold priestly ministry at the cross and His intercessory work in heaven after His ascension, while Philip Melanchthon

---

[14]Spalding, *Footprints of the Pioneers*, p. 82.

[15]O.R.L. Crozier, quoted by J.N. Loughborough to A.W. Spalding, Aug. 2, 1921, Spalding Correspondence, Collection 10, Box 1, Folder 2, CAR, JWL, AU.

[16]Those Millerites who espoused the Age-to-Come teaching believed that the Second Advent of Jesus would usher in a millennial kingdom during which probation would continue, nations would be converted, and the Jews would play a leading part. One prominent Age-to-Come group was the Messenger Party, led by H.S. Case and C.P. Russell of Jackson, Michigan, in the 1850s.

[17]Spicer, *Pioneer Days*, p. 69.

[18]Crozier, *Daily Messenger*, p. 23.

emphasized Jesus' heavenly ministry as high priest to remove sin and grant eternal life. The Puritans in 17th-century England wrote about not only the earthly tabernacles and temples but also about Christ's high priestly ministry in the heavenly sanctuary on the Day of Atonement. While William Miller mistakenly thought that this earth was the sanctuary to be cleansed by fire in 1844, as a deep student of the Bible, he was well aware of the earthly and heavenly sanctuaries and the roles that the high priest played in the former.[19]

Even in the 19th century, others before Edson studied what the Bible had to say about the earthly and heavenly sanctuaries, atonement, cleansing from sin, and final judgment. These individuals included William Miller in 1836, Josiah Litch in 1841, Samuel Snow in 1842, and Apollos Hale in 1843.[20] Yet the fact that they still expected Christ to come to earth on October 22, 1844, demonstrates that their old paradigm of His imminent appearing contained inherent contradictions and had not entirely shifted to include their new findings of an indefinite period of atonement and judgment in the heavenly sanctuary.[21] On the other hand, in the summer of 1844, Joseph Turner believed that the sanctuary to be cleansed was in heaven and that on October 22, 1844, Jesus as High Priest entered the Most Holy Place there.[22] Nor were Edson, Crosier, and Hahn the only ones sharing the message of a pre-advent judgment after October 22, 1844. Contemporaries who advanced similar views included Enoch Jacobs,[23] Joseph Turner,[24] Apollos Hale,[25] Emily Clemons,[26] and G.W.

---

[19]Fritz Guy, "The Journey of an Idea," *Adventist Heritage* 16, no. 3 (Spring 1995), pp. 9-10.
[20]For a more detailed discussion of these individuals and their views, see Maxwell, *Magnificent Disappointment*, pp. 71-78.
[21]Spalding, "Western Ally," p. 11.
[22]G.C. Dept. of Education, *Story of Our Church*, pp. 175-176.
[23]Enoch Jacobs, *The Day-Star*, Nov. 29, 1844.
[24]Joseph Turner, *The Hope of Israel*, Jan. 1845, and *The Advent Mirror*, Jan. 1845.
[25]Apollos Hale, *The Advent Herald*, Feb./March 1845.
[26]Emily Clemons, *Hope Within the Veil* (1845).

Peavey.[27] Yet when Turner, among others,[28] adopted extremist views after October 22—including the idea that the seventh millennium had commenced and they were all sanctified, so they should not do any work—this erratic behavior cast doubt on the validity of their earlier teachings in the eyes of many.[29]

Therefore, in the autumn of 1844, when Edson, Crosier, and Hahn began their intensive study of the Bible regarding the sanctuary, its services, and symbols as found in the book of Leviticus and explained in the books of Daniel and Hebrews, they were not the only ones searching for answers to the dilemma of the Great Disappointment. Nor were they the only ones suggesting that the answers could be found in a Day of Atonement in the heavenly sanctuary.

The Day-Dawn

As mentioned in the previous chapter, on October 22, Edson and his friends retired to the granary to pray, believing, as Edson expressed it, that "there might be light and help for us in our present distress." The men continued in prayer "until the witness of the Spirit was given that our prayer was accepted, and that light should be given, our disappointment be explained, and made clean and satisfactory."[30]

However, it required months of intense Bible study before "clean and satisfactory" answers came. After all, Edson, Hahn, and Crosier were amateurs. They were not professional theologians or trained

---

[27]G.W. Peavey, in the April 1845 *Jubilee Standard*, connected Daniel 8:14 with Hebrews 9:23-24 and Leviticus 16.

[28]For a more detailed discussion of the views of Turner and other individuals, see George Knight, *Joseph Bates: The Real Founder of Seventh-day Adventism* (Hagerstown, MD: Review and Herald Pub. Assn., 2004), pp. 93-94; Knight, *Search for Identity*, p. 64; and Maxwell, *Magnificent Disappointment*, pp. 72-78.

[29]G.C. Dept. of Education, *Story of Our Church*, p. 176.

[30]Edson, handwritten autobiographical manuscript, available in printed form in Knight, *1844 and the Rise of Sabbatarian Adventism*, p. 125.

scholars, but they believed that sincere study of the Bible, when blessed by God, could lead to the discovery of truth. Like Miller, they used their Bibles, concordances, and the Scottish commonsense reasoning[31] approach prevalent at this time to examine every single text that mentioned the words "sanctuary," "tabernacle," and "temple." As Spalding expressed it, "they pioneered their way into the mazes of the sanctuary question,"[32] becoming what Froom called "platform builders" of the Seventh-day Adventist message. The three men especially focused their attention on Leviticus 4 and 16, Daniel 8, and Hebrews 8 and 9.[33]

Not until many months had passed were they ready to share with the public what they had learned. Edson and Hahn chose 25-year-old Crosier to publish their discoveries in *The Day-Dawn*.[34] While logic would have dictated that Edson should have been the one to explicate his first-person experience in the cornfield, Crosier had by far the better writing style. As Chapter 8 reveals, although Edson had a good grasp of the eight parts of speech and the eight marks of punctuation, his speculative, verbose writing style left much to be desired. His tendency toward obfuscation and creative symbolism often obscured his message.[35]

---

[31] Scottish commonsense reasoning was a realist school of philosophy that originated in the ideas of the 18th-century Enlightenment philosophers Thomas Reid, Adam Ferguson, James Beattie, and Dugald Stewart of Scotland. It emphasized human beings' innate ability to perceive common ideas through their senses, judgment, and common sense. Many of the Millerites' books and articles on Bible doctrines and prophecies reflect the influence of Scottish commonsense reasoning upon their thinking. For more information concerning the Scottish commonsense reasoning approach, see Mark Noll, *America's God: From Jonathan Edwards to Abraham Lincoln* (New York: Oxford University Press, 2002) and E. Brooks Holifield, *Theology in America: Christian Thought from the Age of the Puritans to the Civil War* (New Haven, CT: Yale University Press, 2003).

[32] Spalding, *Origin and History*, vol. 1, p. 106.

[33] Froom, *Movement of Destiny*, p. 88.

[34] Volume 1, number 1 of the 1845 *Day-Dawn*, edited by Crosier and published by Hahn, had been lost for 150 years until Merlin Burt, conducting research in the Canandaigua, NY, Historical Society in 1995, discovered that Crosier's article had been reprinted on the back page of *The Ontario County Messenger* of March 26, 1845.

[35] *Footsteps of the Pioneers* (1981), p. 21. However, Loughborough told Spalding that Edson "had noth-

Crosier's article, entitled "To All Who Are Waiting for Redemption, the Following Is Addressed,"[36] declared that signs in the sun, moon, and stars, as well as the growing wickedness of men, demonstrated that the end of earth's history was near. He then proceeded to explicate and apply several symbols from the parable of the ten virgins in Matthew 25 to contemporary events. These included the Bridegroom (Christ), the tarrying time (August-October 1844), the midnight cry (the 1844 movement), the oil (the Spirit of faith and love), the coming of the Bridegroom (Christ's second advent), and the shutting of the door (the final judgment of saints and sinners).

Regarding the heavenly sanctuary, Crosier argued that since October 22, 1844, Christ has filled the role of Mediator and Advocate in the Most Holy Place, but He will also fill the role of Judge until the close of probation, when He returns to earth as King. While forgiveness for individual sins follows sacrifices in the Holy Place, atonement and cleansing take place in the Most Holy Place, where Christ is the Antitype of the high priest in the earthly tabernacle. On October 22, 1844, when the Jubilee Trumpet sounded in heaven, Christ began His atoning work in the Most Holy Place. This work enables Him to "number His jewels" (faithful saints to be saved), who must remain faithful to the end in order to receive their eternal reward.

While the majority of Shut-Door (or Bridegroom) Adventists (including Samuel Snow and James White) believed in a one-day atonement (October 22, 1844), this article clearly proves that Crosier believed in an extended atonement that could entail several years

---

ing to do with that paper [*The Day-Dawn*] published in Canandaigua." That may have been the case, although at the time he said it in 1921, Loughborough was nearly 90 years old and his memory concerning pre-1852 events was notoriously inaccurate. See J.N. Loughborough to A.W. Spalding, Aug. 2, 1921, Spalding Correspondence, Collection 10, Box 1, Folder 2, CAR, JWL, AU. *The Day-Dawn* apparently lasted for only two volumes between 1845 and 1847 with O.R.L. Crosier listed as editor.

[36] O.R.L. Crosier, "To All Who Are Waiting for Redemption, the Following Is Addressed," *The Day-Dawn*, vol. 1, no. 1, reprinted on the back page of *The Ontario Messenger*, March 26, 1845.

of waiting. Furthermore, Crosier was the principal advocate of this extended atonement view through 1846, a perspective also shared by Hiram Edson, Franklin Hahn, Emily Clemons, and Ellen Harmon.[37]

The Day-Star Extra

On February 7, 1846, editor Enoch Jacobs printed Crosier's *Day Dawn* article, "The Law of Moses," in an "Extra" (or special) issue of his Cincinnati, Ohio, paper, *The Day-Star*, one of the more widely read Adventist publications after the Great Disappointment.[38] In a brief endorsement, Edson and Hahn declared:

> We have prayerfully examined the subject presented by Brother Crosier in the light of God's word, and are fully satisfied it is meat in due season, and if properly examined and understood will settle many difficulties in the minds of many brethren at this time.
>
> In order to get it before the brethren, it becomes necessary to loan the money for its publication, with the expectation that all who feel interested and have the means will aid in the expense. The expense as near as we can now ascertain will be about $30. Brethren here, as in most other places, are poor, (but rich in faith) but we can bear one-half of the expense, and will [bear] more if necessary.
>
> If more should be refunded than the other half, it will be sent to Bro. Jacobs, or as brethren may direct. The subject, brethren, is now before you, and we do pray you will examine

---

[37]Merlin D. Burt, "The *Day Dawn* of Canandaigua, New York: Reprint of a Significant Adventist Journal," *Andrews University Seminary Studies* 44 (2006), pp. 331-338.

[38]Gale, *Urgent Voice*, p. 128.

it carefully by the word. May the Lord add His blessing. The brethren will please direct [funds] to F.B. Hahn, Canandaigua, Ont. Co., N.Y.[39]

The two men kept their word and paid $15, half the cost of printing 2,000 copies of the issue, appealing to the readers to donate the remaining $15. To help her husband come up with his half of the $15, Esther Edson sold some of the solid silver spoons they had received as a wedding present seven years earlier.[40]

Before discussing the main points raised in Crosier's *Day-Star* article, it may be helpful to mention some curious omissions that Fernand Fisel noted several decades ago. First, Crosier failed to credit Edson with the initial inspiration for writing his two articles on the sanctuary. Second, Crosier likewise omitted any mention of Edson in his subsequent articles on that topic in *The Day-Star, The Day-Dawn, Voice of Truth,* and the *Harbinger and Advocate* in 1845. Third, although Edson presumably understood that Christ had begun a work of cleansing in the Most Holy Place on October 22 and shared that view with Crosier, yet Crosier did not discuss this aspect of Christ's ministry in any of his articles. Finally, although most post-1844 Adventists avoided date-setting, it is interesting that Crosier and Edson believed for a while that the end of this world would occur in April 1845. Crosier published his prediction in several Adventist papers, including the *Ontario Messenger, Voice of Truth, The Day-Dawn,* and *Hope of Israel* from 1845 to 1847. Altogether, between 1844 and 1854, Crosier wrote at least 60 articles, studies, and letters and published at least one pamphlet dealing with a variety of biblical and prophetic topics.[41]

---

[39] Hiram Edson and Franklin Hahn, *The Day-Star* Extra, Feb. 7, 1846, p. 44.
[40] Gale, *Urgent Voice*, pp. 128-129.
[41] Fisel, "Three Early Visions," p. 5, and Fisel, "Fission or Fiction?" pp. 26-28. See also Hiram Edson to

Regarding the first two points, as Chapters 1 and 2 illustrate, those who professed to have visions and dreams were unpopular with many American citizens; some who laid claim to supernatural phenomena were harassed (as in the case of Hiram Edson and Joseph Smith in 1844, although the latter was also charged with treason and polygamy).[42] In light of this, it could be that Crosier, Hahn, and Edson preferred to emphasize the scriptural basis rather than any visionary origins for their views on the sanctuary. Furthermore, as mentioned in Chapter 3, knowledge of Edson's supernatural presentments was apparently widespread in Ontario County; he had already been mocked in print by Joseph Marsh for them. As for Crosier's omission of Christ's cleansing ministry in the Most Holy Place, it is possible that neither he nor Edson fully understood the ramifications of that teaching until later in the 1850s when articles about the Day of Atonement and the investigative judgment by J.N. Andrews, Uriah Smith, James White, and others appeared in the *Advent Review and Sabbath Herald*.

Crosier's major points

In his article "The Law of Moses," Crosier emphasized several key points. Although as discussed above, probably few of these ideas originated with him, taken together they represented a major paradigm shift in post-Disappointment thinking.[43] First, Crosier asserted that a

---

S.S. Snow, *Jubilee Standard*, May 29, 1845, pp. 90-91.

[42]Clark, *1844*, vol. 1, pp. 128-129, 158-172. While the general public hated Joseph Smith and Mormons in general for their polygamy, the immediate cause of Smith's death was the charge of treason for ordering his Nauvoo Legion to destroy the printing establishment of the *Nauvoo Expositor* in Nauvoo, Illinois, in June 1844, thus undermining freedom of speech.

[43]L.E. Froom, in two letters to A.W. Spalding, Nov. 13 and Dec. 3, 1945, asserted that Crosier had given "a wonderful summary of ten points in the *Voice of Truth* long before" he wrote his Feb. 7, 1846, article in *The Day-Star* Extra. Spalding agreed, asserting in a Nov. 28, 1945, letter to Froom that Crosier's article had first appeared in *The Day-Dawn* in the winter of 1845 (he assumed sometime before March 1845), then in the *Voice of Truth* sometime later in 1845, and finally in *The Day-Star* Extra of Feb. 7, 1846. In a subsequent Dec. 12, 1945, letter to Froom, Spalding revised the date for *The Day-Dawn* article as "in

literal sanctuary exists in heaven. Second, he stated that the Hebrew sanctuary system on earth, a complete visual representation of the plan of salvation, was patterned after the heavenly sanctuary. Third, he explained that the priests in the wilderness tabernacle and Christ in the heavenly sanctuary had a two-phase ministry in the Holy Place and in the Most Holy Place and that the latter phase in heaven began on October 22, 1844. Fourth, he declared that on that date, Christ had "come to the marriage" (Matthew 25:10) and received His kingdom from the Ancient of Days (Daniel 7:13-14), God the Father. Fifth, he believed that while the first phase of Christ's ministry in the Holy Place had dealt with forgiveness, the second phase in the Most Holy Place involved the blotting out of sins and cleansing the heavenly sanctuary and individual believers. Sixth, he said that this cleansing (referred to in Daniel 8:14) is accomplished by Christ's blood, not by fire. Seventh, he predicted that Christ would not return to this earth until He had completed the second phase of His cleansing ministry in the Most Holy Place (Luke 12:35-37).[44]

Consequently, Crosier, Edson, and Hahn came to the realization that the atonement in heaven was not completed in a day as some Millerite writers suggested; instead, this anti-typical day of atonement would last many years, and no one knew exactly how many. In time, they further identified the scapegoat (Azazel) as Satan, not Christ, and realized that at the end of time, Satan would bear the ultimate guilt for the sins he had caused God's people to commit and would finally be destroyed in the lake of fire at the end of the millen-

---

March or April" of 1845. Unfortunately, this earlier *Voice of Truth* article is no longer extant. A.W. Spalding Correspondence, Collection 10, Box 1, Folder 2, CAR, JWL, AU.

[44]Crosier, *The Day-Star* Extra, Feb. 7, 1846, pp. 37-44. For further discussion of these points, see Knight, *Search for Identity*, pp. 63-64; Knight, *Anticipating the Advent*, p. 23; and Andrew Mustard, *James White and Seventh-day Adventist Organization: Historical Development, 1844-1881* (Berrien Springs, MI: Andrews University Press, 1987), pp. 93-94.

nium. It was only in 1857, however, that Sabbatarian Adventist writers Elon Everts and James White explored the significance of Christ's
ongoing investigative judgment work in heaven and the final judgment of the wicked during the millennium following Christ's second
coming. It wasn't until the 1870s that Goodloe Harper Bell advanced
the idea that the cleansing of the Most Holy Place also involved the
cleansing of the hearts of God's people from sin.[45]

Crosier's two articles soon became more widely available as other
newspapers republished them. His 1845 *Day-Dawn* article, for example, was reprinted in the May 5, 1851, issue of the *Review*, while
his February 7, 1846, *The Day-Star* Extra article appeared in two parts
in the September and October 1852 issues of the same paper. Like
Crosier, editor James White emphasized the scriptural evidence for
the heavenly sanctuary and not Edson's cornfield experience.[46]

The above evidence led Merlin Burt to summarize the role played
by Hiram Edson and his friends in the following statement:

> While Edson may have had the inspiring cornfield experience
> he describes, it seems unlikely, given what we know of Cro-
> sier's thought on the sanctuary in 1845, that Edson's ideas were
> as fully developed as he described them in his recollection....
> Hiram Edson perhaps had a less pivotal role (as revealed in ex-
> tant literature) in the origin of the extended atonement and
> heavenly sanctuary view. He did perhaps play a critical role in
> the linking of the Sabbath to the heavenly sanctuary.[47]

---

[45]For further discussion of these developments, see Schwarz and Greenleaf, *Light Bearers*, p. 60; Merlin
D. Burt, *CHIS674: Development of Seventh-day Adventist Theology* (Berrien Springs, MI: Syllabus for the
Seventh-day Adventist Seminary at Andrews University, 2019), pp. 61-62; and Jud Lake, "The Heart of
Adventist Theology," *Review*, Oct. 5, 2018, p. 35.
[46]Neufeld, "Edson's October 23 Experience," pp. 18-19.
[47]Burt, *Development of SDA Theology*, pp. 66-67.

Therefore, it would appear that Edson's insights received in the cornfield on October 23, 1844, while not fully developed at that time, provided the spark that ignited further Bible study on the part of several men whose subsequent articles in Millerite and Sabbatarian Adventist periodicals explored in greater depth the issues of atonement, cleansing, and judgment in the heavenly sanctuary.

Pioneer reactions

As might be expected, most Adventist contemporaries of Edson, Crosier, and Hahn were enthusiastic about their conclusions. For one thing, this new understanding provided them emotional and psychological relief after the Great Disappointment they had endured in 1844. It renewed their relationship with the larger community, because now that time would continue, they could contribute to society once more. Even more important, however, Crosier's articles gave them convincing biblical evidence in support of an October 22, 1844, cleansing event in the heavenly sanctuary. Seven years later, after abandoning their original shut-door teaching in 1851, they understood their duty to help the poor and homeless and conduct missionary work in foreign countries. In the decades that followed, an inward-looking sect was transformed into an outward-focused, mission-directed denomination.[48]

Ellen White had at least 11 visions concerning the sanctuary between 1844 and 1851.[49] One of them, received at Exeter, New Hampshire, in February 1845, confirmed the conclusions reached by Edson, Crosier, and Hahn. On April 21, 1847, White informed Eli Curtis that Crosier had "the true light on the cleansing of the

---

[48]Barton, "Adventism's Life Raft," pp. 18-19.
[49]Lake, "The Heart of Adventist Theology," p. 36.

sanctuary" as explained in the *The Day-Star* Extra article:

> The Lord shew [*sic*] me in vision, more than one year ago, that Brother Crosier had the true light, on the cleansing of the sanctuary, etc.; and that it was his will, that Brother C. should write out the view which he gave us in the Day-Star Extra, Feb. 7, 1846. I feel fully authorized by the Lord, to recommend that Extra, to every saint.[50]

Likewise, James White, who in September 1850 had included Crosier's article as a one-page insert in the *Review*, stated: "The article on 'The Sanctuary,' by O.R.L. Crozier, is excellent. The subject of the Sanctuary should be carefully examined, as it lies at the foundation of our faith and hope."[51] Joseph Bates was equally supportive. In his pamphlet *The Opening Heavens*, he wrote: "But allow me first to recommend to your particular notice, O.R.L. Crosier's article in the Day Star Extra for the 7th of February, 1846.... In my humble opinion it is superior to any thing of the kind extant."[52]

For these pioneer Adventists, the new light concerning the heavenly sanctuary demonstrated that "the end is not yet." This meant that they had more time to plan, to think, to work, and (after they abandoned the shut-door idea) to spread the gospel and save more souls in God's kingdom. Yet, as Edward Vick pointed out, during the next century and a half, the sanctuary doctrine underwent several permutations as it was reinterpreted to fit changing circumstances. For ex-

---

[50]Ellen G. White to Bro. Eli Curtis, April 21, 1847, in James White, Ellen White, and Joseph Bates, *A Word to the Little Flock* (Brunswick, ME: James White, 1847), p. 12.

[51]James White, "Remarks," *Review* Extra (Special), Sept. 1850.

[52]Joseph Bates, *The Opening Heavens, or a Connected View of the Testimony of the Prophets and Apostles, Concerning the Opening Heavens, Compared with Astronomical Observations, and of the Present and Future Location of the New Jerusalem, the Paradise of God* (New Bedford, MA: Benjamin Lindsey, 1846), p. 25.

ample, a teaching that brought great hope to Adventists in the 1840s, who suddenly realized that they had more time, was reinterpreted in the 20th century to encourage a sense of urgency that the end was very near, because when the sanctuary is fully cleansed of sin and the investigative judgment ends, then the Second Coming and final destruction of the earth will occur. The sanctuary teaching that united Adventists in the 1840s and galvanized them into a community that encircled their wagons to protect the five "S" doctrines (second coming, sanctuary, Sabbath, state of the dead, Spirit of Prophecy) sometimes brought contention and disunity among their descendants.[53]

The legacy of the sanctuary

In 1889, Dudley M. Canright declared: "I feel sure that they [Adventists] are in a great error" regarding the sanctuary message.[54] First, he declared that God's throne has always been located in the Most Holy Place of the heavenly sanctuary. Second, he asserted that Christ entered the Most Holy Place at His ascension in 31 A.D. Third, he argued that Old Testament types were not always fulfilled in New Testament realities, especially relating to Christ's ministry. Fourth, he believed that it was absurd to think that Old Testament Levitical services are being carried out in a heavenly sanctuary. In fact, he concluded, since there is no need for a physical temple in heaven, "the Adventists idea of the sanctuary in heaven is an absurdity."[55]

Although Albion Fox Ballenger disagreed with Canright about the reality of the heavenly sanctuary, in a letter written to Ellen White sometime after 1900, he emphasized that the biblical phrase "within

---

[53]Edward Vick, "Must We Keep the Sanctuary Doctrine?" *Spectrum* 14, no. 3 (Dec. 1983), pp. 52-55.
[54]Dudley M. Canright, *Seventh-day Adventism Renounced* (London and Edinburgh: Fleming H. Revell, 1905), p. 121.
[55]Canright, *Seventh-day Adventism Renounced*, pp. 122-128.

the veil" referred to the second apartment or Most Holy Place and not to the first or Holy Place, as Adventists then taught.[56] Two decades later, he agreed with Canright that God's throne has always been located in the Most Holy Place, and, furthermore, that Christ had taken His place near the mercy seat on the ark in the Most Holy Place at His ascension and had not waited until October 22, 1844 to do so.[57]

In October 1931, Louis R. Conradi, president of the European Division, stood before a group of 27 General Conference officials meeting in Omaha, Nebraska, to answer for his doctrinal deviations concerning the sanctuary message. Over the course of four days, he argued first that Christ's antitypical service of cleansing began at the cross in 31 A.D., not in heaven in 1844. Second, he asserted that this service had been finished before the prophetic seventy weeks ended in 34 A.D. Third, he stated that Christ entered the Most Holy Place in heaven at His ascension. Fourth, he defined the church on earth as the sanctuary to be cleansed in 1844. Fifth, he declared that the 2300-day prophecy referred to the breaking of Muslim power to persecute Christians and not to a time of investigative judgment in heaven.[58] Eight years later in 1939, Conradi not only denied the validity of the Adventists' sanctuary message, he also attacked those pioneers who had advocated it. He called Samuel S. Snow, who first preached the October 22, 1844, date, "fanatical."[59] He also said Millerism was "the counterfeit American movement"[60] and argued that Snow and others

---

[56]Albion Fox Ballenger, "A Letter from A.F. Ballenger to Mrs. White Which Was Never Answered," pp. 1-2, manuscript 006688 (190-), CAR, JWL, AU.

[57]Albion Fox Ballenger, *An Examination of Forty Fatal Errors Regarding the Atonement* (Riverside, CA: Author, 192-), pp. 1, 4, 92.

[58]General Conference of Seventh-day Adventists, "Statement of Conradi Hearing" (Omaha, Neb., General Conference Committee Report, Oct. 13-16, 1931), pp. 1-6, manuscript WDF96, no. 18, CAR, JWL, AU.

[59]Louis R. Conradi, *The Founders of the Seventh-day Adventist Denomination* (Plainfield, NJ: The American Sabbath Tract Society, 1939), p. 9.

[60]Conradi, *Founders*, p. 8.

had made "preposterous claims" for October 22 and the shut door.[61] He also denounced the Seventh-day Adventist teaching about the investigative judgment as "a questionable hypothesis."[62]

Four decades later, in his magisterial two-volume work *Daniel 8:14, the Day of Atonement, and the Investigative Judgment* (1980), Desmond Ford, a theology professor at Avondale College, provided a historical sketch of a dozen Adventist preachers and theologians from Crosier in the 1840s to Froom in the 1940s who had expressed doubt about the Adventist position on the heavenly sanctuary.[63] Ford then listed his own objections. First, he asserted that Hebrews teaches that Christ entered the Most Holy Place at His ascension. Second, he said that the Holy Place was a symbol of the typical era, not a phase of His ministry. Third, he argued that Christ completed His cleansing work at the cross. Fourth, he declared that the day-for-a-year calculation was unbiblical. Fifth, he insisted that Daniel 8's "little horn" referred to Antiochus Epiphanes. Sixth, he stated that Daniel 7 focused on judgment of the little horn, not the saints. Seventh, he believed that Revelation 14 is a judgment of Babylon, not the saints. Eighth, he wrote that the Bible does not teach that our sins defile the heavenly sanctuary or that Christ bears our sins in the Most Holy Place. Ninth, he felt that it is impossible to be dogmatic about prophetic dates. (Ford advocated what he called "the apotelesmatic principle": that prophecies have multiple fulfillments.) Tenth, he pointed out that the Adventist pioneers were wrong about the "shut door" until 1851. Finally, he was convinced that no clear Scriptures taught the

---

[61]Conradi, *Founders*, p. 11.
[62]Conradi, *Founders*, p. 20.
[63]Desmond Ford, *Daniel 8:14, the Day of Atonement, and the Investigative Judgment* (Casselberry, FL: Euangelion Press, 1980), pp. 29-60. This list included O.R.L. Crosier, James White, Dudley Canright, E.J. Waggoner, Albion Fox Ballenger, E.S. Ballenger, W.W. Fletcher, Louis Conradi, W.W. Prescott, L.E. Froom, Harold Snide, and R.A. Greive.

investigative judgment.[64]

In the 21st century, Dale Ratzlaff acknowledged that the cleansing of the heavenly sanctuary and the investigative judgment "is unique to the SDA Church and is the very center of SDA theology," but averred that because "no doctrine is more confusing that this one," "it remains the most difficult doctrine to explain, support, or understand."[65] He argued that linking Daniel 8:14 with Leviticus 16 "is not good exegesis" and that there is "absolutely no basis whatsoever to the Seventh-day Adventist 1844 cleansing of the heavenly sanctuary and the investigative judgment," which he disparages as "minutiae" and "the central problem" of Adventist "history, ethics, and religious experience."[66] Instead, like most sanctuary critics before him, Ratzlaff declares that Christ entered the Most Holy Place at His ascension. He concluded that the Adventist teaching on the sanctuary "is dependent upon a proof-text, context-denying, reading-into-Scripture-what-is-not-there method of interpretation which uses a tenuous string of assumptions, most of which are contrary to the biblical evidence."[67] Edward Vick added that for some, the heavenly sanctuary is an allegorical construct, while others see it as typological or even mythological.[68]

In many respects, these criticisms have enhanced the critical understanding of the sanctuary and investigative judgment. Since the 1980s, scholars such as Frank Holbrook, Richard Davidson, Roy Gane, and the members of the Daniel and Revelation Committee have given the subject deeper study. This examination, church historian

[64]Ford, Daniel 8:14, p. 293.
[65]Dale Ratzlaff, Cultic Doctrine of Seventh-day Adventism: An Evangelical Wake-up Call (Glendale, AZ: Life Assurance Ministries, 2009), pp. 153-155.
[66]Ratzlaff, Cultic Doctrine, pp. 158, 165.
[67]Ratzlaff, Cultic Doctrine, pp. 173-175.
[68]Vick, "Must We Keep the Sanctuary Doctrine?" p. 54.

Jud Lake opines, "has opened new vistas and depths from the biblical data on Christ's ministry in heaven." It has served to validate the pioneers' views; it has revealed that the verdict of the pre-Advent judgment actually favors the righteous; and it has strengthened believers' faith in God's Word and deepened their love for Christ. Consequently, Lake concludes: "The doctrine of the heavenly sanctuary, including its pre-advent investigative judgment has been, and will continue to be, the heart of Adventist theology."[69] Along the same line, theologian Richard Rice called the doctrine of the heavenly sanctuary "the distinctive contribution" of Seventh-day Adventists "to Christian theology" that was developed over a period of 13 years (1844-1857) from William Miller (who contributed the 2300-year timeline) and Hiram Edson (who added the sanctuary being in heaven), to Elon Everts and James White (who focused on the investigative judgment).[70] Although Ratzlaff disparaged the Adventist teaching on the sanctuary, he too admitted that the doctrines of the cleansing of the heavenly sanctuary and the investigative judgment lie at "the very center of SDA theology."[71] In this respect, he agreed with Ellen White when she called these doctrines two of "the old landmarks" and "pillars" of the Advent faith.[72]

In the midst of the theological controversy that followed the 1980 publication of Desmond Ford's book *Daniel 8:14, the Day of Atonement, and the Investigative Judgment*, many Adventist theologians presented a more positive view of these "old landmarks." Fritz Guy asserted in 1983: "The consummation of atonement and reconciliation that is described as 'judgment' is the confirmation of salvation.

---

[69]Lake, "The Heart of Adventist Theology," p. 36.
[70]Richard Rice, "The Relevance of the Investigative Judgment," *Spectrum* 14, no. 1 (Aug. 1983), pp. 32-34.
[71]Ratzlaff, *Cultic Doctrine*, pp. 153-154.
[72]Ellen White, *Counsels to Writers and Editors* (Nashville: Southern Pub. Assn., 1946), pp. 30-31, 44.

It is the final recognition and revelation of our acceptance of God's ultimate gift. At that point, God's continuing initiative on behalf of humanity has reached its objective."[73] That same year, Rice stated: "Christ's ministry in the heavenly sanctuary concludes with a review of the ultimate impact of God's saving activity in human history." This review, he added, is comprehensive and in effect shows the true character of God's sovereignty, demonstrating that His deeds are "great and wonderful, that his ways are just and true (Rev. 15:3)." Consequently, according to Rice, the focal point of the investigative judgment is the sovereignty of God and His character, not human beings or the unfallen beings of other worlds. It proves that God deserves to be God because He is loving, just, and fair. Rice concluded by declaring: "The specific concern of the investigative judgment is the cumulative impact of God's saving activity in history." It therefore "removes all doubt about the nature and desirability of God's sovereignty."[74]

Consequently, Adventists in the 21st century are left with two competing realities. On the one hand, as the author Clifford Goldstein pointed out, "The 1844 judgment—more than the state of the dead, the Sabbath, the second coming [of Christ]—establishes the validity of Adventism," because "Adventists are the only people who have the 1844 investigative judgment truth," which constitutes "our calling, our purpose, or our mission."[75] Furthermore, he declared, "if 1844 is not biblical, our message is false—we are a false church teaching a false message and leading people down a false path. Either 1844 is true and we have truth, or it's false and we have inherited and peddled lies."[76]

---

[73]Fritz Guy, "Good News From the Sanctuary in Heaven: God's Continuing Initiative," *Spectrum* (Aug. 1983), p. 45.

[74]Rice, "Relevance," pp. 32-36.

[75]Clifford Goldstein, *1844 Made Simple* (Boise, ID: Pacific Press Pub. Assn., 1988), p. 10.

[76]Goldstein, *1844 Made Simple*, p. 11.

On the other hand, this doctrine that many have called the heart, the center, and the mission of the Seventh-day Adventist Church is waning in popularity among many of its members. Whereas the 1990 Valuegenesis study of Adventist academy students, conducted by V. Bailey Gillespie and Roger Dudley, showed that 45 percent of Adventist youth agreed with the statement that "the investigative or pre-advent judgment in heaven began in 1844,"[77] only 27 percent of youth responded positively to this statement in the 2000 follow-up study. Yet this may also reflect more a lack of knowledge than opposition to the belief.[78] Another survey conducted in the 1990s by Dr. Glen Greenwalt, professor of theology at Walla Walla College, discovered that while 78 percent of retired church members believed that the investigative judgment was "extremely important" or "very important" to their faith, only nine percent of Adventist college sophomores shared the same enthusiasm for that doctrine. Instead, 95 percent of Adventist youth felt that the church should "stop trying to prove time prophecies altogether and move on to bigger, more important issues...to push ahead in the spirit of the pioneers of our discovery of new truths and landmarks."[79] Greenwalt pithily concluded: "To idolize the past is to give up the journey along the way."[80]

In 1846, Edson was determined to neither idolize his past nor abandon the journey that lay ahead as he and a growing number of former Millerite Adventists began coming together to investigate what Ellen White would later call "the truth as it is in Jesus."[81] Dur-

[77]Roger Dudley and V. Bailey Gillespie, *Valuegenesis: Faith in the Balance* (La Sierra, CA: La Sierra University Press, 1992), p. 85.

[78]V. Bailey Gillespie, Michael J. Donahue, Ed Boyatt, and Barry Gane, *Valuegenesis Ten Years Later: A Study of Two Generations* (Riverside, CA: Hancock Center Publication, 2004), p. 157 (see table).

[79]Greenwalt, "Sanctuary," pp. 42-49.

[80]Greenwalt, "Sanctuary," p. 43.

[81]Ellen White, *Christ's Object Lessons* (Mountain View, CA: Pacific Press Pub. Assn., 1900; Washington, D.C.: Review and Herald Pub. Assn., 1941), p. 129.

ing the late 1840s, Hiram and Esther Edson not only participated in frequent "Sabbath Conferences," they also hosted them, as Chapter 6 shows.

Hiram and Esther Edson

Edson Home in Port Gibson

Luther Edson's 1840s barn

Port Gibson, NY, c. 1946

E. Peck, printer.

Erie Canal Aqueduct at Rochester

Tabor Corners in the
1850s was on the main
stage line from Bath

Rochester-Canandaigua Stagecoach

O.R.L. Crosier—*The Day-Dawn* and *The Day-Star* newspapers

Washington Hand Press, 1852

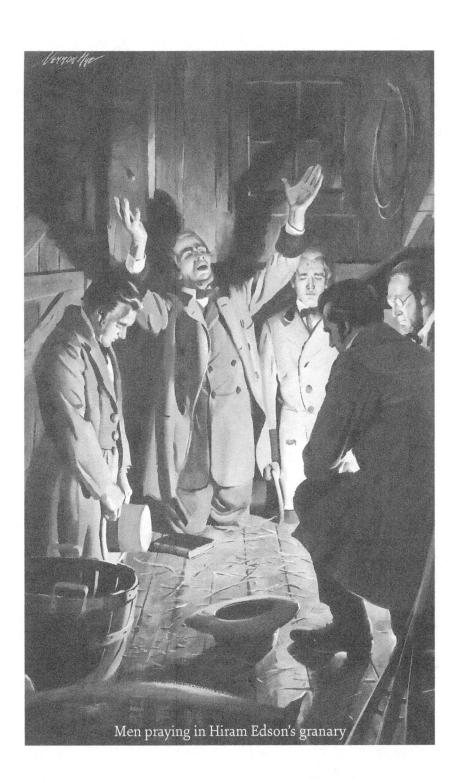

Men praying in Hiram Edson's granary

Hiram Edson and Owen Crosier crossing the cornfield

O.R.L. Crosier—photo found in *The Founders of the Seventh day Adventist Denomination*, by Richard Conradi (1939)

Port Gibson School

Hiram and Esther Edson's Grave

Blossom's Hotel in Canandaigua

Troy Coach

Chapter 6

Active Layman

A fter the Great Disappointment, the Millerites split into two major camps: a larger group that abandoned any belief in the prophetic significance of the October 22, 1844, date and a smaller group that believed Christ had begun His cleansing work in the Most Holy Place of the heavenly sanctuary on that date. Although the latter sect proudly called themselves the "Shut-Door Adventists," in recent years they have been renamed the "Bridegroom Adventists" due to their emphasis on the parable of the bridegroom and the ten virgins related in Matthew 25.[1] By 1845, further splintering produced the spiritualizers (who believed Christ had come to earth secretly in 1844), led by Orlando Squires, who published the newspaper *Voice of the Shepherd* in Utica, New York; and the literalists (who believed Christ would actually return bodily to this earth at some future time), led by Enoch Jacobs, who published the newspaper *The Day-Star* in Cincinnati, Ohio.[2] Ellen Harmon, James White, Crosier, Hahn, Edson, and many others identified with this second group. Finally, among those who still believed in a heavenly sanctuary, some (like Samuel Snow and John Pearson) taught that Christ's atoning work in the Most Holy Place had been completed on October 22, while others (includ-

---

[1]Burt, *Development of Seventh-day Adventist Theology*, p. 44.
[2]Burt, *Development of Seventh-day Adventist Theology*, pp. 53-54.

ing Crosier, Edson, Hahn, Bates, Ellen Harmon, and Emily Clemons) believed His atonement could last for a few more months or years.[3]

Even within this latter group, who called themselves "the remnant" or "the little flock," "internecine squabbles" arose concerning the state of the dead, the existence of hell, the biblical Sabbath, the ordinance of foot washing, the nature of the millennium and the judgment, and the fulfillment of various prophecies.[4] How could such sharp differences of opinion be resolved and unity achieved? The solution, many felt, was to hold weekend meetings in which the participants could, through prayer and intense Bible study, hash out their disagreements and come into harmony with one another. Because these gatherings met on weekends and frequently discussed the Sabbath truth, they have been called "Sabbath Conferences," although a few of them met on weekdays as well.

1846 Port Gibson gathering

As mentioned in Chapter 3, the Edsons hosted several gatherings of Millerites at their home in Port Gibson prior to October 22, 1844. Located on the Erie Canal, Port Gibson was a convenient stopping place for Adventists traveling by packet boat.[5] After reading Crosier's article in *The Day-Star* Extra, James White and Joseph Bates, convinced of its truth, wrote to Edson requesting the privilege of meeting at his home for a conference of believers. Although Edson had never met Bates, the two had become somewhat acquainted through their correspondence.[6] At least eight people attended this meeting in the autumn of 1846: the Edsons, the Whites, Bates, Crosier, and the Hahns.[7]

---

[3]Burt, *Development of Seventh-day Adventist Theology*, p. 55.
[4]Gaustad, *Rise of Adventism*, pp. 178-179.
[5]Collins, *Heartwarming Stories*, Book 1, p. 33.
[6]Viah Cross to P.Z. Kinne, "Hiram Edson's Experience," p. 7.
[7]Collins, *Heartwarming Stories*, Book 1, pp. 35-37.

As the participants opened their Bibles, Crosier presented the subject of the cleansing of the heavenly sanctuary, perhaps with occasional comments from Edson and Hahn.[8] When Crosier finished, Bates read to the group from his pamphlet *The Seventh Day Sabbath, a Perpetual Sign*, which argued that Saturday was still the Lord's Sabbath day as it had been in Bible times.[9] When Bates finished reading, Edson rose to his feet and exclaimed, "Brother Bates, that is light and truth! The seventh day is the Sabbath, and I am with you to keep it." Crosier demurred, telling the attendees, "We don't want to step on any new planks until we know they'll hold us up." Edson responded, "I've been studying the Sabbath question for a long time. As for me, I've put my weight upon it, and I know it's a plank that will hold us up."[10] As a result of Bates' Bible study, the Edsons, Hahns, and Crosier accepted the seventh-day Sabbath. While the Edsons kept the Sabbath for the rest of their lives, Crosier and Hahn later abandoned it and returned to Sunday keeping by 1848.[11]

When Edson read the second edition of Bates' pamphlet in March 1847, he wrote a letter to *The Day-Dawn* recommending it "to all such as are willing to *do* the commandments of God" and go to heaven. In this lengthy letter, Edson emphasized that the Law of Moses was carnal, limited, faulty, and a law of bondage. It was therefore nailed to the cross. Thereafter, the gospel covenant, which took the place of the Mosaic law, was "the perfect law of liberty," spiritual, holy, just, and good. All who fulfilled its demands would be justified, blessed, and saved eternally. Consequently, all "the true

---

[8]Damsteegt, *Foundations*, p. 139.

[9]Knight, *Joseph Bates*, pp. 99-100.

[10]This conversation is recreated in Collins, *Heartwarming Stories*, Book 1, pp. 36-37.

[11]Knight, *Joseph Bates*, pp. 100-101. Hiram Edson had apparently read T.M. Preble's tract on the Sabbath sometime before Oct. 22, 1844, but he did not at that time see its importance for contemporary Christians. See Damsteegt, *Foundations*, p. 140. James and Ellen White had already accepted the Sabbath after reading Bates' 1846 pamphlet.

children of Israel" (which he called "bible [sic] Jews") would keep the seventh-day Sabbath "for a PERPETUAL COVENANT" and a "sign between God and his people forever." Thus, all those "that DO his commandments" will enter in through the gates into the city [the New Jerusalem in heaven]."[12]

The results of the 1846 Port Gibson gathering and subsequent Sabbatarian Advent publications proved highly significant, because they forged a consensus around several key Adventist doctrines. They helped to unify a tiny band of believers who accepted October 22, 1844, as the commencement of the Day of Atonement in the Most Holy Place of the heavenly sanctuary; who kept the seventh-day Sabbath; who accepted the Spirit of Prophecy as manifested in Ellen White; and who saw themselves fulfilling the three angels' messages of Revelation 14.[13] The scattered saints were thus united theologically and geographically by the preaching of the sanctuary message (representing western New York), the Sabbath doctrine (representing Massachusetts and New Hampshire), and the Spirit of Prophecy (representing Maine)—a sort of "three-legged stool" that could now stand on its own.[14] Furthermore, according to George Knight, in Bates' revised pamphlet, he connected all these doctrinal dots by showing how the Sabbath, the heavenly sanctuary, and the seal of God[15] were linked in the setting of a Sabbatarian Advent prophetic movement heralded by the three angels' messages.[16]

---

[12]Hiram Edson, Letter of March 1, 1847, to *The Day-Dawn*, April 2, 1847, pp. 7-8; emphasis his.
[13]Merlin D. Burt, "Remember the Mighty Acts of God," *Adventist World*, July 2017, pp. 24-25.
[14]Froom, *Prophetic Faith*, vol. 4, p. 845.
[15]In his 1848 tract *A Seal of the Living God, a Hundred Forty-Four Thousand of the Servants of God Being Sealed in 1849* (New Bedford, MA: Benjamin Lindsey, 1849), Bates identified those who kept the seventh-day Sabbath as having the seal of God.
[16]Bates, *The Seventh Day Sabbath, a Perpetual Sign* (New Bedford, MA: Benjamin Lindsey, 1847). For further discussion of Bates' tract, see Knight, *Millennial Fever*, pp. 310-312, and Knight, *Search for Identity*, p. 70.

1848 Volney gathering

The 1846 meeting at Edson's home proved so successful that the growing group of Adventists decided to hold several more conferences in 1848:

> April 20-24, 1848, at Albert Belden's home in Rocky Hill, Connecticut
>
> August 18, 1848, at David Arnold's carriage house in Volney, New York
>
> August 27-28, 1848, at Hiram Edson's barn in Port Gibson, New York
>
> September 8-9, 1848, at Albert Belden's home in Rocky Hill, Connecticut
>
> October 20-22, 1848, at Stockbridge Howland's home in Topsham, Maine
>
> November 18, 1848, at Otis Nichol's home in Dorchester, Massachusetts.[17]

While it does not appear that Edson attended the first Sabbath Conference at Rocky Hill, he did attend the second one in Volney. David Arnold had joined the Methodist Episcopal Church in 1821 and then accepted the Millerite message in the 1840s.[18] More than 40 individuals attended this second gathering, including the Whites, Bates, Stephen Pierce, Heman S. Gurney, E.L.H. Chamberlain, and about 35 others from western New York.[19] Edson sent the Whites money to help pay their travel expenses, and James earned another

---

[17]Froom, *Prophetic Faith*, vol. 4, pp. 1021-1023.
[18]Froom, *Prophetic Faith*, vol. 4, p. 1023 (see footnote 8).
[19]Froom, *Prophetic Faith*, vol. 4, p. 1022.

$40 by mowing hay with a scythe for a week at 87.5 cents an acre.[20]

Ellen White described the attendees as searching "for the truth as for hidden treasure." They sometimes studied their Bibles late into the night, and occasionally, through the entire night.[21] Once again, Bates discoursed on the seventh-day Sabbath while James White preached about the parable of the bridegroom and the wedding feast in Matthew 25.[22] Unfortunately, unlike the 1846 gathering at the Edson home, harmony did not prevail at this meeting. Instead, Ellen White bemoaned the fact that hardly two of the attendees agreed on any topic they discussed.[23] To borrow a colorful contemporary phrase used by New Yorkers and popularized by Lydia Maria Child in the 1840s: "They have put my mind and body both in a confounded muss."[24] Arnold, for example, thought that the thousand years of Revelation 20 lay in the past, that the Lord's Supper and foot-washing services should be held only once a year like the ancient Passover celebration, and that the 144,000 mentioned in Revelation 7 and 14 would be raised at Christ's second coming.[25]

Their contention so alarmed White that she fainted and lay unconscious for some time. A few of those present, fearing that she was dying, prayed over her prostrate body, and she revived and went into vision. When the vision ended, she pointed out individuals' errors and urged the group to yield them to Bible truth. They did so, and in her words, "Our meeting closed triumphantly. Truth gained the victory. Our brethren renounced their errors and united upon the third angel's message."[26]

---

[20]Ellen White, *Life Sketches of Ellen G. White* (Mountain View, CA: Pacific Press Pub. Assn., 1915), pp. 108-110.

[21]Ellen White to J.H. Kellogg, Nov. 20, 1903, quoted in Knight, *Joseph Bates*, p. 153.

[22]Froom, *Prophetic Faith*, vol. 4, pp. 1022-1023.

[23]Ellen White, *Life Sketches*, p. 110.

[24]Child, "Letter XIII," *Letters from New York*, p. 129.

[25]Ellen White, *Life Sketches*, pp. 110-111.

[26]Ellen White, *Life Sketches*, p. 111.

1848 Port Gibson gathering

At this third Sabbath Conference there were so many participants that they could not all fit inside the house, so the women slept in the house and the men bedded down in the haymow. The meeting was held in the spacious main floor of the barn.[27] Unlike the contentious Volney meeting, union and harmony prevailed at this gathering.[28] While there were some significant differences expressed, the attendees agreed to submit their disagreements to biblical evaluation and unite on the platform of Bible truth. Consequently, if some teaching could not be proved from Scripture, it was abandoned.[29] As a result, the attendees eventually came to complete agreement regarding the seventh-day Sabbath and the sanctuary message, linking these two doctrines as key components of the third angel's message. Thus, according to Merlin Burt, this meeting constituted "the theological birthplace of the Seventh-day Adventist Church," because it linked together those in New England teaching the Sabbath with those in New York teaching the sanctuary.[30]

Following this meeting, Bates and the Whites boarded an Erie Canal line boat and headed for New York City. As they attempted to jump from the line boat to a passing packet boat near Centerport, Bates caught his heel on the edge of the boat and fell backwards into the water, holding onto his pocketbook and hat, but losing his dollar fare. Fortunately for him, however, the canal was only four feet deep in that section. The Whites and a sopping wet Bates walked to the nearby home of the Harris family, and while Bates' clothing was hung to dry, the Whites gave Mrs. Harris a temperance lecture about

---

[27]Viah O. Cross, "Recollections of the Message," *Review*, April 1, 1920, p. 23.
[28]Froom, *Prophetic Faith*, vol. 4, p. 1023.
[29]Ellen White, *Life Sketches*, pp. 111-112.
[30]Burt, *Adventist Pioneer Places*, pp. 130-131.

her use of snuff and her visiting friend's penchant for gaudy jewelry. In time, the entire Harris family converted and became pillars of Sabbatarian Adventism in central New York.[31]

Edson's favorite hymn

In 1849-1850, while the Whites were living in Oswego, New York, James paid Richard Oliphant[32] to publish several copies of a new hymnbook, *Hymns for God's Peculiar People*.[33] Included in its pages were 53 gospel songs that had been sung by the Millerites earlier in the 1840s. One of those hymns, "Here Is No Rest," had become one of Edson's favorites, and he was often heard singing it. The words of its four stanzas and choruses are as follows:

Stanza 1:   Here o'er the earth as a stranger I roam,

Here is no rest—is no rest;

Here as a pilgrim I wander alone,

Yet I am blest—I am blest.

Chorus 1:   For I look forward to that glorious day,

When sin and sorrow will vanish away,

My heart doth leap while I hear Jesus say,

There, there is rest—there is rest.

Stanza 2:   Here fierce temptations beset me around;

Here is no rest—is no rest;

Here I am griev'd while my foes me surround;

Yet I am blest—I am blest.

---

[31]Ellen White, *Life Sketches*, pp. 112-114.
[32]Richard Oliphant was a printer whose second-floor establishment was located at West First Street in Oswego. Richard's brother, Henry Oliphant, was a printer in Auburn, New York. Both printed many Sabbatarian Adventist tracts, pamphlets, and newspapers in the 1840s and 1850s.
[33]James White, comp., *Hymns for God's Peculiar People, That Keep the Commandments of God, and the Faith of Jesus* (Oswego, NY: Printed by Richard Oliphant, 1849).

Chorus 2:   Let them revile me, and scoff at my name,

Laugh at my weeping—endeavor to shame;

I will go forward, for this is my theme;

There, there is rest—there is rest.

Stanza 3:   Here are afflictions and trials severe;

Here is no rest—is no rest;

Here I must part with the friends I hold dear;

Yet I am blest—I am blest.

Chorus 3:   Sweet is the promise I read in his word;

Blessed are they who have died in the Lord;

They will be call'd to receive their reward;

Then there is rest—there is rest.

Stanza 4:   This world of cares is a wilderness state,

Here is no rest—is no rest;

Here I must bear from the world all its hate—

Yet I am blest—I am blest.

Chorus 4:   Soon shall I be from the wicked released,

Soon shall the weary forever be blest,

Soon shall I lean upon Jesus' breast—

Then there is rest—there is rest.[34]

In many ways, this song reflects Edson's personal experience. As described in stanza 1, he, too, was a pilgrim, not only as a descendant of the original Pilgrims of 1620, but also as a spiritual pilgrim whose journey from Methodism to Millerism and finally to Sabbatarian Adventism garnered him both friends and enemies along the way. Like the words of stanza 2, in the 1840s, Edson had been grieved by the mocking of his fellow citizens regarding the Great Disappointment

---

[34]"Here Is No Rest," Hymn No. 23 in White, *Hymns for God's Peculiar People*, pp. 24-25.

and by the slander of Joseph Marsh against his good name. Mirroring the words of stanza 3, he, too, had been abandoned by former friends (like Crosier and Hahn) who now opposed the seventh-day Sabbath and sanctuary doctrines they had once discovered together. Likewise, chorus 4's reference to "the wicked" paralleled his family's experience with the mob who had invaded their home and assaulted their guests in 1844. Given the unending rigors of year-round farming, Edson undoubtedly yearned for the rest promised in the four choruses. He needed rest on several levels—physical, mental, emotional, and spiritual. And yet, he found little rest as he endeavored several times to locate Samuel Rhodes and persuade him to return to active ministry.

Rescuing Samuel Rhodes

Hiram Edson described Samuel W. Rhodes as "one of the most faithful, and self-sacrificing lecturers on the Second Advent, that ever labored in this region [New York]."[35] Active in the Millerite movement, Rhodes had donated much of his property and personal belongings to that cause in order to provide funds for the distribution of Adventist publications and to pay the expenses of field agents and lecturers. He also paid his own expenses as he traveled from place to place, preaching the message of Christ's imminent return. By October 22, 1844, his personal means had been entirely exhausted.[36]

It was not the prospect of poverty that broke Rhodes' spirit, however, but the verbal abuse that former friends heaped upon him after the Great Disappointment. He also felt that God had forsaken him. Deeply depressed, he decided to abandon human society and

[35]Hiram Edson, Nov. 26, 1849, Letter to *Present Truth*, Dec. 1849, p. 34.
[36]D.E. Robinson, "The Gift of Tongues in Early Advent History," p. 1, undated manuscript 032461, CAR, JWL, AU.

flee, as the prophet Elijah had once done, to some secluded place.[37] For three years (1847-1849), he hid himself amidst the wilderness of the Adirondack Mountains of northern New York, sustaining himself by hunting deer and fowl in its forests and catching fish in its streams.[38] Fifteen miles from the nearest settlement, he lived the life of a hermit.[39]

Even though Rhodes lived in solitude, he was not forgotten. Edson twice attempted to find Rhodes in order to return him to active Adventist ministry, but he failed both times. On November 7, 1849, he made a third journey, hiking 14 miles roundtrip, but he did not find his friend. Edson nevertheless refused to give up his quest.[40] Eight days before attending a meeting at the Harris home in Centerport, New York, on November 17-18, 1849, Edson dreamed of entering a room in which six discouraged people were praying. One of them had said to him, "Oh! Bro. Edson, I am in the dark!" Edson believed this dream was fulfilled when he entered the Harris parlor and heard Richard Ralph express uncertainty regarding whether they should try to find Rhodes yet again.[41]

When Edson asked Ellen White's advice about this quest, she expressed skepticism about the practicality of trying to find a man who did not want to be found. During a prayer session asking God for some indication of His favor for this enterprise, Edson reported that the Holy Spirit "settled upon us so that the place was awful and glorious." Ralph began speaking in an unknown tongue.[42] Providing the

---

[37]Robinson, "Gift of Tongues," p. 1.
[38]A.W. Spalding to T.E. Unruh, Feb. 25, 1946, A.W. Spalding Correspondence, Collection 10, Box 1, Folder 3, CAR, JWL, AU.
[39]James Nix, William Fagal, Lewis Walton, and Richard Walton, "What Hath God Wrought?" compact disc (Harrisburg, PA: American Cassette Ministries, c. 2006), disc 4.
[40]"What Hath God Wrought" CD, disc 4.
[41]Edson, Nov. 26, 1849, Letter to *Present Truth*, Dec. 1849, p. 36.
[42]Robinson, "Gift of Tongues," p. 2.

interpretation for those kneeling in prayer, he said that God wanted Edson and Ralph to go after Rhodes.[43] After receiving another vision the following morning, White granted her approval for the mission, instructing them to tell Rhodes that God loved him; that "there had been no guile" in his mouth when he had opposed the seventh-day Sabbath and the shut-door teachings; that there was "hope and mercy for him"; and that angels would protect him if he returned with Edson and Ralph.[44]

The two men left on Monday, November 19, and traveled 14 miles, much of it on foot, following trails blazed by Indians, hunters, and fishermen. At last, they found Rhodes working in a field near the Black River. Like most hermits, he was somewhat the worse for wear. Rhodes shared a surprise with his friends. Two or three nights earlier, he had dreamed that the two men were seeking him.[45] As they prayed with him, sharing White's message of God's mercy and love, Ralph once again began speaking in tongues.[46] Taking that as a sign of God's approval, Rhodes agreed to return to civilization. Thus, Edson and Ralph not only rescued Rhodes from his wilderness hermitage but also from the cloud of despondency in which he had lived since 1844.[47]

Subsequently, Rhodes became "a blazing star in evangelism."[48] When he attended the November 22-23, 1849, Sabbath Conference held in David Arnold's carriage house at Volney, New York, his friends rejoiced to see him. As Edson reported in *The Present Truth*:

---

[43] Robinson, "Gift of Tongues," p. 2 and "What Hath God Wrought?" CD, disc 4.
[44] Ellen White, "Beloved Brethren, scattered abroad," *Present Truth*, Dec. 1849, p. 35.
[45] Edson, Nov. 26, 1849, Letter to *Present Truth*, Dec. 1849, p. 36.
[46] Robinson, "Gift of Tongues," p. 3.
[47] Edson, Nov. 26, 1849, Letter to *Present Truth*, Dec. 1849, p. 36.
[48] Spalding, "House of Refuge," *Review*, March 9, 1950, p. 11.

They were all rejoiced to see Bro. Rhodes. Tears of joy and
tenderness flowed freely as they greeted each other. We had a
sweet, heavenly sitting together during the meeting, and Bro.
Rhodes' faith and hope are fast increasing. He stands firm in
all the present truth; and we heartily bid him God speed, as
he goes to search out and feed the precious, scattered flock
of Jesus.[49]

During the winter of 1849-1850, Rhodes and George Holt traveled together, preaching the third angel's message throughout New
York State. An editorial in the March 1850 *Present Truth* described
the spiritual and emotional euphoria the two men felt after several
months of successful ministry:

[They had returned to Oswego] in good health, and strong in
faith. Their labors for a few weeks past, have been effectual,
in bringing out the precious jewels [converts], and establishing them in the present truth. About forty have embraced the
Sabbath within a few weeks where they have labored. They
feel that they cannot rest; but must go as fast as possible, and
hunt up the scattered "sheep" who are perishing for want of
spiritual food. Brethren, let them have your prayers; also, be
careful to see that their temporal wants are supplied.[50]

Like Bates, Rhodes was a trailblazer for Sabbatarian Adventism.
He was the first evangelist to go to Wisconsin—some two years before
Joseph Bates went there—and also entered Michigan, Illinois, and In-

---

[49]Edson, Nov. 26, 1849, Letter to *Present Truth*, Dec. 1849, p. 36.
[50]"Conference," *Present Truth*, March 1850, p. 56.

diana.[51] Brave and self-denying, he could also be impulsive. On one occasion, when he and the Whites were confronted by "white-robed fanatics," Rhodes dragged them in their chairs from the meeting-house onto the lawn so that they could no longer disrupt the meetings.[52] Church leaders appointed Rhodes to the Review and Herald Publishing Committee, but he was too erratic and impulsive for committee work and did not remain in that position more than a year.[53] In later years, Joshua V. Himes, William Miller's public relations agent, accused Rhodes of "spiritual wifery" (having more than one female partner), but Ezra P. Butler, the father of General Conference president George I. Butler, cleared him of those charges.[54] Rhodes once exclaimed to James White: "Be of good courage, my dear tried brother, and in Jesus' name, press the battle to the gate. I mean to go to heaven with you."[55]

Spalding called Rhodes "a trial to his brethren in his later career," adding that James White had once said "some very stiff things" about Rhodes at Oswego, New York. Nonetheless, Rhodes was also "swift to repent and confess" his sins and mistakes and express his remorse in letters to the *Review*.[56] Rhodes moved to Battle Creek, Michigan, in 1867, but he later lived in nearby Marshall, where he died of paralysis in 1883. He was buried in an unmarked grave in Battle Creek's Oak Hill Cemetery, surrounded by many early Adventist friends.[57] Doubtless his old friend Hiram Edson would have considered his many

---

[51]A.W. Spalding to T.E. Unruh, Feb. 25, 1946, Spalding Correspondence, Collection 10, Box 1, Folder 3, CAR, JWL, AU.
[52]Spalding to Unruh, Feb. 25, 1946.
[53]Spalding to Unruh, Feb. 25, 1946.
[54]Spalding to Unruh, Feb. 25, 1946.
[55]Samuel Rhodes, quoted in Spalding to Unruh, Feb. 25, 1946.
[56]A.W. Spalding to C.L. Taylor, June 20, 1948, Spalding Correspondence, Collection 10, Box 2, Folder 1, CAR, JWL, AU.
[57]A.W. Spalding to W.P. Elliott, July 16, 1946, Spalding Correspondence, Collection 10, Box 1, Folder 3, CAR, JWL, AU.

treks to rescue Rhodes well worth the time and energy invested.

During the 1850s, however, Edson traveled more than 1,000 miles as he teamed up with several ministerial colleagues. Chapter 7 explores why he was chosen for this task and how successful he was in working with many early Adventist evangelists.

Chapter 7

Ministerial Partners

In response to an invitation from Hiram Edson, James and Ellen White journeyed from Middletown, Connecticut, to New York in November 1849 and rented Elias Goodwin's large two-story house on the corner of Circular and Phila streets in Oswego,[1] a growing industrial town on the shores of Lake Ontario.[2] Here they frequently boarded J.N. Andrews, Stephen Belden, Annie Smith, G.W. Holt, and other traveling Sabbatarian Adventists.[3] Their primary purpose for moving there was to find a reliable printer to publish the little paper, *The Present Truth*. Between July and September 1849, James White had already produced four issues of this semimonthly paper at Middletown. But Edson knew a better printer in Oswego who would charge less to print the paper.[4]

His name was Richard J. Oliphant, and, like Edson's ancestors, the Oliphants had emigrated from England to America. One Oliphant had served in the British Parliament; another had been Attorney General of South Africa; a third had been a soldier of fortune, trekking

---

[1]Spalding, *Origin and History*, vol. 1, pp. 201, 403 (note 12).
[2]Cross, *Burned-over District*, pp. 63, 65, 69.
[3]See J.N. Andrews' address, *Review*, Sept. 2, 1851, p. 24; Stephen Belden, letter to the *Review*, Oct. 21, 1851, p. 48; Annie Smith and G.W. Holt, letters to the *Review*, Nov. 25, 1851, pp. 53, 56.
[4]See mastheads for *Present Truth*, vol. 1, nos. 1-4 (July, Aug., and Sept. 1849).

through the Central American jungle with the famous 19th-century filibuster (adventurer) William Walker, the self-proclaimed "President of Nicaragua." In the United States, the Oliphants had first settled in Brocton, New York, a town near Lake Erie, but over time they had spread their wings.[5] Two brothers, both printers, would play crucial roles in publishing Sabbatarian Adventist papers: Richard Oliphant,[6] in Oswego, produced the next six issues of *Present Truth* between December 1849 and May 1850;[7] Henry Oliphant, in Auburn,[8] printed the first four issues of the *Review* in August and September 1850. Both were Christian men who trusted the members of the publishing committee to find the funds to pay their expenses.[9]

James White had been the sole editor and producer of *The Present Truth* in Middletown; he and Edson wrote most of the articles as well. But in 1850, a five-man publishing committee was established that included Hiram Edson, David Arnold, George Holt, Samuel Rhodes, and James White.[10] As discussed in more detail in Chapter 8, one of Hiram Edson's lengthy articles completely filled the *Review* Extra issue of September 1850.[11] Edson served on the publishing committee for the *Second Advent Review and Sabbath Herald* from the August 5, 1851, issue to the March 23, 1852, issue, but he was dropped with volume 3 and never appeared again.[12]

[5] Carl Cramer, *Listen for a Lonesome Drum: A York State Chronicle* (New York: D. McKay, 1950 [1936]), pp. 252-253.

[6] Roger H. Ferris, "Roosevelt Seventh-day Adventist Church History," April 15, 1959, pp. 59-60; typed manuscript in the author's possession.

[7] *Present Truth*, vol. 1, nos. 5-10 (Dec. 1849-May 1850).

[8] Ferris, "Roosevelt," p. 60.

[9] *The Advent Review*, vol. 1, nos. 1-4 (Aug.-Sept. 1850).

[10] See masthead of the *Review*, Aug. 1850, p. 1.

[11] Arthur L. White, *Ellen G. White*, vol. 1, p. 181.

[12] See mastheads for *The Advent Review and Sabbath Herald*, vols. 1-3 (1850-1852). The *Review* was printed in Paris, Maine, from Nov. 1850 to June 9, 1851; in Saratoga Springs, NY, from July 21, 1851, to March 23, 1852; and in Rochester, NY, from May 6, 1852, until May 1855 when the publishing committee set up the Washington Hand Press in Battle Creek, Michigan.

The Edsons sell their farm

The most likely explanation for dropping Edson's name from the publishing committee was that he no longer lived close enough to serve on it. Following Ellen White's advice to move away from Port Gibson, in 1850 Hiram and Esther Edson sold their flock of sheep for $150 and their 56-acre farm in Manchester Township to Warren and Ann Hyde for $2,200.[13] Edson gave some of this money to James White to help defray the traveling expenses of Joseph Bates, J.N. Andrews, J.N. Loughborough, George Holt, and Samuel Rhodes.[14] The Edsons then moved east to Oswego, a burgeoning town with numerous flour mills and grain elevators and the formidable Fort Ontario in Grampus Bay, where they rented a farm for a couple of years.[15] Then in 1852 they purchased another farm in Port Byron, a tiny village of a thousand residents on the Erie Canal.[16] Before the end of 1852, Hiram had sold that farm for $3,500, donating $650 to James White to help pay for the new Washington Hand Press, type, and other equipment at the Review and Herald press.[17] As Gerald Wheeler quipped, "Edson seemed to have a farm to sell whenever the believers needed money."[18]

While Hiram and Esther were moving east to Oswego and Port Byron, however, the Review and Herald staff was moving west to Rochester in 1852. First located in the home of Jonathan T. Orton on the corner of Union and Monroe streets, the Washington Hand Press was next moved to a larger two-story building (rented for $175 a year) at 124 Mount Hope Avenue that could accommodate the en-

---

[13]Indenture (deed), April 3, 1850; handwritten document in the author's possession.
[14]Froom, *Prophetic Faith*, vol. 4, p. 890.
[15]Terrance H. Prior and Natalie J. Siember, *Images of America Around Oswego* (Charleston, SC: Arcadia Publishing, 1996), pp. 9, 18.
[16]Spalding, *Captains*, pp. 186-187 (footnote 18).
[17]Spalding, *Footprints*, p. 79.
[18]Wheeler, *James White*, p. 83 (footnote 2).

tire publishing staff and the printing equipment. In 1853, however, the headquarters moved again, this time to 21 South St. Paul Street (the site of the first Adventist Sabbath School), where it remained until the staff moved to Battle Creek, Michigan in 1855.[19]

Ministerial partners

In addition to moving farther away from the Review and Herald headquarters, an even more important reason why Edson could no longer serve on the publishing committee was because he was often traveling with older preaching colleagues and training younger ministerial recruits as a kind of "minister without portfolio"—free to travel wherever he wished with whomever he chose.[20] Regarding his training efforts on behalf of younger preachers, Edson allegedly used the phrase "breaking them in," much as one would break a pair of oxen to pull the plough or a pair of horses for pulling a wagon.[21]

But why was Hiram Edson chosen for this important task? Unlike James White and Joseph Bates, he was not an ordained minister; he did not become a local church elder until 1855. Nor did he have seniority over some of the men with whom he traveled. Bates (born in 1792) and Byington (born in 1798), for example, were many years older than he. Unfortunately, there are no extant primary documents that provide information concerning this question. We can only speculate that perhaps the answer lies in certain character traits that the Whites and others admired in him.

First, Edson was dependable. He could always be relied upon to keep his word, to follow through on his promises, and to finish the

---

[19]Henry Uhl, "Church and State," *Atlantic Union Gleaner*, Aug. 27, 1974, pp. 3-4.

[20]Campbell and Lake, eds., *Pocket Ellen G. White Dictionary*, p. 64.

[21]For the names of early Advent preachers who traveled the circuit with Edson, see Strayer, *Loughborough*, pp. 73-74, and Strayer, "Presentation at the Hiram Edson Farm," Oct. 2019, pp. 1-5, typewritten manuscript.

tasks assigned him, no matter what the weather threw at him. He had demonstrated that he was not intimidated by climate, physical threats, or other hardships.

Second, he was orthodox. Once he accepted the seventh-day Sabbath, the heavenly sanctuary, the second coming of Jesus, the Spirit of Prophecy, and the state of the dead teachings, Edson never once deviated from preaching this present truth and assisting others in sharing it also. When it came to doctrine, Hiram was—to borrow a 19th-century Victorian phrase—"steady as a pump handle."

Third, he was hard-working. As a farmer, he knew what it was like to rise early in the morning to milk the cows, feed the sheep, plant the fields, harvest the crops, and perform dozens of other tasks rural folk faced in those days before the appearance of electricity and gas-powered machinery. On the gospel trail, he refused to allow summer heat, autumn rains, winter blizzards, or spring floods to thwart his mission.

Fourth, he was gregarious, polite, good-humored, and cooperative most of the time. But he was not the type of person who felt comfortable in administrative positions, sitting behind an office desk, or serving on committees; instead, he liked to be out in the field working one on one with his ministerial colleagues.

Fifth, he was understanding. No doubt the younger men that he mentored made many mistakes. Yet Edson patiently corrected their missteps and commended their achievements, often in his reports to the *Review*. And those recruits never forgot what he had done for them. Decades later, John Andrews, John Byington, John Loughborough, and Samuel Rhodes, among others, would remember him in the diaries, letters, articles, and books they wrote.[22]

---

[22]Strayer, "Presentation at the Hiram Edson Farm."

Travels with George Holt and J.N. Andrews

Although some of Edson's trips would include visits with Sabbatarian Adventists—often called "the scattered sheep," "the little flock," and "the remnant"—most were missionary journeys in search of former Millerites and "Strangers" (as non-Adventists were then called).[23] Having preached the third angel's message with Joseph Bates in Canada West (Ontario) and Canada East (Quebec) in 1850, Edson remembered how friendly the Canadians had been. So, in November 1851 he decided to return with George Holt to visit the "scattered sheep" (former Millerite Adventists).[24] During their three-week journey,[25] the two men covered hundreds of miles, frequently wading through deep snow—sometimes for only a couple of miles, at other times for up to 40 miles at a stretch.[26]

Returning to the United States, Edson and Holt traveled through western New York, covering Yates and Steuben counties in February. There they discovered "precious jewels," both former Millerites and Strangers, who eagerly accepted the third angel's message. In Wheeler, New York, they fellowshipped with the Lockwood family on Sabbath, and the father, mother, and son agreed to witness for their new-found faith throughout the region. "We had a glorious time of special refreshing from the presence of the Lord," Edson wrote in the *Review*. "It was a time of victory, complete, perfect, and entire. Free and full 'Hallelujahs' ascended to God and he was glorified in praise,

---

[23]Seventh-day Adventists have employed a variety of terms to refer to those not within their denomination. Between 1850 and 1900, Adventists in Indiana called them "Strangers." From around 1900 to the 1950s, they were referred to as "Outsiders." From the 1960s to the present, however, they have been called "Non-Adventists." See A.W. Spalding to V.G. Anderson, April 18, 1949, Spalding Correspondence, Collection 10, Box 2, Folder 2, CAR, JWL, AU, and Brian E. Strayer, "'The Cause Is Onward': The History of Seventh-day Adventism in Indiana, 1849-1900," p. 162, CAR, JWL, AU.

[24]Cooper, *Great Advent Movement*, p. 155.

[25]George Holt, letter to the *Review*, Feb. 1851, p. 48.

[26]Cooper, *Great Advent Movement*, p. 155.

love and adoration."[27] In a few places, they faced opposition, but the men quickly discovered that "Our opponents are doing more for us than against us. Praise the Lord."[28]

Travels with Samuel Rhodes, H.S. Case, and J.N. Andrews

Few of Edson's colleagues proved more enthusiastic about facing the hardships of a peripatetic ministry than Samuel Rhodes, who was seven years younger than Hiram. After returning to civilization in 1849 following his self-imposed isolation in the Adirondack Mountains, Rhodes was eager to reenter the Adventist ministry. When Ellen White encountered him in December 1849, she wrote:

> Dear Brother Rhodes was with us in our last conference. It was good to see his face once more and cheering to hear him talk the plain cutting truth of God from the Bible.... Brother Rhodes has now gone in company with Brother John Andrews to the eastern part of the State [New York] to hunt up the scattered sheep. We have received two letters from them. God is at work and is bringing souls from the rubbish to the clear light of truth.[29]

In July 1851, Edson, Rhodes, H.S. Case, and about 20 active laymen convened in Bath, New York, to worship together on Sabbath. Following a sermon on the Sabbath, Sanctuary, and Law of God, they celebrated the Lord's Supper and foot-washing service before setting forth to witness for their faith. In a letter to the *Review*, Rhodes signed himself, "Yours to suffer with the saints a little while, and then to

---

[27]Edson, letter to the *Review*, Feb. 1851, p. 48.
[28]George Holt, letter to the *Review*, Feb. 1851, p. 48.
[29]Ellen White to Bro. and Sr. Loveland, Dec. 13, 1850, in *Manuscript Release*, vol.6, p. 252.

reign in glory with you for all eternity."[30]

One month later, Edson and J.N. Andrews set forth on a six-week, 600-mile preaching circuit that took them from Niagara Falls west to Erie and then through Potter and Tioga counties in Pennsylvania and back north into Allegheny, Cattaraugus, Chautauqua, Erie, Niagara, Monroe, Wayne, and Ontario counties, New York, in search of both former Millerites and Strangers.[31] According to Edson's report in the *Review*, they traversed rugged mountains and climbed steep-sided valleys, crossed rutted roads and Indian trails often blocked by fallen trees, scrambled over cradle knolls and stumps, and clambered through slough-holes and rough log-ways—eating and sleeping in a tent, even when the nights grew cold in September. Along the way, they visited former Sabbath-keepers and held meetings with several Seventh Day Baptists. Although they occasionally faced prejudice and opposition, they also encountered many families who accepted their teachings. Despite these hardships, Edson wrote optimistically: "The truth is mighty and will prevail."[32]

Upon their return, Edson and Andrews joined Holt, Rhodes, and about 30 other Sabbath-keepers for a general conference in Pitcher, New York. At this gathering, "the testimonies of the saints to the truth were sweet and refreshing," Rhodes wrote. "That the blessing of the latter rain may soon refresh God's waiting saints is my earnest prayer."[33]

Travels with Joseph Bates

Joseph Bates had been a Millerite agent for *Signs of the Times* and a peripatetic preacher throughout New England and the Mid-

---

[30]Samuel Rhodes, July 15, 1851, letter to the *Review*, Aug. 5, 1851, pp. 7-8.
[31]Gilbert M. Valentine, *J.N. Andrews: Mission Pioneer, Evangelist, and Thought Leader* (Nampa, ID: Pacific Press Pub. Assn., 2019), pp. 132-133, 208.
[32]Edson, letter of Aug. 20, 1851, to the *Review*, Sept. 2, 1851, p. 24.
[33]S.W. Rhodes, Sept. 23, 1851, letter to the *Review*, Oct. 7, 1851, p. 40.

west since 1844. Nearly 60 years old, he was 14 years Edson's senior. Nonetheless, these two champion walkers teamed up in the winter of 1851-1852 for a marathon ministry that would take them hundreds of miles on foot and by horse and buggy.[34] Meeting in Auburn, New York, at the end of November 1851, they headed north to the St. Lawrence River and crossed into Canada West (Ontario). Completely circumnavigating Lake Ontario on foot, they visited the "scattered sheep" in the back settlements, sometimes wading through two or three feet of snow. On some days they covered 40 miles, on others, only two miles, but they kept going for five freezing weeks. In January 1852, they reached Toronto, Ontario, and then headed west, trekking along the shores of Lake Huron and Lake Erie to Mariposa and Scewgog Lakes, also in Ontario. Along the way, they rejoiced when 20 Strangers accepted the third angel's message.[35] Moving west to Kingston, Ontario, they next trekked south across the Canada-United States border to Centerport, a tiny village west of Weedsport, New York, on the Erie Canal. As a result of their missionary journey, about 100 individuals expressed an interest in the Adventist message, and 50 or more subscribed to the *Review*.[36]

Not content to rest on their laurels, however, the two men headed for the Southern Tier, visiting Potter and Allegany counties in Pennsylvania before returning to New York. During their 13-week trip, they preached the gospel in Batavia, Fredonia, Gerry, and Jamestown; held a baptism in Mill Grove; debated the seventh-day Sabbath with a Sunday-keeping minister in Laona; and gave Bible studies in Buffalo, Jamestown, Ellington, Busti, and Napoli, New York, before returning

---

[34]Joseph Bates, report to the *Review*, Nov. 25, 1851, p. 56.
[35]Bates, Jan. 1, 1852, letter to the *Review*, Jan. 13, 1852, p. 80.
[36]Bates, reports to the *Review*, Feb. 17, 1852, p. 96, and May 6, 1852, pp. 6-7.

to Rochester and Marion in early March.[37] In his previous report to the Review, Bates declared, "We believe that God has precious jewels [souls] in Canada West."[38]

Edson had little time to rest after this marathon missionary journey, however, for he was expected to attend the conference held in the parlor of Jesse Thompson's home at Ballston Spa, near Saratoga Springs, New York, from March 12 to 15.[39] Thompson, a lawyer, farmer, and generous contributor to the Advent cause, had been a Christian Connexion[40] minister for two decades before converting to Sabbatarian Adventism. Others in attendance besides Hiram Edson included Joseph Bates, J.N. Andrews, Samuel Rhodes, W.S. Ingraham, Frederick Wheeler, Washington Morse, Joseph Baker, and the entire publishing staff.[41] Unlike many of the previous Sabbath Conferences, however, greater unanimity prevailed among the attendees. According to the report in the Review, "The brethren came together with a desire to be benefited and to benefit each other. Not to establish any peculiar views of their own, but to be united in the TRUTH."[42]

By a unanimous vote, they decided to purchase a new Washington Hand Press[43] and type. They also voted to move their printing es-

---

[37]Bates, report to the Review, May 6, 1852, pp. 6-7.
[38]Bates, report to the Review, Jan. 13, 1852, p. 80.
[39]Spalding, Captains, p. 186.
[40]Although it is now acceptable to spell this Christian church's name "Connection," I am following the quaint but conventional spelling that its members used in the 19th century. James White, Joseph Bates, and several other Sabbatarian Adventists once belonged to the Christian Connexion church.
[41]M. Ellsworth Olsen, Origin and Progress of Seventh-day Adventists (Washington, D.C.: Review and Herald Pub. Assn., 1925), p. 211.
[42]"The Conference [at Ballston Spa]," Review, March 23, 1852, p. 108.
[43]In 1829 Solon Rust received a patent for inventing the Washington Hand Press. Subsequently, he sold it to the Hoe Company of New York City where over 6,000 presses were manufactured between about 1830 and 1910. Adventists used this first Washington Hand Press in Rochester, New York, from 1852 to 1855 and again in Battle Creek, Michigan, for several years after the 1855 relocation of their headquarters. Once the new steam press was installed in the 1860s, however, the old manual press was placed in storage. On Dec. 30, 1902, this nearly half-century old artifact was destroyed in the fire that burned down the Review and Herald buildings. [Robert Allen], "The Washington Hand Press"; undated one-page manuscript in the author's possession.

tablishment, which had been in Paris, Maine, (November 1850-June 1851) and Saratoga Springs, New York, (July 1851-March 1852) to Rochester in May 1852,[44] and to form a three-man publishing committee to oversee this move and solicit funds to pay for it. Hiram Edson, E.A. Pool, and Lebbeus Drew were appointed to this committee.[45] As mentioned earlier, Hiram and Esther sold their farm in Port Byron for $3,500 and loaned James White the $650 needed to purchase the press and to ship their paper stock, printed pamphlets, and personal belongings to Rochester; they anticipated being repaid as donors sent money to the *Review*.[46] In addition, the attendees chose Edson, Holt, and Rhodes to be in charge of planning future conferences in New York and Canada West.[47] The session closed with Bates, the perpetual health and temperance advocate, making a request that "plain food" rather than "rich food" be prepared at future conferences. Otherwise, he would be compelled to offer his unique blessing: "Lord, bless [only] the clean, nutritious, wholesome, lawful food."[48]

Travels with George Holt and J.N. Andrews

Three months after the Ballston Spa conference, Edson and Holt teamed up a second time for a marathon preaching tour across Canada and New England.[49] In June they went to Champlain, New York, and then across the St. Lawrence River into Canada East (Quebec), preaching at Farnham and Melbourne while residing at Asa Hasel-

---

[44]Wheeler, *James White*, p. 67.

[45]"The Conference," *Review*, March 23, 1852, p. 108.

[46]Accounts vary somewhat regarding exactly how much of the $3,500 Edson loaned White: Nix ("Edson," p. 61) says the amount was $650; Spalding (*Origin and History*, vol. 1, p. 205) states the amount more precisely at $652.93; while Krug ("Phase One," *Atlantic Union Gleaner*, Nov. 2008) estimates the amount at $752.

[47] "The Conference," *Review*, March 23, 1852, p. 108.

[48]Joseph Bates mentioned this prayer to Ellen White in a letter he wrote her two decades later on Feb. 14, 1872, in which he referred to participating in a July 4 picnic in Vassar, Michigan, in his "Report from Bro. Bates," *Review*, July 24, 1866, p. 61.

[49]John Lindsey, report to the *Review*, May 27, 1852, p. 16.

tine's home.[50] Heading south into New York, they held meetings in Bangor, which resulted in several converts "firmly settled in the present truth."[51] Speaking in schoolhouses, homes, and other denomination's churches, they shared the Advent message in Chateaugay and Champlain, New York, and in Irasburg, Vermont.[52] Heading west into northern New York, they held meetings in Potsdam Township, the home of the large Byington family.[53] Following these services, Holt baptized John and Catharine Byington and three of their children, Martha, Fletcher, and Luther, in the nearby Grasse River. Then the team moved south to Lorain and Sandy Creek before reaching home on July 8.[54] Bursting with optimism, Holt told readers of the *Review*: "The work of the Lord in this message is progressing. Prejudice is giving away where the truth is presented, and the honest are seeking for light."[55]

One month later, Edson took the newly converted John Andrews out on the gospel trail across upstate New York. Hiram listened to John preach his first sermons at Fredonia on August 14 and 15, 1852, at meetings that were "thinly attended."[56] Andrews then accompanied Edson, Holt, and Rhodes to a September conference at Pultney, where they preached about gospel order and unity, then ameliorated some friction that existed among Sabbath-keeping Adventists in Bath, Wheeler, and Pultney.[57] Andrews faced a real test of his abilities during a grove meeting attended by 500 Strangers who wanted to know what Adventists believed. Apparently, Andrews proved more

---

[50]G.W. Holt, report to the *Review*, June 24, 1852, p. 32.

[51]Edson, report to the *Review*, June 10, 1852, pp. 22-23.

[52]Holt, reports to the *Review*, July 8, 1852, p. 39 and July 22, 1852, p. 46.

[53]Holt, report to the *Review*, July 22, 1852, p. 46.

[54]Brian Strayer, *John Byington: First General Conference President, Circuit-Riding Preacher, and Radical Reformer* (Nampa, ID: Pacific Press Pub. Assn., 2018), pp. 93, 97.

[55] Holt, report to the *Review*, July 8, 1852, p. 39.

[56]John Hamilton, letter to the *Review*, Sept. 2, 1852, p. 70.

[57]Holt, report to the *Review*, Sept. 16, 1852, p. 80.

successful at that gathering, for Holt reported in the *Review*: "I do rejoice to see the work of the Lord prosper."[58]

Travels with J.N. Loughborough

Another couple in Rochester—John Loughborough, an Arnold Patent Sash Locks salesman and former Advent Christian preacher, and his seamstress wife, Mary—also rejoiced in the truths they had been learning during Bible studies with Edson and Andrews. After some startling dreams and faith healings had convinced them to worship with the Advent band at 124 Mount Hope Avenue, John was impressed that he should stop selling sash locks and start seeking souls for God's kingdom.[59] However, as a new convert and barely 20 years old, he did not feel ready to go out on his own in the fall of 1852.

Meanwhile, Hiram Edson, finally free to relax at home, was leading out in family worship on Sabbath when he suddenly felt impressed that he was needed in Rochester. When he spoke to Esther about this, she told him that she, too, had felt impressed that he should go and had already packed his bag. After the sun set that evening, Hiram traveled by train the 40 miles to Rochester. When he found James White, Edson asked him if there was anything he wanted him to do. White told him to take John Loughborough on a six-week tour of southwestern New York and Pennsylvania and teach him how to preach among Strangers.[60] Perhaps sensing Hiram's reluctance, Ellen White encouraged him to "take his place" in the church and not to hesitate for fear of "getting out of his place."[61]

To make their travel more pleasant, the Whites loaned Hiram and

---

[58]Holt, report to the *Review*, Sept. 16, 1852, p. 80.
[59]Strayer, *Loughborough*, pp. 67-68.
[60]Olsen, *Origin and Progress*, p. 220.
[61]Ellen White testimony to Hiram Edson, handwritten manuscript, quoted in Nix, "Edson," p. 75.

John their horse, "Old Charlie," who pulled the wagon containing their personal belongings, books, and tracts,[62] as well as handbills proclaiming "these that have turned the world upside down are come hither also [to preach] the commandments of God and the faith of Jesus."[63] As the Southern Tier counties had no canals, railroads, or paved roads at the time, they mostly walked or rode in the wagon, preaching in homes, schoolhouses, and isolated churches. When the winter snow proved too deep for the wagon, the men converted it into a "pung" (a primitive box sled with runners).[64]

During a blizzard, Hiram noticed that John had no warm winter coat, so he bought him one. So that Charlie could pull the pung more easily, the two men walked 40 miles from Buffalo to Rochester. During their six-week tour, Edson and Loughborough covered hundreds of miles from Buffalo to southern New York and eastern Pennsylvania, visiting a dozen Sabbath-keeping groups and numerous Strangers.[65] According to John Hamilton of Fredonia, New York, wherever the two men preached, they strengthened the faith of their listeners.[66] At the end of their journey, Edson took the train from Rochester to Port Byron while Loughborough rode Charlie the 50 miles to Orangeport, New York, to hitch him to a carriage and return him to the Whites.[67] John also returned with many sheaves of notes he had taken while interviewing Hiram about his early Advent experiences in the 1840s—notes he would later consult while writing his 1892 book *Rise and Progress* and his 1905 book *The Great Second Advent Movement.*[68]

---

[62]J.N. Loughborough, report to the *Review*, March 17, 1853, p. 176.
[63]J.N. Loughborough, "The Church," *Pacific Union Recorder*, Aug. 19, 1909, p. 1.
[64]Strayer, *Loughborough*, pp. 74-75.
[65]Loughborough, "The Church," *Pacific Union Recorder*, Aug. 19, 1909, pp. 1-2.
[66]John Hamilton, letter to the *Review*, Sept. 2, 1852, p. 70.
[67]Loughborough, report to the *Review*, March 17, 1853, p. 176.
[68]Strayer, *Loughborough*, pp. 328, 392.

Repacking his bags, Edson then set out alone in February 1853 on a month-long tour of upstate New York to visit the scattered Sabbath-keeping bands in Cayuga, Oswego, Jefferson, and Lewis counties. Along the way, he appealed for someone to preach the gospel in Watson, Lewis County, and rejoiced to find faithful believers in Copenhagen, New York, including one man with the Bunyanesque name of Harvey Goodenough, whom Edson felt certain was "capable of holding up the standard of truth."[69]

After only a few weeks' respite tending to his farm chores in Port Byron that summer, in September 1853 Edson headed northeast to Potsdam for yet another conference in the Byington's home, arriving much fatigued, but gratified to find nearly 80 other believers in attendance, including the Whites and Andrews.[70]

Travels with Horace W. Lawrence

Then in October and November, Edson teamed up with Horace Lawrence for yet another extended evangelistic tour of upstate New York. The two men headed east into Dutch country, where Edson preached to a few believers in present truth in Copenhagen while Lawrence enjoyed the rare privilege of being invited to speak in an Advent Christian chapel in Martinsburg. Their meetings among Seventh Day Baptists in Watson and Lorain were also well attended, with people tramping miles through mud and snow to hear them speak and then purchasing the literature they offered for sale.[71] Edson rejoiced to find the saints in Lorain "holding fast the truth, and stiving

---

[69]Hiram Edson and H.W. Lawrence, report to the *Review*, Nov. 8, 1853, p. 143. In 1678 the English Puritan pastor John Bunyan wrote his famous allegory *Pilgrim's Progress*, which he filled with memorable characters, some of whom (e.g., Evangelist, Wiseman, Discretion, Prudence) assisted Christian on his journey to the Celestial City while others (e.g., Obstinate, Pliable, Worldly Wiseman) hindered his progress. The name "Goodenough" might well have fit somewhere in Bunyan's plot.

[70]James White, "Eastern Tour," *Review*, Sept. 20, 1853, pp. 84-85.

[71]Hiram Edson and H.W. Lawrence, report to the *Review*, Nov. 8, 1853, p. 143.

to make their way to Mount Zion."[72] But he expressed shock and dismay a few months later after learning about the apostasy of H.S. Case and C.P. Russell in Jackson, Michigan, so soon after believers there had erected the first meetinghouse built by Sabbath-keeping Adventists in March 1854. "I am grieved on hearing of the unrighteous course of some who have formerly been with us but are now separated from us. I sincerely pity them, but cannot countenance them nor have any union with their present course." He hoped that "they may yet see their folly" and repent. But if not, he hoped James White "will not go down into the plains of Ono, and so let the building of the walls of Zion cease" (an allusion to Nehemiah 6:1-3). Instead, he should "be making up the hedge and repairing the breach." He closed his letter with a benediction: "May the Lord give you grace, wisdom, understanding, judgment, and his Holy Spirit, to guide, sustain and uphold you, is our prayer."[73]

Edson ordained

From December 14 to 16, 1855, Edson, now 49, attended a conference in Oswego, New York, that had as its primary purpose finding ways to establish "further order in the churches in Central New York" so as to avoid the turmoil that Case and Russell had caused in Michigan. One method of accomplishing what James White called "Gospel Order" was to appoint more deacons and elders in the fledgling congregations.[74] Therefore, at this gathering, both Hiram Edson and David Arnold were ordained by the laying on of hands as the first local elders in the state, with responsibilities over several upstate

---

[72]Edson, March 10, 1854, letter to the *Review*, March 21, 1854, p. 71.
[73]Edson, Nov. 20, 1854, letter to the *Review*, Dec. 5, 1854, p. 127. For more information concerning the Case and Russell defection and the formation of the Messenger Party, see Fortin and Moon, eds., *Ellen G. White Encyclopedia*, s.v. "Messenger Party," pp. 974-976.
[74]Loughborough, report to the *Review*, Dec. 27, 1855, p. 101.

churches.[75] Although this ordination did not in any way limit Edson's ability to travel widely as a preacher of the gospel, it was not the same as being ordained or credentialed as a minister, something Edson received only later in 1870 when he was 64 years old.[76]

It was also at this Oswego gathering, following a spirited revival meeting one night, that Hiram's 12-year-old daughter Ophelia expressed a desire to be baptized. Her father pointed out that because it was mid-December, Lake Ontario already had a fringe of ice along the shoreline; besides, it was dark outside. Nevertheless, she insisted on being baptized. J.N. Loughborough (who was 5'4" tall and weighed about 120 pounds), perhaps not feeling up to the task himself, asked Roswell F. Cottrell to immerse the girl. One member carried a single lantern, while others broke the ice with hatchets and axes so that Cottrell and Ophelia could descend into the frigid water. Later, donning warm clothing, Ophelia returned home with her father to Port Byron wrapped in heavy blankets in the cutter, "happy in the Lord."[77]

Only three months earlier on September 19, Hiram had given his eldest daughter, Susan Frances Edson, age 20, in marriage to Chester R. Wells during a ceremony held in Charlotte, New York. However, since this service was presided over by the Reverend Moses Wallace, it is possible that Susan, unlike her younger half-sister Ophelia, was not a Sabbath-keeping Adventist. It is likely that Hiram's joy at seeing his daughter's marital happiness was tinged with sadness that she had not married someone who shared his commitment to present truth.[78]

Edson demonstrated his commitment to the cause in 1855 when an appeal was issued for funds to purchase the first tent for evange-

[75]Loughborough, report to the *Review*, Dec. 27, 1855, p. 101.
[76]Collins, *Heartwarming Stories*, Book 1, p. 37.
[77]J.N. Loughborough to R.M. Kelley, Dec. 13, 1910, DF3006, manuscript no. 8, CAR, JWL, AU.
[78]Nix, "Edson," p. 68.

listic meetings across New York.[79] He and Esther gave five dollars.[80] A few months later, they gave a dollar and a half to help pay the expense of moving the Review and Herald press from Rochester, New York, to Battle Creek, Michigan.[81]

The Edsons move—again

Having already undergone two moves in two years from Port Gibson to Oswego in 1850 and from Oswego to Port Byron, New York, in 1852, the family relocated once again during the summer of 1856. This time Hiram purchased rather than rented a farm in Martville, New York, five miles from Hannibal in the northern section of Cayuga County.[82] Just weeks later, on July 30, something unusual occurred with the birth of Lucy Jane Edson. In an era when the average lifespan was about 45, Hiram was past 50 years of age and his wife Esther was already 46. Doubtless this unexpected blessing was appreciated all the more for arriving so late in her parents' lives.[83]

Hiram's lengthy letter to the *Review* that announced his family's relocation also expressed concern for those believers who were experiencing trials. "Many are the cares, anxieties, and trials of the remnant in this time of their patient waiting for Christ," he wrote. To endure such "tribulations" required having "the patience of the saints." Yet the "fiery trial" also developed patience, experience, and hope within the Christian; trials also purified God's people. Edson applied this spiritual lesson specifically to those in the publishing work, many of whom had already encountered anxieties and trials. Therefore, he urged Sabbath-keeping Adventists everywhere to support and to pray for the

---

[79]James White and J.N. Loughborough, "Tent for New York," *Review*, Feb. 20, 1855, p. 182.
[80]"Receipts," *Review*, June 26, 1855, p. 256.
[81]"Receipts," *Review*, Jan. 17, 1856, p. 128.
[82]Edson, June 15, 1856, letter to the *Review*, June 26, 1856, p. 71.
[83]Wurst, et al., *Archaeological-Historical Investigations*, p. 27.

Review and Herald employees that God would grant them wisdom and strength for their tasks. Perhaps once again referencing H.S. Case and C.P. Russell's apostasy in Jackson, Michigan, he reminded readers that Satan's work is to divide and "scatter the flock" by bringing confusion into God's work. To thwart his efforts, believers needed to stop complaining and unite their efforts to combat the enemy. "United we stand, divided we fall," he exclaimed. In conclusion, he hoped that God would bring unity, destroy pride, and bring "self-abasement" among the remnant so that "the light of his [God's] reconciled countenance [may] shine more clearly upon us."[84]

Eight months later, in a ceremony at Clifton Springs (a few miles south of Edson's former farm in Port Gibson), his second oldest daughter, 22-year-old Belinda Adelaide Edson, married William W. Cobb on February 3, 1857. Although the presiding minister's name is unknown, it is likely that this wedding, like that of Belinda's older sister Susan Frances two years earlier, was not blessed by a Sabbatarian Adventist minister and did not establish a Sabbath-keeping home.[85]

Conferences bring unity

Holding conferences, or general gatherings of believers, proved to be one of the most effective means of bringing about the unity that Hiram Edson sought. Consequently, he attended as many as he could. In October 1856, he traveled once again to Bucks Bridge for a conference at the home of John and Catharine Byington. Leading Sabbatarian Adventist ministers such as C.W. Sperry, A.S. Hutchins, and Samuel Rhodes preached during the three-day gathering, which was attended by several believers from New York and Vermont. The

---

[84]Edson, June 15, 1856, letter to the *Review*, June 26, 1856, p. 71.
[85]Nix, "Edson," p. 70.

meetings proved "a great blessing to the church" as many confessed their "wanderings" and "lukewarmness" and accepted the message to the Laodicean Church in Revelation 3:14-22 as applicable to their present spiritual condition. "God manifested himself in power," John Byington reported in the *Review*.[86]

Four months later in a letter to the *Review*, Edson likewise accepted the Laodicean rebuke and recognized its application for his fledgling church. "We are lukewarm," he declared, so God will "spue us out of his mouth." Members needed to examine themselves to see if they were reprobate or if Christ lived within their hearts. On a deeply personal level, Hiram feared that he did not truly realize his "wretched, and miserable, and poor, and blind and naked" condition. Therefore, he, like every Sabbath-keeping believer, needed God's eye salve, white raiment, and gold tried in the fire. Summing up, he viewed the Laodicean message as a call to repentance "now or never," a summons to receive salvation from God "now or never," because "the day of grace is closing; the mystery of God is almost finished."[87]

Another effective method of bringing salvation, both to Laodicean Adventists and to Strangers, was through tent evangelism. To further this cause, Edson met with Samuel Rhodes and Frederick Wheeler (then based in New Hampshire) at Oswego late in February 1857 to make preliminary plans for "running the tent" (as Sands Lane phrased it[88]) across central New York. In order to accomplish this, Edson and Rhodes asked Wheeler to join the New York preaching team, which he agreed to do.[89] The following spring, Edson boarded the train from Martville to Syracuse and then took a stagecoach to

---

[86]John Byington, "Conference at Buck's Bridge, N.Y.," *Review*, Nov. 27, 1856, p. 32.
[87]Edson, March 21, 1857, letter to the *Review*, April 9, 1857, p. 182.
[88]Sands Lane, *General Conference Bulletin*, March 7, 1899, p. 169.
[89]"Conference at Oswego," *Review*, Feb. 12, 1857, p. 120.

Central Square in Roosevelt to attend a conference.[90] The delegates decided to send a team of tent evangelists into the field throughout the summer and fall of 1858 "if suitable laborers" could be found and if believers in both New York and Pennsylvania agreed to support it with their prayers and donations. Hiram Edson, David Arnold, and A. Robinson were chosen to recruit qualified workers; Roswell Cottrell was appointed treasurer to receive donated funds; and all local church deacons were tasked with raising money in their congregations for the tent efforts.[91]

Travels with Frederick Wheeler and William S. Ingraham

Although he was now 52 years old and showing signs of aging, Edson was not yet ready to forsake the blessings that came with a circuit-riding ministry. Despite the harsh winter weather in January and February 1858, he teamed up with Frederick Wheeler for a four-week tour on horseback through upstate New York and western Pennsylvania. The two men traversed Jefferson and Lewis counties, strengthening the faith of Sabbath-keepers and holding evangelistic meetings with Strangers. At Watson they gave seven discourses on Adventist beliefs to a group of Seventh Day Baptists, made three more presentations at the New Bremen schoolhouse, followed by six more lectures on God's Ten Commandment Law at the Indian River Settlement. After tramping eight miles through thick forest, they arrived at Diana and Pitcairn in northern New York's St. Lawrence County; then they preached to a full schoolhouse at Harrisville, reaping several converts and finding "honest souls famishing for the bread of life."[92] Despite his physical weariness, Edson said, "We feel new courage to still visit the 'highways

---

[90]Hiram Edson and Frederick Wheeler, report to the *Review*, Jan. 21, 1858, p. 88.

[91]Wheeler and Edson, report to the *Review*, March 11, 1858, p. 133.

[92]Edson and Wheeler, report to the *Review*, Feb. 11, 1858, pp. 110-111.

and hedges,' and with this last compelling message labor to rescue the honest from the destruction that is soon coming on the earth."[93]

Later that spring, Edson took William S. Ingraham out on the gospel trail along the Southern Tier and western Pennsylvania. They had enjoyable visits with the scattered Sabbatarian Adventists and converted about 20 Strangers. But somewhere along the way, "some of our enemies" (as Edson phrased it) poisoned Ingraham's eight-year-old horse, and it sickened and died. Mortified that anyone could stoop so low, Hiram wrote a letter to the *Review*, emphasizing that the horse had been certified healthy by a physician; that it was worth between $125 and $150; and that Ingraham depended on it for transportation. Then, putting his money where his mouth was, Edson gave William three dollars and called for 50 *Review* subscribers to donate three dollars each to raise the $150 needed to replace the horse. He directed them to send their gifts to Ingraham at Ulysses, Potter County, Pennsylvania.[94]

Hiram and Esther's generosity

Such generosity, far from being the exception, was typical of Hiram and Esther Edson throughout their lives. As previously shown, in 1850 and 1852 they had donated hundreds of dollars from the sale of two farms to advance the cause of evangelism and publishing in the Northeast and Midwest. In September 1858, when Edson's young protégé John Andrews left his farm in Marion, Iowa, and returned to full-time ministry, Hiram and Esther offered to pay the expenses for George Amadon's travel from Battle Creek to Waukon and then pay his wages to take John's place on the farm.[95]

---

[93]Edson and Wheeler, report to the *Review*, Feb. 11, 1858, p. 111.
[94]Edson, March 1858 letter to the *Review*, April 1, 1858, p. 159.
[95]Edson, letter to the *Review*, June 16, 1859, p. 32. The exact amount that Edson contributed to George

Edson also gave generously of his time to help establish new churches in New York and Pennsylvania.[96] During the 1850s, frequent tent meetings were held in the area with upwards of 500 people attending.[97] When the Sabbatarian Adventists in Roosevelt decided to erect a meetinghouse in 1858, they purchased a half-acre of land from Lyman Drake for $32. Edson donated his time to help them build their "House of Prayer," which contained a large pulpit, a rostrum with a railing around it, plain board pews, and a wood-burning stove, but no organ, piano, or melodeon (except for weddings and funerals). For three decades, men entered by the right door and women through the left door (until 1885 when the two doors became windows and a large middle door was created).[98] Today this tiny chapel is the oldest original Seventh-day Adventist church building in which Sabbath services have been held continuously for nearly 165 years.[99]

Yet while Hiram liberally supported the work, not only in New England and New York but also in the Midwest, he never visited the church headquarters in Battle Creek. When a conference was convened there in May 1859 to discuss the proposed Systematic Benevolence Plan (nicknamed "Sister Betsy"), he wanted to go, "but [I] did not see my way clear," he told *Review* readers. Nonetheless, he testified, he had "felt some freedom, and a measure of the Spirit frequently, while praying for the great Head of the Church [Jesus Christ] to preside at the Conference." He hoped that this gathering "would be the dawning of a new era in the Third Angel's Message" and that "the spirit of sacrifice may be revived in the church throughout." Con-

Amadon's wages is not known in part because James White assured him that Adventists in Michigan would "cheerfully and fully" pay Andrews' expenses, so Edson should donate his funds to support the work in New York instead. See James White's response in the *Review*, June 16, 1859, p. 32.

[96]Krug, "October Morn," pp. 11-12.

[97]Ferris, "Roosevelt SDA Church History," pp. 1-2.

[98]Ferris, "Roosevelt SDA Church History," pp. 2-3.

[99]Roosevelt Historical Tour brochure (1990), p. 1; document in the author's possession.

cluding his letter, Hiram exclaimed, "I very much desire the Lord to give a new impetus to the cause of present truth." While across the landscape of Europe, "the mighty men of the earth are waking up and preparing [for] war," the saints needed to awake and prepare for "the battle in the day of the Lord."[100]

For some unknown reason, however, Edson did not attend the first meeting convened inside the new Roosevelt meetinghouse in June 1859. According to Frederick Wheeler's report, "It was easy praying and a free place to preach the word."[101] In addition to Wheeler, C.W. Sperry and Eri L. Barr (the first Black ordained Sabbatarian Adventist minister) preached at this gathering and baptized three converts. On Sunday, so many Adventists and Strangers came to worship that the pews were full and many sat outside in wagons and on horseback listening through the open windows.[102] Edson also missed another meeting held at the Roosevelt church from August 26 to 28, 1859, perhaps due to illness.[103]

Yet it is also possible that the family was too preoccupied with packing crates and boxes for their next move. Sometime in 1859 or 1860, Hiram and Esther, with their two daughters, 16-year-old Ophelia and three-year-old Lucy Jane, left Martville and settled on a small farm in Palermo in Oswego County. According to the 1860 Federal Census, Hiram owned $1,000 in real estate and $225 in personal possessions; nevertheless, he was still one of the poorest landowners in the area, having given much of his accumulated wealth to advance the cause of present truth.[104]

One of Hiram Edson's little-known methods of spreading present

---

[100]Edson, letter to the *Review*, June 16, 1859, p. 32.
[101]Frederick Wheeler, report to the *Review*, June 30, 1859, p. 48.
[102]Wheeler, report to the *Review*, June 30, 1859, p. 48.
[103]James White, "Roosevelt, N.Y. Conference," *Review*, Sept. 15, 1859, p. 132.
[104]Wurst, et al., *Archaeological-Historical Investigations*, p. 28.

truth was through his pen. During the 1850s and 1860s, he wrote a dozen lengthy articles for *The Present Truth* and the *Review*. These articles filled multiple pages in each issue in which they appeared; furthermore, many of them were printed as a series in several issues of the *Review*. Chapter 8 examines Edson's writings, seeking to understand them in their historical and theological context.

Chapter 8

Speculative Theologian

F ew individuals have attempted to analyze the difficult prose in Edson's articles in *The Jubilee Standard, Present Truth,* and *Advent Review* between 1849 and 1867. Clifton Taylor told A.W. Spalding that since Edson "had such startling success in his study of the sanctuary question, it appears to have encouraged him to willingly attack any subject."[1] Spalding agreed, adding, "Edson was sometimes a trial to his brethren, because he made interpretations of prophecies and other Scriptures which were not orthodox."[2]

Nevertheless, LeRoy Froom praised Edson for helping to clarify how the "little book" of Revelation 10 described Adventists' experience before and after the Great Disappointment; the Kings of the North and South; the two-horned beast; the Laodicean Church; the "deadly wound"; the seven heads of Revelation 17; and the "willful king" of Daniel 11.[3]

In his 1971 seminary paper, Jim Nix likewise acknowledged that some of Edson's ideas "were thought to be important enough to be

[1]Clifton Taylor to A.W. Spalding, Nov. 19, 1947, Spalding Correspondence, Collection 10, Box 1, Folder 4, CAR, JWL, AU.
[2]A.W. Spalding to C.L. Taylor, June 20, 1948, Spalding Correspondence, Collection 10, Box 2, Folder 1, CAR, JWL, AU.
[3]Froom, *Prophetic Faith,* vol. 4, pp. 1038, 1082-1086.

the lead article in that particular issue of the Review."[4] In an undated manuscript, Fernand Fisel called Edson the writer "prolific" and "verbose," and he considered his writings to be "lengthy, fanciful, and unclear."[5] Yet this begs the question: How was a farmer with no more than an elementary education able to publish some 20 articles and pamphlets during two decades? Where did Edson find his inspiration? The answers to these questions lie embedded in the Millerite movement itself.

Numerologist and symbologist

Millerite Adventism was nurtured on numerology and saturated with symbolism. In 1841, when Joshua Himes published his "Explanation of Prophetic Figures" list, he enumerated 143 biblical symbols that had prophetic significance for modern times.[6] In the same work, Himes explicated 10 biblical time predictions, including the 1260-, 1290-, 1335-, 2300-, and 2520-day prophecies.[7]

Between 1842 and 1844, William Miller, employing what critic Donald Casebolt has called "a fanciful, arbitrary, allegorical-typological-historical methodology,"[8] likewise made apocalyptic applications for "Babylon,"[9] "the Day of God's Vengeance,"[10] and "the Laodicean Church,"[11] as well as explaining symbols like "the Red Dragon," "the

---

[4]Nix, "Edson," p. 115.

[5]Fisel, "Three Early Visions," p. 4.

[6]Joshua V. Himes, *Views of the Prophecies and Prophetic Chronology, Selected from Manuscripts of William Miller; with a Memoir of His Life* (Boston: Moses A. Dow, 1841), pp. 25-32.

[7]Himes, "A Dissertation on Prophetic Chronology," in *Views of the Prophecies*, pp. 40-53.

[8]Donald E. Casebolt, *Father Miller's Daughter: Ellen Harmon White* (Eugene, OR: Wipf & Stock, 2022), p. x.

[9]William Miller, *A Lecture on the Typical Sabbaths and Great Jubilee* (Boston: Joshua V. Himes, 1842), pp. 16-21.

[10]Miller, *Lecture on the Typical Sabbaths*, pp. 8-12.

[11]William Miller, *Evidence from Scripture and History of the Second Coming of Christ about the Year 1843* (Boston: Joshua V. Himes, 1842), p. 127.

Lamb," "the Leopard,"[12] and the "Beast with seven heads and ten horns."[13] His mathematical calculations explained the 1260-,[14] 1290-, 1335-, 2300-, and 2520-day prophecies.[15] Yet even Seventh-day Adventist apologist Francis D. Nichol considered many of Miller's interpretations "far-fetched" and "fanciful."[16] Nonetheless, Miller set the tone and established the methodology employed by other Millerite, Advent Christian, and Sabbatarian Adventist expositors of biblical prophecies during the 1840s and 1850s.

As early as 1838, Josiah Litch had predicted that Christ would return to earth in 1844. Yet he, like Miller, could bury readers in choking detail concerning the ancient historical correspondence of the "King of the North" (Seleucus of Syria) and the "King of the South" (Ptolemy of Egypt).[17]

In 1843, Charles Fitch produced his "Chronological Chart of the Visions of Daniel and John" to illustrate his colleagues' prophetic predictions. He showed four different ways of arriving at the Second Coming in 1843.[18] Fitch also discussed the apocalyptic significance of the "false prophets" in Jeremiah 5;[19] the "wicked power" in Daniel

---

[12]William Miller, *Dissertations on the True Inheritance of the Saints, and the Twelve Hundred and Sixty Days of Daniel and John* (Boston: Joshua V. Himes, 1842), pp. 30-36.

[13]William Miller, *Remarks on Revelations Thirteenth, Seventeenth, and Eighteenth* (Boston: Joshua V. Himes, 1844), pp. 5-16.

[14]Miller, *Remarks*, pp. 6-8.

[15]Miller, *Evidence*, pp. 103, 261. For the 15 different ways in which Miller showed that Christ's second coming would be in 1843-1844, see William Miller, "Synopsis of Miller's Views," *Signs of the Times* (Jan. 25, 1843), p. 147.

[16]Francis D. Nichol, *The Midnight Cry: A Defense of the Character and Conduct of William Miller and the Millerites, Who Mistakenly Believed that the Second Coming of Christ Would Take Place in the Year 1844* (Takoma Park, Washington, DC: Review and Herald Pub. Assn., 1944), Appendix L, pp. 522-524.

[17]Josiah Litch, *The Probability of the Second Coming of Christ About A.D. 1844* (Boston: David H. Ela, 1838), pp. 1-8.

[18]Charles Fitch, "Chronological Chart of the Visions of Daniel and John (1843)," reproduced in Spalding, *Origin and History*, vol. 1, p. 90. The four ways of arriving at 1843 included subtracting 677 years from the 2520 years; subtracting 457 years from the 2300 years; adding 45 years to 1798 A.D.; and adding 1335 years to 508 A.D.

[19] Charles Fitch, *A Wonderful and Horrible Thing* (Boston: Joshua V. Himes, 1842), p. 3.

7;[20] the sixth and seventh trumpets;[21] and the "woman clothed with the sun" in Revelation 12.[22]

Rochester was the headquarters of the Advent Christians, led by the former Millerite Joseph Marsh. The fact that Edson's articles occasionally referenced Marsh's views indicated that Hiram was reading Advent Christian literature. In two prominent works, Marsh explicated the seventy-week and 1260-, 1335-, 2300-, and 2520-day prophecies, ending them in 1843.[23]

The former Millerite agent and Sabbatarian Adventist preacher Joseph Bates, who became Edson's preaching partner in the 1850s, significantly shaped his writing style. In 1847 his *Second Advent Waymarks and High Heaps* explored the meanings of the seven trumpets, the ten virgins, and the "Mystery of God" in Paul's epistles.[24] In addition, Bates applied creative interpretations for such biblical terms as "the third woe" (Revelation 8:13), "marriage of the Lamb," and the "shut door" (Matthew 25:10).[25] Bates, like Edson, was one of the few Sabbatarian Adventist preachers to discourse on "the times of the Gentiles" in connection with the 2520-year prophecy.[26] Finally, when Christ did not return in 1844, Bates set a new date—1851—based on adding seven years to 1844 (for "seven drops of blood" sprinkled before the altar in Leviticus 4:6, 17 and Leviticus 16:14, 19).[27]

---

[20]Charles Fitch, *The Glory of God in the Earth* (Boston: Joshua V. Himes, 1842), p. 6.

[21]Fitch, *A Wonderful and Horrible Thing*, p. 11.

[22]Fitch, *Glory of God in the Earth*, p. 30.

[23]Joseph Marsh, in "The World's End in 1843" (Portland, ME: n.p., 1843), pp. 6-8, and *The Bible Doctrine: or True Gospel Faith Concerning the Gathering of Israel, the Millennium, Personal Coming of Christ, Resurrection, Renovation of the Earth, Kingdom of God, and Time of the Second Advent of Christ* (Rochester, NY: Advent Harbinger and Bible Advocate Office, 1848), pp. 52-53, briefly covers all the above time prophecies.

[24]Joseph Bates, *Second Advent Waymarks and High Heaps: Or a Connected View of the Fulfillment of Prophecy, by God's Peculiar People, From the Year 1840 to 1847* (New Bedford, MA: Benjamin Lindsey, 1847), pp. 40-41.

[25]Bates, *Second Advent Waymarks*, pp. 45-55, 63-68.

[26]Bates, *Second Advent Waymarks*,, pp. 43-45.

[27]Joseph Bates, *An Explanation of the Typical and Anti-typical Sanctuary by the Scriptures* (New Bedford,

The Jubilee Standard

Edson's first published venture was a lengthy letter he wrote on May 29, 1845, to *The Jubilee Standard*, a Millerite Adventist paper published by Samuel Snow in New York City. Edson argued that the 1335-day prophecy of Daniel would most likely end in August 1845, because all the types had met their antitypes.[28] Although it was written only seven months after Hiram's experience in the cornfield on October 23, 1844, Edson made no reference to that experience. He never mentioned the new understanding that he and his friends, Crosier and Hahn, had received regarding the heavenly sanctuary or the role that the cleansing and final judgment in the Most Holy Place would play in end-time events. And while he used the word "Sabbath" several times, he and Esther did not accept the seventh-day (Saturday) Sabbath until the following year.[29]

Final return of the Jews

In 1849, Edson wrote his first pamphlet, *An Exposition of Scripture Prophecy, Showing the Final Return of the Jews in 1850.* The idea that the scattered Jews would soon be reunited in Palestine was widely popular in the 1840s, especially among the Advent Christians.[30] Despite the fact that Ellen White and the majority of Sabbatarian Adventists did not share this belief,[31] Edson believed that Christians needed to do more to help the Jewish people. He also felt that Adventists had not incorporated the Jews into their

---

MA: Benjamin Lindsey, 1850), pp. 10-11.
[28]Hiram Edson, May 21, 1845, letter to *The Jubilee Standard*, May 29, 1845, pp. 90-91.
[29]Edson, letter to *The Jubilee Standard*, p. 91.
[30]Spicer, *Pioneer Days*, p. 224.
[31]Ellen White, *Early Writings*, p. 213. White believed that God had forsaken the Jews as a nation but that individual Jews could be saved.

prophetic timelines, and he intended to correct that omission.[32]

Edson argued that Zechariah 14:2-14 and other Old Testament texts taught that the literal Jews would return to a literal Palestine sometime after the 2300-day prophecy ended in 1844 but "before the coming of the Lord." God would accomplish this very soon when "the Seventh JUBILEE trumpet" sounded and the "chains of the Jews" would be broken.[33]

After the Jews occupied Jerusalem, the "Battle of the great day of God Almighty" would occur. Then this "remnant of the House of Jacob" would become a mission field for Christian endeavor, especially by Sabbath-keeping Adventists, who would show them how the Old Testament promises were fulfilled in Jesus Christ and then share the sealing message with them.[34]

The Time of the End

Edson's second tract, The Time of the End, was published by Henry Oliphant in Auburn, New York. Addressed "To the Scattered Flock—the Remnant,"[35] it explicated several last-day symbols found in Daniel and Revelation. These included "the time of the end"; the fifth and sixth trumpets; the King of the South (Egypt) and the King of the North (Russia); and the seven trumpets.[36]

The three angels of Revelation 14 began giving their messages in 1840 (first angel), 1843 (second angel), and 1844 (third angel), when the "time of trouble" commenced. Edson predicted future wars in Eastern Europe and the Balkans, after which Christ would

---

[32]Hiram Edson, An Exposition of Scripture Prophecy; Showing the Final Return of the Jews in 1850 (Canandaigua, NY: Printed at the Office of the Ontario Messenger, 1849), pp. 1-41.

[33]Edson, Return of the Jews, pp. 2-9.

[34]Edson, Return of the Jews, pp. 10-31.

[35]Hiram Edson, The Time of the End; Its Beginning, Progressive Events, and Final Termination (Auburn, NY: Henry Oliphant, 1849), p. 3.

[36]Edson, Time of the End, pp. 3-8.

return to rescue His saints on May 19, 1850.[37] When that date passed, Edson never again set a time for Christ's return.

Advent Review Extra article

Edson in September 1850 paid for an "Extra" (special) issue of the *Review* entitled "An Appeal to the Laodicean Church" and devoted entirely to prophetic and symbolic insights. In its 16 pages, buttressed with lengthy quotes from Joseph Marsh's August 13, 1845, *Voice of Truth*, Edson identified the Sardis Church as nominal Christians, the Philadelphia Church of Revelation 3 as Millerite Adventists who had come out of the Sardis Church, and the Laodicean Church as those who continued to reject present truth. Edson defined the "Shut Door"[38] of Matthew 25 as applying solely to non-Adventists, while the door to the Most Holy Place was now open to Sabbath-keeping Adventists. He explicated such symbols as Jezebel (the Roman Catholic Church) and her horrible death (the destruction of Babylon portrayed in Revelation 13); Balaam (the greedy popes in Rome); and Elijah's prophecy that there would be no rainfall in Israel for three and a half years, paralleling the "famine in the land" for God's Word from 1844 to 1848.[39]

Edson then asked: "Who can be saved now?" His answer was surprisingly broad: It encompassed all those who were living up to all the light they had; those who had "a sacred reverence for God and His word" but belong to no denomination; and young children.[40]

---

[37]Edson, *Time of the End*, p. 14.

[38]The "Shut-Door" belief, first advanced by Joseph Turner at the Millerite camp meeting in Woodstock, Maine, taught that on the tenth day of the seventh month (Oct. 22, 1844), a door in the heavenly sanctuary would be shut, barring further conversions. Isaac Wellcome recalled hearing Ellen Harmon speak in support of this shut-door teaching in the 1840s. He also claimed to have twice caught her in his arms when she went into vision so that she would not fall to the floor. See Wellcome, *History of the Second Advent Message and Mission* (Portland, ME: B. Thurston, 1874) p. 397.

[39]Hiram Edson, "An Appeal to the Laodicean Church," *Review* Extra, 1850, pp. 1-16. White and Bates endorsed Edson's views on the three churches of Revelation 3. See James White, *Review*, Nov. 1850, and Joseph Bates, *Review*, Aug. 19, 1851, pp. 13-14.

[40]Edson, "Appeal," p. 3.

Edson then drew parallels between the Israelite bondage in Egypt and end-time scenarios (persecution); Ahab and Roman Catholicism; Balaam and the pope; God's Sabbath and the pope's Sunday; and Elijah's rainfall and the Latter Rain of the Spirit.[41] He warned readers that there was no biblical foundation for the Age-to-Come Adventists' teaching of a second probation; instead, this was a device of Satan to draw attention away from the third angel's message.[42]

"The Sixty-Nine Weeks and 2300 Days"

In March 1851, Edson submitted a manuscript examining two prophetic periods: the Sixty-Nine Weeks and the 2300 Days. He stated that the 2300-day prophecy ended on October 22, 1844, not in 1850 (his own view in 1849) or in 1851 (Bates' view). Christ was anointed by the Holy Ghost as the Messiah during His immersion in the Jordan River by John the Baptist in 27 A.D. (at the end of the 69 prophetic weeks); He died "in the middle of the week" in 31 A.D. The Christian message had been preached first to the "house of Israel" (the Jews) and, after 34 A.D. (the end of the Seventy Weeks prophecy), to the Gentiles.[43]

"The Holy Covenant"

In a May 5, 1851, article to the *Review*, Edson stated that God's law was unchanging and eternal; it existed long before He gave it to Moses on Mt. Sinai. Human beings, he added, can neither abolish nor

---

[41]Edson, "Appeal," pp. 4-10.

[42]Edson, "Appeal," pp. 12-16. For further information concerning Edson's views on the Seven Churches, see Robert Leo Odom, "Philadelphians or Laodiceans?" *Review*, Jan. 5, 1956, pp. 4-5. A 48-page article on the "Shut Door" edited by Hiram Edson, David Arnold, George Holt, Samuel Rhodes, and James White in the *Review-Extra* of Sept. 1850, declared: "We are down through 'the shut door' in that representation of Advent History [based on Matthew 25]. My language to many has been, I believe in the shut door just as you have *experienced it*. Precisely so." *Review-Extra*, Sept. 1850, p. 27; emphasis in the original.

[43]Hiram Edson, "The 69 Weeks and 2300 Days," *Review*, March 1851, pp. 49-50.

improve God's law, for it is perfect, holy, just, and good. Indulging his love for numerology, Edson estimated (based on Psalm 90:10) that God's law would last for a thousand generations—and given 70 years per generation, that would mean 70,000 years.[44]

"The Two Laws"

In an October 1851 article, Edson had more to say about the ceremonial laws (temporary) and the moral law (eternal). He described the moral law as "the government of God," which was founded on "holy, just and righteous principles" and based on love. The Ten Commandments, including the Sabbath, were part of God's moral law, still binding upon humanity.[45]

The ceremonial law was a "law of types and shadows" given to the Israelites because they had failed to obey the moral law. The seventh-day Sabbath was not part of the ceremonial law and was not abolished at the cross. Here Edson opposed Joseph Marsh and the Age-to-Come Adventists who argued exactly the opposite based on their interpretation of Hebrews 4:4-9.[46]

"The Ten Commandments of God"

Edson's article, "The Commandments of God," appeared as a three-part series in the September 2, 16, and 30, 1852, issues of the *Review* and covered about nine pages total.

In part one he argued that the Sealing Angel of Revelation 7 and the Third Angel of Revelation 14 were the same being and that God's wrath will be poured out on the wicked after these three angels give their messages. He then explicated the seven last plagues, the four

---

[44]Hiram Edson, "The Holy Covenant," *Review*, May 5, 1851, p. 80.
[45]Hiram Edson, "The Two Laws," *Review*, Oct. 7, 1851, pp. 36-37.
[46]Edson, "Two Laws," pp. 38-40.

vials, the four winds loosed by the four angels, the identity of the 144,000, and the "time of trouble."[47]

In part two Edson countered arguments advanced by a certain "E.D.C." in *The Harbinger* of March 27, 1852, concerning the Ten Commandment Law.[48] He argued that God's seal (the Sabbath) revealed His identity as Creator and His authority to make laws. Without this seal, the other nine commandments were "a dead letter." The "Little Horn" (papacy), by changing the day of worship from Saturday to Sunday, had attempted to nullify God's law and establish the "mark of the beast," exalting traditions above the Bible.[49]

Part three contrasted true knowledge and wisdom with worldly wisdom, with God's law being the true "well-spring of wisdom." Without the fourth commandment, people would have no knowledge about or fear of God as the Supreme Ruler and Creator, and this is "the beginning of wisdom" in contrast with rejecting His law, which is "the beginning of FOLLY." In conclusion, Edson called upon the faithful to "cry aloud" against the "trampling" of God's Sabbath day and to warn Sunday-keepers that they risked receiving the "mark of the beast" and being lost eternally.[50]

"The Times of the Gentiles"

Edson's next articles for the *Review*, "The Times of the Gentiles and the Deliverance and Restoration of the Remnant of Israel from the Seven Times, or 2520 Years of Assyrian or Pagan and Papal Captivity Considered," appeared between January 3 and February 28,

---

[47]Hiram Edson, "The Commandments of God, and the Mark of the Beast Brought to View by the Third Angel of Rev. XIV, Considered in Connection with the Angel of Chap. VII, Having the Seal of the Living God," *Review*, Sept. 2, 1852, pp. 65-67.

[48]Edson, "Commandments," *Review*, Sept. 16, 1852, p. 74.

[49]Edson, "Commandments," *Review*, Sept. 16, 1852, pp. 73-75.

[50]Edson, "Commandments," *Review*, Sept. 30, 1852, pp. 81-84; emphasis in the original.

1856, and filled nearly 20 pages. Edson advocated a 2520-year time-line (based on Leviticus 26) that few of his colleagues supported. At the top of part one, Uriah Smith added this caveat:

> The following article was received from Bro. Edson some time since; but we have not yet had time to examine it thoroughly. Many of the ideas presented are new, and we think it proper to publish them for the consideration of the brethren, letting the writer remain responsible for the views presented.[51]

Part one explicated the following type-antitype analogies: The entrance of Israel into the Promised Land (the entrance of the saints into heaven); the destruction of the Antediluvians in the Flood (the destruction of the wicked at the end of the world); and Elijah's message to Israel (the Millerite Adventists' warnings of 1844). Referencing Luke 21:24 for "the times of the Gentiles," he then mined the Old Testament for every prediction regarding the future of the Gentiles.[52]

Part two constituted a meandering journey through several biblical types and symbols, including the "seven times" of Assyrian (pagan) and papal captivity that ended in 1798 (Daniel 8-12); the papacy as "mystery Babylon"; and the identities of the King of the North and the King of the South. Then Edson explained that the 2520 prophetic days actually began in 723 B.C. with the imprisonment of Israel's King Hoshea by the pagan Assyrians, and it ended in 1798 A.D. with the overthrow of the pope by Napoleon I.[53]

In part three, Edson briefly explained the interrelationship of the

---

[51]Uriah Smith, *Review*, Jan. 3, 1856, p. 105.
[52]Hiram Edson, "The Times of the Gentiles and the Deliverance and Restoration of the Remnant of Israel from the Seven Times, or 2520 Years of Assyrian or Pagan and Papal Captivity Considered," *Review*, Jan. 3, 1856, pp. 105-107.
[53]Edson, "Times of the Gentiles," *Review*, Jan. 10, 1856, pp. 113-115.

1260-, 1290-, 1335-, and 2300-day prophecies before highlighting some of the end-time events that brought about the end of the "indignation": the rise of Protestantism, the increase in Bible translations, and the outpouring of the Holy Spirit in revivals.[54]

Part four expressed Edson's exultation that Protestantism was in the ascendancy over the Papal See and that religious persecution ended when Napoleon I "overthrew the throne of the Papal beast" in 1798, when "the time of the end" began and the books of Daniel and Revelation, previously "sealed," were now open for all to read and understand. Half a century later, however, the "deadly wound was healed" in 1848-1849 when the "beast in the bottomless pit" came forth and the papacy revived.[55]

Part five constituted a diatribe against the papacy and Catholicism in general. Edson explained centuries-old symbols often applied to the papacy, among them the seven-headed beast, the little horn power, and the healing of the deadly wound. Roman supremacy, he argued, had manifested itself through several phases—pagan, imperial, barbarian, papal, and now Napoleonic power—all of them Catholic in one form or another.[56]

Part six focused primarily on the role of the United States in prophecy as the great Protestant counterweight to Catholicism. Edson saw the establishment of a republican government in the U.S. as a fulfillment of several biblical references. America was the two-horned gentle lamblike beast that arose from the land (symbolizing emptiness) rather than from the sea (symbolizing dense populations). He believed that the U.S. Constitution and republicanism were a "heaven-ordained government, which was established by di-

[54]Edson, "Times of the Gentiles," *Review*, Jan. 17, 1856, pp. 121-123.
[55]Edson, "Times of the Gentiles," *Review*, Jan. 24, 1856, pp. 129-131.
[56]Edson, "Times of the Gentiles," *Review*, Feb. 14, 1856, pp. 153-155.

vine appointment."[57]

Part seven argued that under God's blessing, Protestantism had achieved "her glorious triumph" in America. God had guided a remnant people from all areas where Babylon, Persia, Greece, Rome, and the papacy had once held power to come to the "wilderness," the "land toward the west" (Isaiah 11:11-16 and 59:19) where civil and religious freedom reigned supreme.[58]

Although part seven closed with the words "To be continued," implying that Edson had yet another section to add to the series, subsequent issues of the *Review* carried no eighth part. One can only surmise that perhaps readers had grown weary of Edson's theological speculations or that Uriah Smith as editor felt that some of his scriptural interpretations were too "fancy" and allegorical to be of much theological benefit to subscribers.

"Daniel Standing in His Lot"

"Daniel Standing in His Lot" appeared in the July 30, 1857, *Review*. Edson explained that "Daniel's Lot" meant a "time of judgment" for the whole human family when the eternal destiny of all will be determined by divine providence. In that Day of Judgment, the ungodly "shall not stand," while the godly will be acquitted and saved. This judgment day occurred at the close of both the 1335- and 2300-day prophecies, which ended on October 22, 1844.[59]

"The Shortening of the Days"

In the summer of 1867, Edson penned "The Shortening of the Days, And Typical Bearing of the Forty Years Sojourn of Israel in the

---

[57]Edson, "Times of the Gentiles," *Review*, Feb. 21, 1856, pp. 162-163.
[58]Edson, "Times of the Gentiles," *Review*, Feb. 28, 1856, pp. 169-170.
[59]Hiram Edson, "Daniel Standing in His Lot," *Review*, July 30, 1857, p. 101.

Wilderness," a two-part essay. In part one, he likened the 40 years of Israel's wandering in the wilderness to the 40 years prior to 1844, when most Christians were still uncertain what all the end-time prophecies meant. He argued that while Ancient Israel was the type, Sabbath-keeping Adventists were the antitype fulfilling these prophecies during "the period of the indignation" from 1798 to 1844.[60]

In part two, he asserted that the civil and religious liberties guaranteed by the Constitution had attracted thousands of immigrants to America after 1798. Fulfilling Bible prophecy, these refugees came "into the wilderness" seeking religious freedom. Finally, just as the Israelites (type) forgot the true Sabbath during their 400 years of Egyptian bondage, but had it restored to them during their 40 years of wilderness wandering, so Adventists (anti-type) after 1849 had restored the truth of God's seventh-day Sabbath by preaching the third angel's message to the world.[61]

In conclusion, these extremely short summaries of Edson's lengthy articles demonstrate that his speculative theological mindset mirrored the "allegorical-typological-historical method" advanced by William Miller and endlessly repeated by contemporary Millerite writers such as Joshua V. Himes, Josiah Litch, Charles Fitch, Joseph Turner, Samuel Snow, and Joseph Marsh as well as by Sabbatarian Adventist writers like O.R.L. Crosier, Joseph Bates, Ellen Harmon, James White, Uriah Smith, and J.N. Andrews. As members of the "Apocalyptic Club," they all emphasized "biblical math" (but did not always agree on their timeline prophecies)[62] and "fanciful" interpreta-

---

[60]Hiram Edson, "The Shortening of the Days, And Typical Bearing of the Forty Years Sojourn of Israel in the Wilderness," *Review*, July 30, 1867, pp. 102-103.

[61]Edson, "Shortening of the Days," *Review*, Aug. 6, 1867, p. 118.

[62]For a more detailed discussion of the similarities and differences among Millerite and Sabbatarian Adventist interpretations of biblical prophecies, see Casebolt, *William Miller's Daughter*, pp. 15, 22-32, 35-42, 48-51, 56-57, 185-191, and 213-219.

tions of biblical imagery (that sometimes clashed with their contemporaries' views).[63]

Although Hiram Edson is traditionally credited with introducing the heavenly sanctuary message to Sabbatarian Adventists, the above articles clearly reveal that it was not the dominant subject of his articles and tracts. Instead, several of his colleagues actually did the biblical spadework to establish that teaching in the 1850s, as Chapter 9 reveals.

---

[63]For a more detailed discussion of the similarities and differences among Millerite and Sabbatarian Adventist interpretations of biblical imagery, see Casebolt, *William Miller's Daughter*, pp. 15, 52-56, 69-71, 76-82, 96-101, 112-119, 130-140, and 159-161.

Chapter 9

Sanctuary Expositors

Given the fact of Hiram Edson's first-person experience in the cornfield on October 23, 1844 (see Chapter 4) in which he understood that the sanctuary was in heaven, it would have made logical sense for *Review* editors James White and Uriah Smith to ask him to write a series of articles on the subject, but they did not. As Chapter 8 shows, Edson seldom alluded to the heavenly sanctuary in any of his articles or pamphlets penned between 1849 and 1867. Furthermore, his bent for speculative theology, his love of type/antitype analogies, and his yen for interpreting biblical symbolism in unorthodox ways may have made him unsuitable in the editors' eyes to explicate such key concepts as the heavenly sanctuary, the atonement, and the investigative judgment with clear, concise prose.

Consequently, during the 1850s, the editors chose six authors to explicate the meaning of the heavenly sanctuary: Owen Crosier, James White, J.N. Andrews, Uriah Smith, C.W. Sperry, and Elon Everts. Between 1850 and 1859, their articles filled 136 multi-column pages of the Review. In 1850-1851, sanctuary articles amounted to eight percent of all doctrinal articles; in 1852-1853, 13 percent; in

1854-1855, 12.5 percent; and in 1857, 12 percent.[1] While the subject matter in their articles sometimes overlapped, it is noteworthy that each of these six authors also made some unique contributions and that no one of them encompassed the full breadth and depth of the subject matter. Like pieces of a jigsaw puzzle, their different perspectives, when combined, form a more complete picture of the sanctuary teaching. This chapter briefly analyzes those different viewpoints by grouping together the various articles written by each author.

Owen R.L. Crosier

Six issues of the *Review* between September 1850 and October 1852 carried sanctuary articles written by Crosier. To a great extent, these are reprints of his February 7, 1846, *Day-Star Extra* article on the same topic.[2] It may seem paradoxical that James White chose Crosier as the lead contributor on the sanctuary, a teaching (along with the seventh-day Sabbath) that Crosier rejected in 1848 and continued to oppose in print thereafter. (See Chapter 5). Almost certainly Crosier was not consulted before his articles ran in the *Review*.

Crosier's scope in these articles is rather broad and is based on references to 50 Bible texts.[3] He discusses the furnishings in the earthly and heavenly sanctuaries and the roles of the priests and high priest in great detail.[4] He also refutes those who teach that the sanctuary is this earth or Palestine.[5] He shows how Catholicism has "polluted" God's heavenly services by substituting the pope for Christ and priestly con-

---

[1] Brian E. Strayer, "Charts Analyzing the Number of Articles on the Sanctuary in *The Advent Review and Sabbath Herald* for volumes 1-15 (1850-1876)" (Berrien Springs, MI: typed manuscript, 1974-1975), 49 sheets in the author's possession.

[2] Compare O.R.L. Crosier, "The Law of Moses," *The Day-Star* Extra, Feb. 7, 1846, with Crosier, "Sanctuary," *Review-Extra*, Sept. 1850, pp. 42-47, 57-64.

[3] Crosier, "The Sanctuary," *Review* Extra, Sept. 1850, pp. 42-47.

[4] Crosier, "Sanctuary," *Review* Extra, Sept. 1850, pp. 42-47, 57-63.

[5] Crosier, "Sanctuary," *Review*, May 5, 1851, pp. 78-80.

fession for Christ's forgiveness. He also focuses on Christ's ministry in the Most Holy Place from 1844 to the end of time.[6] In addition, he explicates such topics as the Day of Atonement,[7] the identities of the two goats,[8] the various sanctuaries in Jewish history,[9] and several type/antitype analogies between the earthly and heavenly sanctuaries.[10] One key point Crosier made in 1846 that is repeated in his September 30, 1852, article is that Christ's death on the cross was not part of His atonement for humanity. Only His ministry in the Most Holy Place in heaven constitutes His atoning work—a position with which most 19th-century Seventh-day Adventists would have agreed.[11]

James Springer White

Likewise, six issues of the *Review* between January 1851 and January 1859 carried sanctuary articles by James White. But whereas Crosier was simply explicating what to him was a newly understood subject, White was writing to refute the erroneous views advanced by Ira Fancher,[12] Apollos Hale,[13] and others in the *Advent Herald*, the *Gospel Herald*, and the *Second Advent Manual*. White denies their assertions that the sanctuary is this earth, the land of Canaan, or the Christian Church rather than being in heaven;[14] that the 2300-day prophecy ended in 1851 rather than 1844;[15] and that Christ entered the Most Holy Place (rather than the Holy Place) at His ascension in

---

[6]Crosier, "The Priesthood of Christ," *Review*, Sept. 16, 1852, pp. 76-77.

[7]Crosier, "Sanctuary," *Review* Extra, Sept. 1850, pp. 42-47.

[8]Crosier, "Priesthood," *Review* Extra, Sept. 1850, pp. 47, 57-63.

[9]Crosier, "Sanctuary," *Review*, May 5, 1851, 78-80, and Crosier, "Sanctuary," *Review*, Sept. 2, 1852, pp. 68-69.

[10]Crosier, "Priesthood," *Review*, Sept. 16, 1852, 76-77 and Crosier, "Priesthood," *Review*, Oct. 14, 1852, pp. 90-91.

[11]Crosier, "Priesthood," *Review*, Sept. 30, 1852, pp. 84-85.

[12]James White, "To Ira Fancher," *Review*, March 1851, pp. 52-53.

[13]White, "The Sanctuary," *Review*, March 31, 1853, p. 181.

[14]White, "To Ira Fancher," *Review*, March 1851, pp. 52-53.

[15]White, "The Sanctuary and 2300 Days," *Review*, March 17, 1853, pp. 172-173.

31 A.D.[16] Like Crosier, he also condemned the Catholic Church for substituting priestly confession for Christ's forgiveness and the mass for His atoning work in heaven.[17]

But to a greater extent than Crosier, White focused on the unfolding of the 2300-day prophecy in Daniel 8, highlighting the importance of such dates as 457 B.C., 27, 31, 34, and 1844 A.D., and explained the significance of the seventy weeks.[18] His January 29, 1857, article, by contrast, is based on 1 Peter 4:17-18 which deals with God's judging the righteous and the wicked prior to His second coming and the subsequent opening of heaven's books during the millennium so that the saints can examine the records of the wicked as well.[19]

It is also in this January 29, 1857 issue that White uses the term "investigative judgment" (which he borrowed from Elon Everts as shown below) to describe Christ's work in the Most Holy Place of the heavenly sanctuary after October 22, 1844. This, he explained, is the antitypical Day of Atonement.[20] The term "investigative judgment" would become part of the doctrinal lexicon of Seventh-day Adventists for the next century and a half. Moreover, White identified the heavenly books containing the records of human deeds as the book of life (for the saved) and the book with sins recorded (for the damned).[21]

John Nevins Andrews

Between December 1852 and February 1856, the *Review* published nine articles penned by J.N. Andrews focusing on the sanctuary. Like White, Andrews devoted much space to refuting the positions

---

[16]White, "Sanctuary," *Review*, March 31, 1853, p. 181.
[17]White, "Our Present Position," *Review*, Jan. 1851, pp. 27-30.
[18]White, "Sanctuary," *Review*, March 17, 1853, pp. 172-173.
[19]White, "The Judgment," *Review*, Jan. 29, 1857, p. 100.
[20]White, "Judgment," *Review*, Jan. 29, 1857, p. 100.
[21]White, "Judgment," *Review*, Jan. 29, 1857, p. 101.

advanced by the *Advent Herald*;[22] therefore, he carefully explained the historical significance of key dates (457 B.C., 27, 31, 34, 1844 A.D., the seventy-weeks prophecy, the 2300-days prophecy, etc.).[23]

Unlike Crosier and White, however, Andrews devotes more attention to explicating the symbols relating to the sanctuary (i.e., the ram, the two goats, the "Little Horn," "the Desolation," the "trodding of the host underfoot," the "mystery of iniquity," the dragon, the beast, etc.).[24] Ever the historian, he also traces the development of the various tabernacles erected by Moses, Solomon, Ezra and Zerubbabel, and Herod—down to the destruction of the latter in 70 A.D.[25]

He also argues that the 2300-day prophecy ended on October 22, 1844, and is not ongoing;[26] that the seventy-weeks prophecy and the 2300-days prophecy have the same (not different) starting dates;[27] that the sanctuary is a literal edifice in heaven (not Palestine, this earth, or merely metaphorical);[28] and that Daniel 8 and 9 and Hebrews 8 and 9 prove that the cleansing takes place in the heavenly (not earthly) sanctuary. Instead, the services in the earthly tabernacle and temples were but "shadows" of those yet to come in the heavenly sanctuary.[29]

Uriah Smith

As the editor of the *Review* for nearly half a century, Uriah Smith naturally had the opportunity to write several thousand articles and

---

[22]J.N. Andrews, "Position of the *Advent Herald* on the Sanctuary Question," *Review*, May 12, 1853, pp. 204-205; Andrews, "The Antitypical Tabernacle," *Review*, July 7, 1853, pp. 25-28; Andrews, "Antitypical Tabernacle," *Review*, Aug. 28, 1853, pp. 60-61.

[23]Andrews, "Position of the *Advent Herald*," *Review*, May 12, 1853, pp. 204-205.

[24]Andrews, "The Sanctuary," *Review*, Dec. 23, 1852, pp. 121-125.

[25]Andrews, "Sanctuary," *Review*, Jan. 20, 1853, pp. 137-139.

[26]Andrews, "Sanctuary," *Review*, Dec. 23, 1852, pp. 121-125.

[27]Andrews, "Position of the *Advent Herald*," *Review*, May 12, 1853, pp. 204-205.

[28]Andrews, "Antitypical Tabernacle," *Review*, July 7, 1853, pp. 25-28.

[29]Andrews, "The Sanctuary and Its Cleansing," *Review*, Oct. 30, 1855, pp. 68-69, and Andrews, "The Cleansing of the Sanctuary," *Review*, Feb. 21, 1856, pp. 164-165.

editorials covering a wide range of subjects. Between March 1854 and March 1858, he devoted 20 of those articles to topics related to the sanctuary. Like Andrews and White, he focused much of his attention on the prophetic timelines (particularly the 1260-day and 2300-day prophecies)[30] as well as the symbols found in Daniel 8 and 9 (goat, ram, Little Horn, Seventy Weeks).[31] Also like his colleagues, Smith explained the significance of such dates as 457 B.C., 27, 31, 34, and 1844 A.D.[32]

Like Andrews, he traced the history of the earthly sanctuaries from Moses to Herod and explicated the spiritual significance of each item of interior furniture they contained (the table of shewbread, the seven-branched candlestick, the altar of incense, and the ark of the covenant) as well as the roles filled by the priests and High Priest.[33] Also like his predecessors, Smith sought to refute positions advanced by the *Advent Herald, Advent Watchman, Advent Harbinger, World's Crisis,* and the *Christian Reformer* regarding the shut and open doors, the scapegoat's (Azazel) role, and the identity and placement of the heavenly sanctuary. (It was not the earth, Canaan, or the Christian Church.)[34] Moreover, the 2300-day prophecy ended on October 22, 1844, not in 1845, 1851, or 1854 as some had claimed.[35]

---

[30]Uriah Smith, "The Sanctuary," *Review*, March 21, 1854, pp. 69-70; Smith, "Sanctuary," *Review*, Feb. 18, 1858, pp. 116-117.

[31]Smith, "Sanctuary," *Review*, March 21, 1854, pp. 69-70; Smith, "Sanctuary," *Review*, April 4, 1854, pp. 84-86; Smith, "Synopsis of the Present Truth," *Review*, Feb. 25, 1858, pp. 124-125; Smith, "Sanctuary," *Review*, March 11, 1858, p. 132.

[32]Smith, "Sanctuary," *Review*, March 21, 1854, pp. 69-70; Smith, "Sanctuary," *Review*, April 4, 1854, pp. 84-86; Smith, "Sanctuary," *Review*, Feb. 18, 1858, pp. 116-117.

[33]Smith, "Sanctuary," *Review*, March 28, 1854, pp. 77-78; Smith, "History of the Worldly Sanctuary," *Review*, Aug. 21, 1856, p. 124; Smith, "History," *Review*, Aug. 28, 1856, p. 132; Smith, "History," *Review*, Sept. 4, 1856, pp. 140-141; Smith, "History," *Review*, Sept. 11, 1856, p. 148; Smith, "History," *Review*, Sept. 18, 1856, pp. 156, 160.

[34]Smith, "Sanctuary," *Review*, April 4, 1854, pp. 84-86; Smith, "The Sanctuary: A Novel Argument," *Review*, Jan. 9, 1855, pp. 156-157; Smith, "A Comprehensive View of the Sanctuary," *Review*, Jan. 24, 1856, p. 132.

[35]Smith, "Sanctuary," *Review*, March 21, 1854, pp. 69-70; Smith, "Sanctuary," *Review*, April 4, 1854, pp. 84-86; Smith, "Synopsis of the Present Truth, No. 14," *Review*, Jan. 24, 1858, p. 132.

Regarding Christ's role as high priest in the Most Holy Place of the heavenly sanctuary, Smith described and explained the meaning of His cleansing and judging ministry as depicted in Hebrews 9 and His intercessory work on behalf of human beings.[36] He drew parallels and highlighted differences between the earthly priests' shedding of the blood of lambs, goats, and calves to atone for human sins and Christ's shed blood atoning for sins in the Most Holy Place of the heavenly sanctuary. By so doing, Smith declared, Jesus forgives our sins, removes our guilt, and imputes His righteousness to us. Human sins (and guilt), he added, will be laid on Satan (the antitype of the goat Azazel) at the end of the millennium.[37]

Yet Smith also advanced two views not suggested by his colleagues. For example, he asserted that when the Babylonians burned Solomon's Temple in 586 B.C., they also destroyed the ark of the covenant.[38] In an article based on Revelation 6:12-17 and 8:1, Smith explained that the "silence in heaven for half an hour" does not occur during the cleansing of the heavenly sanctuary under the Sixth Seal but at the time of the opening of the Seventh Seal after Christ has finished His cleansing work in the Most Holy Place.[39] However, he agreed with the majority of 19th-century *Review* writers in declaring: "No part of Christ's ministry can be performed on the earth," including at the cross. Only in the heavenly sanctuary did His atoning ministry begin, in the Holy Place following His ascension to heaven in 31 A.D., and in the Most Holy Place beginning on October 22, 1844.[40]

---

[36]Smith, "Sanctuary," *Review*, March 28, 1854, pp. 77-78; Smith, "The Cleansing of the Sanctuary," *Review*, Oct. 2, 1855, pp. 52-54.

[37]Smith, "The Sanctuary of the New Covenant," *Review*, Oct. 2, 1856, pp. 172-173; Smith, "The Scapegoat," *Review*, Nov. 27, 1856, pp. 28-29; Smith, "Is the Silence in Heaven During the Cleansing of the Sanctuary?" *Review*, Dec. 18, 1856, p. 52.

[38]Smith, "History," *Review*, Sept. 11, 1856, p. 148. Ellen White, in *Prophets and Kings*, p. 453, asserted that the ark of the covenant was hidden in a cave.

[39]Smith, "Silence," *Review*, Dec. 18, 1856, p. 52.

[40]Smith, "Synopsis," *Review*, Feb. 25, 1858, p. 125.

In his final "Synopsis of the Present Truth, No. 14," a summary of his 20 sanctuary articles, Smith indulged in what for him was a rare exclamation. He stated that the sanctuary doctrine was the "grand nucleus around which cluster the glorious constellations of present truth!"

> Its importance can neither be overdrawn nor overestimated... We venture the assertion that it is impossible for a person to entertain correct and scriptural views on the subject of the Sanctuary, and yet be at variance with any of the fundamental points of what we consider Present Truth.... It is the great safeguard against all those bewildering errors, which since the passing of the time in 1844, have torn and scattered the once harmonious body of Advent believers.... Thus the Sanctuary becomes a great bulwark of the truth on every hand.... Never lose sight of the Sanctuary.... In hours of darkness, trial, temptation and persecution, look to the Sanctuary.[41]

Charles W. Sperry

Raised as a Baptist, Charles Sperry joined the Millerite movement at 23 in 1843. In 1851, he and his wife, Rachel Sperry, née Gardner, were among the first converts to Sabbatarian Adventism in Vermont. Although they both suffered from lung disease (likely tuberculosis) for many years, they remained faithful witnesses for present truth during their short lifetimes. Charles died in 1861 at about 41 and Rachel died in 1863 at 32.[42]

Five years before his death, Sperry penned a short one-page ar-

---

[41]Smith, "Synopsis," *Review*, March 25, 1858, p. 148.
[42]*Ellen G. White Encyclopedia*, s.v., "Sperry, Charles W. and Rachel Ann (Gardner)," p. 518.

ticle for the *Review* entitled "The Sanctuary."[43] While not as profound
in its scope or its breadth as the articles written by White, Andrews,
and Smith, nonetheless, it contained an interesting insight concerning Christ's work of cleansing in the heavenly sanctuary. Sperry
maintained that the work of cleansing was also a work of justifica-
tion to restore the moral rectitude of human beings, to cancel their
debt of sin and guilt, and to remit their punishment. The services in
the earthly tabernacle and temples involved daily animal sacrifices to
atone for sins and a once-per-year sacrifice and cleansing on the Day
of Atonement. In the heavenly sanctuary, Christ, who made a once-
for-all sacrifice on the cross, now carries on a continual atonement
for humans in the Most Holy Place, interceding on behalf of sinners
who confess their sins and accept His atoning blood. By contrast with
Crosier, White, Andrews, and Smith, therefore, it appears that Sperry
may have recognized that Christ's death on the cross constituted part
of His atoning ministry which, after His ascension, He continued in
the heavenly sanctuary. If this was the case, then Sperry stood virtu-
ally alone in sharing this insight in the 1850s.[44]

Elon Everts

Like Charles and Rachel Sperry, Elon and Anna Maria Everts, née
Rider, were Vermonters who converted to Sabbatarian Adventism in
1851. Elon then traveled throughout New England as an agent for
the *Review*. The couple assisted in several general conferences held
near their home, and in 1853, at age 46, Elon was ordained to the
gospel ministry. In 1855 the Everts moved to Round Grove, Illinois,
where they became prosperous farmers. The following year, Elon ac-

---

[43]C.W. Sperry, "The Sanctuary," *Review*, Feb. 7, 1856, p. 148.
[44]C.W. Sperry, "The Sanctuary," *Review*, Feb. 7, 1856, p. 148.

companied James and Ellen White on their perilous midwinter sleigh ride across the melting ice on the Mississippi River to Waukon, Iowa, where Ellen preached the Laodicean message and reclaimed J.N. Loughborough and J.N. Andrews for full-time ministry. Anna died in 1856 and Elon died at 51 in 1858.[45]

But one year before his death, Elon Everts wrote a letter to the *Review* in which he quoted Revelation 14:6-7 ("The hour of his judgment is come") and Daniel 8:14 (concerning the cleansing of the sanctuary). He asserted that this cleansing was also an act of judgment.[46] On October 22, 1844, Christ had begun a work of judgment in the Most Holy Place, first considering the deeds of the righteous dead from Adam onwards. Then in a key sentence, Everts stated: "It appears that the order is, that the righteous dead have been under *investigative judgment* since 1844."[47] This is the first time that the term "investigative judgment" appeared in any Sabbatarian Adventist publication. Everts then explained that while in 1844 Adventists had lived in the era of the Philadelphia Church of Revelation 3 characterized by hope, love, and zeal, since then they have lived under the Laodicean Church, which is lukewarm and worldly. Everts concluded by accepting this message on his own behalf and resolving, with Christ's help, to "be zealous and repent."[48]

Five months later, in "A Few Thoughts on the Cleansing of the Sanctuary," Everts focused once again on the cleansing of the earthly tabernacle by the blood of animals and the cleansing of the heavenly sanctuary (Daniel 8:14) by Christ's blood shed on the cross. Once again, he declared that Christ is currently carrying on the "investi-

---

[45]*Ellen G. White Encyclopedia*, s.v., "Everts, Elon and Anna Maria (Rider)," p. 373.
[46]Elon Everts, "Communication from Bro. Everts," *Review*, Jan. 1, 1857, p. 72.
[47]Everts, "Communication," *Review*, Jan. 1, 1857, p. 72; emphasis mine.
[48]Everts, "Communication," *Review*, Jan. 1, 1857, p. 72.

gative judgment" in the Most Holy Place of the heavenly sanctuary. When He has completed His work, He will return the second time to earth.[49] James White, as editor of the *Review*, was so delighted with the aptness of the term "investigative judgment" that four weeks later, he used the term four times in his article "The Judgment" in the January 29, 1857 *Review*. Others would also incorporate that term into their articles on Daniel 8:14 until it eventually became a key component of sanctuary exegesis.

At least 96 more articles concerning the earthly and heavenly sanctuaries would appear in the *Review* between 1861 and 1876 written by Uriah Smith (56 articles) and Joseph Waggoner (40 articles).[50] But from the evidence provided by the above six men in the articles they wrote in the 1850s, it appears that nearly all of the important elements of the sanctuary teaching had been assembled by 1860, with the exception of the later addition that Christ's death on the cross had indeed been an important part of His atoning work on earth even as His cleansing and judging ministry in the Most Holy Place of the heavenly sanctuary is an ongoing atonement work today. In that sense, Adventists in the 20th century would come to recognize that Christ's atonement on the cross was complete, but not yet completed.

---

[49]Elon Everts, "A Few Thoughts on the Cleansing of the Sanctuary," *Review*, June 11, 1857, p. 45.
[50]Strayer, "Charts."

Chapter 10

Sunset Years

The 1860s was a decade of tragedy and turmoil for the United States. A bloody Civil War (1861-1865) devastated the South and resulted in over a million soldiers and civilians killed in action or from disease, besides those who were wounded or missing.[1] Meanwhile out in Minnesota, a six-week Sioux uprising in 1862 killed upwards of 800 whites and an undetermined number of Dakota.[2] Then on April 14, 1865, John Wilkes Booth shot Abraham Lincoln at Ford's Theater in Washington, D.C., the first assassination of a United States president.[3]

Within Sabbatarian Adventism, the 1860s also witnessed tensions and conflicts as the nascent movement struggled to become a denomination.[4] Despite opposition to "Gospel Order" from anti-organization individuals, James and Ellen White, Joseph Bates, J.N. Loughborough, John Byington, and others moved forward in choosing an official name in 1860,[5] forming state conferences after 1861 and a General Conference in 1863,[6] and legally incorporating the

---

[1]Bailey, *American Pageant*, p. 457.
[2]Williams, *The Union Sundered*, p. 153.
[3]Bailey, *American Pageant*, p. 456.
[4]Schwarz and Greenleaf, *Light Bearers*, pp. 83-90.
[5]Schwarz and Greenleaf, *Light Bearers*, pp. 91-92.
[6]Schwarz and Greenleaf, *Light Bearers*, pp. 92-94.

Review and Herald press, the Western Health Reform Institute (later Battle Creek Sanitarium), and other institutions.[7] Scores of new congregations throughout the Northeast and Midwest also organized, "covenanting to keep the commandments of God and the faith of Jesus Christ."[8] To support a burgeoning evangelistic outreach, church members after 1859 implemented the Systematic Benevolence Plan of tithing their increase from year to year.[9]

Move to Palermo, New York

Hiram Edson, now in his late 50s, supported all of these organizational endeavors with his voice, pen, and pocketbook. Yet he, too, faced new challenges, particularly to his health and finances. Perhaps in an effort to reduce these stressors, Hiram and Esther sold their farm in Martville and moved to a rural location near Palermo, a tiny village in Oswego County about eight miles southwest of Mexico, New York.[10] On January 6, 1860, Levi and Sarah Chapel sold Hiram and Esther 147.5 acres located on Lot 19 for $550.[11]

Edson's letters to the *Review* clearly revealed that he needed physical rest and medical attention. In 1861 he informed readers that although he found the church paper "a welcome messenger," severe illness had prevented him from reading much of it over the past year (1860-1861). Indeed, his health had been declining for years, he said, but it had grown much worse over the past 14 months (March 1860-June 1861). In fact, he had been unable "to labor, read, or write but a trifle." While his overall health had improved somewhat in February

[7]Schwarz and Greenleaf, *Light Bearers*, pp. 92, 108-111.
[8]Schwarz and Greenleaf, *Light Bearers*, p. 93.
[9]Schwarz and Greenleaf, *Light Bearers*, pp. 86-87.
[10]Hiram Edson, report to the *Review*, July 26, 1864, p. 72.
[11]Indenture (deed) for Hiram and Esther Edson's purchase of property in Palermo, New York, Jan. 6, 1860, Deeds Book 85, pp. 276-277, Hannibal, New York; document in the author's possession.

1860, it had grown worse in March and April.[12]

Yet he assured *Review* readers that "my faith is unshaken in the third angel's message. I believe we are nearing the loud cry, and the closing scenes." He then expressed his confidence in church workers who "have borne the heat of the burden of the day," for they were of "much value and worth to the church."[13] He heartily endorsed the Systematic Benevolence Plan (often nicknamed "Sister Betsy" by 1860s Adventists[14]) as "in the order and counsel of heaven." He believed widespread support of this plan would bring the "latter rain." But his optimism belied the one regret he felt. "I feel bad at times," he wrote, "that I am so bound that I am of no service in the blessed cause I love. Though unworthy, I hope to share in the prayers of such as have power and can prevail with God." He closed his letter, "Your unworthy brother in affliction."[15]

Two months later, James White informed readers of the church paper that "Bro. Edson had been unable to labor for about a year and a half in consequence of failing strength."[16] As if to counter that gloomy report, Edson's letter to the October 22, 1861, *Review* assured his friends that his health was actually improving, despite some relapses, "one rather serious of late." He thanked James and Ellen White for "your friendly visit with us, the precious seasons we enjoyed with you around the family altar, and also in the public congregation. We know your prayers availed much in our behalf."[17] Edson was especially grateful for "the manifestation given through the gift of the Spirit, while you were here," which "has been a source of comfort and en-

---

[12]Hiram Edson, letter to the *Review*, June 11, 1861, p. 23.
[13]Edson, letter to the *Review*, June 11, 1861, p. 23.
[14]Schwarz and Greenleaf, *Light Bearers*, p. 86.
[15]Edson, letter to the *Review*, June 11, 1861, p. 23.
[16]James White, report to the *Review*, Aug. 20, 1861, p. 92.
[17]Hiram Edson, letter to the *Review*, October 22, 1861, p. 167.

couragement to us." He assured readers that "I am trying to lean upon the arm of the Lord." At the same time, he asked them for a favor: "If we come into mind in your seasons of prayer, still pray for us."[18]

Edson also expressed strong support for church unity and the organization of local congregations. This, he affirmed, would "move forward...into the unity of the faith." "There must be order in the church or house of God," he insisted. Then, perhaps recalling the Messenger Party defection, he added, "Have we not tried anti-organization until we have confusion, Babel, Babylon, enough?" In conclusion, he signed his letter, "Yours as ever, in hope, though wading through deep waters."[19]

Edson's organizational efforts

Although it is generally believed that Hiram Edson played a significant role in organizing several local congregations throughout New York and Pennsylvania in the 1850s and 1860s, the names of most of these churches are unknown, perhaps because busyness or personal modesty prevented him from mentioning them in his reports. But his role in organizing the Roosevelt, New York, church is well documented. A one-page affidavit signed by C.B. Preston and Hiram Edson on March 11, 1861, and recorded by Oswego County Special Judge D.W.C. Peck on December 10, 1862, states that on January 15, 1861, "the male persons of full age belonging to a religious Society in which divine worship is celebrated according to the rites of the Seventh-day Advent Society," formed what would subsequently be named the Roosevelt Seventh-day Adventist Church.[20] As men-

---

[18]Edson, letter, October 22, 1861, p. 167.
[19]Edson, letter to the *Review*, October 22, 1861, p. 167; emphasis his.
[20]Hiram Edson and C.B. Preston, "Certification of Roosevelt Church, January 15, 1861," Oswego County, New York; document in the author's possession.

tioned in Chapter 7, Edson had also helped local believers erect their chapel and other outbuildings in 1858.

On August 3-4, 1861, Edson and the Whites convened "a day of fasting, humiliation and prayer" at the Roosevelt Church, pleading with God to humble and unite His people for the spreading of present truth.[21] Two months later, however, when the New York-Pennsylvania Conference was formed during another gathering at the Roosevelt Church, presided over by J.N. Andrews, Edson's poor health prevented him from attending.[22]

Extreme prostration

Over the next three years (1861-1864), however, no letters, reports, or articles by Hiram Edson appeared in the *Review* to update concerned readers as to the state of his health and his evangelistic activities. Consequently, it must have come as somewhat of a shock to many when J.N. Andrews stated in the July 26, 1864, *Review* that Edson "is at this time in a state of extreme prostration, from nervous debility." Andrews also informed subscribers that at present, Hiram was reduced to "slender means for the support of his family" and, given his physical prostration, "to helplessness."[23] Hoping to inspire their benevolence, James White reminded readers that Edson's "sacrifices at an early stage of the cause were great, in traveling extensively from Maine to Michigan, and in the Canadas [Ontario and Quebec], at his own expense, and blessing with his means God's poor ministers." Then he made his appeal: "[Will] God forsake such a man, who trusts in him? Never! A statement of his condition will kindle a fire

---

[21] James White, report to the *Review*, Aug. 20, 1861, p. 92. It is also likely that during this day of fasting the members pleaded with God to bring an end to the Civil War then raging.
[22] J.N. Andrews, report to the *Review*, Nov. 4, 1862, p. 182.
[23] J.N. Andrews, report to the *Review*, July 26, 1864, p. 72.

of love and benevolence in a thousand sympathizing hearts at once... Let such send their fives and tens right along."[24]

Andrews also informed subscribers that funds were being raised (without Edson's knowledge or consent) to send him to Dr. James Caleb Jackson's Water Cure in Dansville, New York, for several weeks of hydrotherapy treatments. John and Angeline Andrews gave ten dollars; James and Ellen White donated ten dollars; their son Edson White contributed five dollars; and John and Mary Loughborough sent five dollars.[25] Altogether, Adventists sent $243.04 to Battle Creek to pay Hiram's transportation and medical expenses for several months at this rapidly growing health spa.[26]

Our Home on the Hillside

In 1858, Dr. James Caleb Jackson, a nationally famous American health reformer, in association with Dr. Harriet Austin, had purchased a defunct water cure establishment high on a hillside overlooking the town of Dansville, New York. Renaming it "Our Home on the Hillside," Jackson and Austin introduced a strict health regimen that included two vegetarian meals a day, health lectures, water treatments, physical exercises, and evening amusements. Regular patients paid five dollars a week; ministers, however, received a 50 percent discount at two and a half dollars a week.[27]

Jackson based his beliefs on 10 health principles: fresh air, nutritious food, clean water, sunlight, loose-fitting garments, physical exercise, regular rest and sleep, positive social influence, mental forces, and moral forces. According to his advertisements, daily treatments

---

[24]James White, report to the *Review*, July 26, 1864, p. 72.
[25]J. N. Andrews, report to the *Review*, July 26, 1864, p. 72.
[26]Hiram Edson, letter to the *Review*, Feb. 13, 1866, p. 87.
[27]*Ellen G. White Encyclopedia*, s.v., "Jackson, James Caleb," pp. 424-425.

included "half-baths, packs, sitz baths, plunges and dripping sheets," but never any drugs.[28] This water cure establishment proved so popular that during its first four years of operation (1858-1862), an estimated 4,000 patients were treated at Our Home.[29] Although many objected to some of Dr. Jackson's restrictions (no strenuous mental activities, no meat, salt, or spices on the tables), nearly everyone who submitted to his regimen left enjoying far better health than they had when they entered.[30]

During the year 1864-1865, a regular caravan of sick Seventh-day Adventists (what Uriah Smith dubbed "the Adventist invalid party"[31]) registered for treatment at Our Home. The first to do so was the 32-year-old John Andrews, and following his restoration to full health, he quickly spread the word to other ailing Adventists.[32] In addition to Andrews and Edson, this "invalid party" included James and Ellen White, Horatio S. Lay, Uriah Smith, John Loughborough, Daniel Bourdeau, and Mary F. Maxson.[33] At one time, three-fourths of the General Conference Committee members were lying flat on their backs in Jackson's sick wards. Some Adventists, like Edson, spent several months in the water cure; others were released after only a few weeks.[34]

Given the rather strict, moralistic lifestyles most Victorian-era Adventists followed, they no doubt objected to some of Dr. Jackson's practices: Phrenological readings (mapping the bumps of the head to determine one's character) upon admission, dancing, card playing, and intermingling of the sexes at musical soirees.[35] Yet the ideas

---

[28]*Ellen G. White Encyclopedia* s.v., "Jackson, James Caleb," p. 424.

[29]*Ellen G. White Encyclopedia*, s.v., "Jackson, James Caleb," p. 424.

[30]*Ellen G. White Encyclopedia*, s.v., "Jackson, James Caleb," pp. 425-426.

[31]Uriah Smith, quoted in *Ellen G. White Encyclopedia*, s.v., "Jackson, James Caleb," p. 425.

[32]*Ellen G. White Encyclopedia*, s.v., "Jackson, James Caleb," p. 424.

[33]Strayer, *Loughborough*, pp. 150-151.

[34]See James White, "Eastern Tour," *Review*, Nov. 22, 1864, p. 205; Edson, letter to the *Review*, Feb. 13, 1866, p. 87; and Strayer, *Loughborough*, p. 151.

[35]*Ellen G. White Encyclopedia*, s.v., "Jackson, James Caleb," p. 425.

Horatio Lay, James and Ellen White, and J.N. Loughborough gleaned during their weeks of rehabilitation at Our Home better prepared them to establish their own church-sponsored sanitarium, the Western Health Reform Institute at Battle Creek in 1866.[36]

In a one-page letter sent to the *Review* in February 1866, Edson thanked those who had donated funds to pay his expenses at Dansville's "Health-reform institution" (as he called it) and promised to repay the entire $243 "to our common cause." He assured readers that his health was improving, yet because "I have been long impairing my health," "nature would require time to restore [it]." He confessed that in the summer of 1865, "I was brought near the dark valley and shadow of death, beyond the reach of human skill or power." But in answer to "fervent, effectual prayer" by God's people, God had raised him up so that at present, he was "on the up-hill grade, my health amending." There is some indication that, after his release from Our Home, Hiram may have altered some of his dietary habits, for he concluded by saying, "I am thankful for the light on health reform received while at Dansville, and from the publications [Ellen White's six pamphlets], *How to Live*."[37] Furthermore, when James White, following his first stroke, was rushed to Our Home in the fall of 1865, Edson was among the first to give $10 to help with his expenses.[38]

Happier occasions

On July 17, 1866, Edson, now just five months shy of his 60th birthday, had the pleasure of giving his daughter, Viah Ophelia, 23, in marriage to Washington Cross. This Adventist wedding ceremony,

---

[36] *Ellen G. White Encyclopedia*, s.v., "Jackson, James Caleb," p. 426, and s.v., "Health Reform Institute," p. 862.

[37] Hiram Edson, Jan. 30, 1866, letter to the *Review*, Feb. 13, 1866, p. 87.

[38] James White, "Acknowledgement," *Review*, Nov. 14, 1865, p. 192.

presided over by Elder David Arnold, a close family friend from Volney, probably took place in the Edson parlor in Palermo, New York.[39] This left Esther and Hiram with only one remaining child still living at home, 10-year-old Lucy Jane. The family nest was nearly empty.

Edson's health, while never robust, improved sufficiently during the late 1860s so that he felt able to attend several sessions of the New York-Pennsylvania Conference. He was present for the fifth session on September 28, 1866, when the believers at Roosevelt added 14 feet to their meetinghouse to accommodate the crowd. Nonetheless, between a third and half of the attendees listened from outside through the windows. The delegates voted Edson a ministerial license at this session.[40] This license was renewed at the sixth session, also held at Roosevelt on October 26, 1867.[41]

In July 1867, Edson attended a quarterly meeting (where footwashing and the Lord's Supper were celebrated) at Vernon, New York. There, perhaps for the first time, he met the 27-year-old minister, Dudley Canright, converted eight years before by James White. At that meeting, Canright shared a report concerning the recent General Conference session in Battle Creek.[42] Given the poor state of his health and the great distance between Palermo and Battle Creek, Edson would never attend a General Conference session, so it must have been thrilling for him to hear Canright tell of the progress of the Adventist cause. Then on January 2, 1868, Edson attended a meeting held in Adams Center, New York, with James and Ellen White, Samuel and Mary Abbey, Alexander and Caroline Ross, Frederick and Lydia Wheeler, among others.[43]

[39]Nix, "Edson," p. 80.
[40]Report of the fifth session of the New York-Pennsylvania Conference, *Review*, Oct. 16, 1866, p. 158.
[41]Report of the sixth session of the New York-Pennsylvania Conference, *Review*, Oct. 29, 1867, p. 308.
[42]R.F. Cottrell, "Quarterly Meetings in New York," *Review*, June 11, 1867, p. 307.
[43]James White, report to the *Review*, Jan. 28, 1868, p. 105.

Nine months later Edson was present at the seventh session of the New York-Pennsylvania Conference, this time held at Adams Center on October 23-26, 1868, and once again, his ministerial license was renewed.[44] He also attended the eighth Conference session at Kirkville, New York, on September 16, 1869, and his ministerial license was renewed.[45]

But after Elder Charles Taylor visited Hiram and Esther during the winter of 1868, he expressed shock at seeing Hiram in such poor health. In his report to the *Review*, Taylor stated that Hiram "has been running down for some weeks." The problem seemed to be a combination of terrible colds and typhoid fever, which left him "very weak and helpless." So weak, in fact, did the 62-year-old man appear that Taylor offered his own prognosis: "The earthly toil and labor of this dear brother [is] most over, and his work about done."[46]

But Charles Taylor was wrong. Hiram Edson would recover and live another 14 years. During that time, he would attend many more quarterly meetings, conference sessions, and other gatherings. He would also be ordained as a gospel minister and his ministerial credentials would be renewed well into his 70s, as Chapter 11 shows.

---

[44]Report of the seventh session of the New York-Pennsylvania Conference, *Review*, Nov. 17, 1868, p. 246.
[45]Report of the eighth session of the New York-Pennsylvania Conference, *Review*, Oct. 12, 1869, p. 126.
[46]C.O. Taylor, letter to the *Review*, March 3, 1868, pp. 182-183.

Chapter 11

Dark Days

In 1860, when Hiram, Esther, Ophelia, and Lucy Edson moved from Martville to Palermo, the family owned about $1,000 in real estate and $225 in personal property. A decade later, their farm was worth $1,140 and their personal property amounted to about $500. Despite this slight increase in their net worth, these figures mark them as one of the poorer families in Oswego County in 1870. In addition, Hiram, nearly 64, was not in good health. His frequent coughing fits and high fevers indicated that he suffered from consumption (tuberculosis) and catarrh (inflammation of the nose and throat).[1]

Edson receives ministerial credentials

Nevertheless, he soldiered on, attending as many quarterly meetings and New York-Pennsylvania Conference sessions as his health permitted. When the ninth conference session convened at Oneida, New York, on August 3, 1870, Hiram was there. In recognition of his call from God to ministry and his past generosity and service to the

---

[1]Wurst, et al., *Archaeological-Historical Investigations*, p. 28.

Sabbatarian Adventist movement, the delegates granted him ministerial credentials. He could now officially organize churches, ordain deacons and elders, and baptize new members.[2] In the summer of 1871, Elder Edson immersed perhaps his first baptismal candidate, 16-year-old Byron E. Tefft, in Allegany County, New York. Byron would soon leave the state to enroll as a student in Battle Creek College, after which he would become a colporteur, a missionary to England, and a health care professional, first at Boulder Sanitarium in Colorado and then at Paradise Valley Sanitarium in California.[3]

Yet Henrietta Kolb doubted whether Edson had ever received ministerial ordination or ministerial credentials. In 1948 Kolb, then 79, told Clifton Taylor that as a little girl she had known Edson and that "in his lifetime he was not regarded as such a hero as our historian writers have made of him since his death." Kolb had never heard him referred to as "Elder Edson" until "recent years"; therefore, she questioned whether he had been ordained as a minister.[4]

The answer to Kolb's query can easily be found in the *Review*. When Edson attended the 10th session of the New York-Pennsylvania Conference held at Kirkville on August 9, 1871, his ministerial credentials, granted in 1870, were renewed. He, along with Henry Hilliard and C.W. Taylor, also served on the Committee on Nominations that determined which candidates received ministerial licenses and which ones received ministerial credentials.[5] At the 11th conference session, which also met in Kirkville on August 6, 1872, Edson's credentials were renewed.[6]

---

[2]Report of the ninth session of the New York-Pennsylvania Conference, *Review*, Aug. 23, 1870, p. 78.

[3]J.A. Burden, obituary for Byron Tefft, *Review*, July 4, 1929, p. 29. While it is likely that Edson baptized others, Byron Tefft is his only documented baptismal candidate.

[4]Henrietta Kolb, cited by Clifton L. Taylor to A.W. Spalding, March 17, 1948, Spalding Correspondence, Collection 10, Box 2, Folder 1, CAR, JWL, AU.

[5]Report of the 10th session of the New York-Pennsylvania Conference, *Review*, Sept. 12, 1871, p. 102.

[6]Report of the 11th session of the New York-Pennsylvania Conference, *Review*, Sept. 10, 1872, p. 102.

Although Edson did not attend the 12th conference session in August 1873, his credentials were once again renewed.[7] He also missed the 13th conference session in September 1874 when the delegates passed a unique motion: That "the labors of our aged brethren, [Frederick] Wheeler, [Roswell F.] Cottrell, [Hiram] Edson, and [David] Arnold, in case they received credentials, should be mainly in a local sphere, looking to themselves mainly for their support.[8] Not until 1910 did the denomination create a sustentation fund for retired church workers; therefore, those men and women too old or feeble to continue in active ministry either found alternate means of earning money or boarded with one of their children.[9]

Yet the generosity displayed by Hiram and Esther during the 1870s would seem to indicate that they had found some form of regular income, perhaps from the sale of fruit and vegetables on their farm. In James White's 1873 book *An Appeal to the Working Men and Women in the Ranks of Seventh-day Adventists*, Hiram is listed as buying two shares of stock in the Seventh-day Adventist Publishing Association for $20; Esther had also bought two shares for $20; and their daughters, Lucy and Ophelia, had each purchased one share for $10. Hiram also owned a share of stock in the Battle Creek Sanitarium for which he had paid $25; furthermore, he had donated another $10 to the Book Fund.[10] Three years later, when Battle Creek College owed the Seventh-day Adventist Publishing Association $10,000, the *Review* issued an appeal for 3,000 Adventists to purchase $100,000 in stock to pay off that debt. Edson pledged $10 to that fund.[11]

---

[7]Report of the 12th session of the New York-Pennsylvania Conference, *Review*, Aug. 26, 1873, p. 86.
[8]Report of the 13th session of the New York-Pennsylvania Conference, *Review*, Oct. 13, 1874, p. 127.
[9]*Seventh-day Adventist Encyclopedia* (1996), s.v., "Retirement Plans," p. 440.
[10]James White, *An Appeal to the Working Men and Women in the Ranks of Seventh-day Adventists* (1873), pp. 30, 79, 104.
[11]List of donors, *Review-Supplement*, April 27, 1876, p. 2.

Given this noteworthy record of Hiram Edson's past benevolence and ministerial service to the church, he might have anticipated having his ministerial credentials renewed indefinitely. But when the delegates to the 14th conference session convened in Rome, New York, on September 9, 1875, and voted on the list of candidates to receive ministerial ordination or credentials, Edson's name was not on the list. Despite being asked to serve with James White and Uriah Smith on the prestigious Committee on Nominations that determined who would receive ministerial licenses and who would receive ministerial credentials, he himself had been passed over.[12] Why?

One plausible explanation could have been his age: In 1875 Hiram was already in his 70th year. Yet the Michigan Conference renewed John Byington's ministerial credentials in 1886 when he was 88[13] and the General Conference renewed J.N. Loughborough's credentials in 1922 when he was 90.[14] Another factor might have been his limited range of ministry during his declining years. But Byington's ministerial credentials were repeatedly renewed during the 1880s when he and Catharine were more or less confined to the home of their oldest daughter, Martha, and her husband, George Amadon, in Battle Creek.[15] Meanwhile out in California, Loughborough's credentials were renewed annually even though he was confined to a fifth story room at St. Helena Sanitarium from 1916 to 1924.[16] Still another possibility might have been Edson's physical condition, which prevented him from engaging in active ministry. However, Byington's credentials were regularly renewed despite the fact that he battled lameness, malarial fever, congested lungs, a tumor on his thigh, poor eyesight

---

[12]Report of the 14th session of the New York-Pennsylvania Conference, *Review*, Sept. 30, 1875, p. 103.
[13]Strayer, *Byington*, p. 253.
[14]Strayer, *Loughborough*, p. 466.
[15]Strayer, *Byington*, p. 254.
[16]Strayer, *Loughborough*, p. 450.

and hearing, and almost constant coughing in the 1880s.[17] In his last years, Loughborough suffered from frequent bouts of flu and pneumonia, yet his credentials were also regularly renewed.[18] Therefore, if age, ill health, and living conditions cannot account for Edson's ministerial credentials not being renewed in 1875, what factor may have played a role in that decision?

The Edson manuscript—again

While it is true in a spiritual sense that ministerial credentials are bestowed in recognition of an individual's call from God to the gospel ministry, it is also true that granting such credentials indicates church officials' confidence in the recipient's orthodoxy and their approval of the candidate's life and witness within the church as well as among non-Adventists. Is it possible that church leaders James and Ellen White, Uriah Smith, J.N. Andrews, and J.N. Loughborough had lost confidence in Hiram Edson, and if so, why?

As described in Chapter 4, sometime after October 23, 1844, Edson produced a lengthy manuscript written with pen and ink that contained a brief account of his experience during the Millerite movement, the Great Disappointment, and his cornfield insights. It also included theological speculations (based on Jeremiah 4:7) that the prediction of "the lion [that] is come up from its thicket" portended a key role for England in fulfillment of Bible prophecy. When Edson took the document to the reading committee at the Review and Herald office, they offered to publish the autobiographical material but refused to print his lengthy prophetic speculations as being "too fanciful and unsound." At that point, an argument broke out between

---

[17]Strayer, *Byington*, pp. 259, 260, 263.
[18]Strayer, *Loughborough*, p. 449.

Edson and Andrews, with the former insisting that he had "light from God" while the latter promised to "spoil your light." After telling his colleagues to either publish the entire manuscript or none of it, Edson stormed from the building.[19]

The key issues here are two: When did Edson write the manuscript? When did he submit it to the Review and Herald Reading Committee? His daughter Ophelia insisted that her father had penned the manuscript "immediately after the disappointment of 1844."[20] But as Chapters 8 and 9 show, this is impossible simply because the depiction of the heavenly sanctuary, its cleansing, the judgment, and Adventists' worldwide work as described in the manuscript would not be fully understood until after Sabbatarian Adventists abandoned the shut-door teaching in 1851 and after White, Smith, Andrews, Everts, and others explicated the deeper meaning of the sanctuary message in their articles to the *Review* during the 1850s.[21] Furthermore, Hiram Edson himself remained highly esteemed by church leaders throughout the 1850s and 1860s, and they published his lengthy articles in the church paper even when they disagreed with some of his "fanciful" interpretations. Based on these facts, an argument could be made that his manuscript was probably written not between 1844 and 1869 but sometime after 1870.

Regarding the second issue, when Edson submitted the manuscript to the reading committee, it is a fact that James White, J.N. Loughborough, and J.N. Andrews served on that committee.[22] But White died in August of 1881;[23] Loughborough left for England in

---

[19]See Chapter 4.
[20]Mrs. O[phelia] V[iah] Cross to H.M. Kelley, "The Spirit of 1844," *Review*, June 23, 1921, p. 4.
[21]See the detailed discussion of the sanctuary in the 1850s *Review* articles by these four authors in Chapter 9.
[22]J.N. Loughborough to A.W. Spalding, Aug. 2, 1921, A.W. Spalding Correspondence, Collection 10, Box 1, Folder 2, CAR, JWL, AU.
[23]Wheeler, *James White*, pp. 240-241.

December of 1878;[24] and Andrews left for Europe in September of 1874.[25] Therefore, the only time these three men could have examined Edson's manuscript in Battle Creek would have been between 1870 and 1874. But since Edson's ministerial credentials were renewed in 1871, 1872, and 1873 (see above), it is evident that he still found favor with the "leading brethren" until 1874, when the New York-Pennsylvania Conference delegates voted that he and several other aged ministers should henceforth support themselves. Consequently, a case could be made that Hiram Edson finished writing his lengthy manuscript some 30 years after his October 23, 1844, cornfield experience and submitted it to the reading committee sometime in 1873-1874 before Andrews left for Europe.

Did Edson leave the church?

While some writers take rejection of their manuscripts philosophically, others view disapproval of their writings as a rejection of themselves. There is some evidence that Hiram Edson belonged to the latter group. When White, Andrews, and Loughborough refused to publish his theological speculations, he rigidly held onto his peculiar views, stubbornly insisting that they were light from God. Disappointed and bitter, he continued sharing his unique interpretations of Bible prophecy with Adventists across upstate New York during the 1870s, much to the disappointment of his colleagues and friends.[26] Ellen White, one of his closest friends, was heartbroken as she witnessed Edson's contentious behavior within the church. Writing years later to W.H. Littlejohn, she stated:

---

[24]Strayer, *J.N. Loughborough*, p. 236.
[25]Valentine, *J. N. Andrews*, p. 521.
[26]Nix, "Edson," p. 87.

Brother Edson's production [his 200-page manuscript] was never printed. He was a good man, beloved by all who knew him; but the matter which he had brought together, was not the subject that should appear, not meat in due season for the flock of God. It was of a character that would start into life erroneous theories that would be nourished by human agents, and would bear fruit in dissension and discord.[27]

Yet after burning the manuscript, Edson had second thoughts. So once again he wrote out his ideas and left money for his wife Esther to publish them after his death. But after consulting with church leaders, she withdrew the manuscript from publication. After asserting, "We ought to have given Sister [Esther] Edson a vote of thanks" for retrieving her husband's manuscript, Ellen White repeated her commendation: "He [Edson] was a good man, beloved of God and all who knew him."[28]

After a visit to the Roosevelt Seventh-day Adventist Church in 1877 (where the Edsons had their membership), Dudley Canright reported in the *Review*:

As is well known to all our brethren in the State [of New York], father Edson for eight or ten years [since 1867 or 1869] has not seen his duty in the same light that his brethren have, but has had a different burden from what they thought God designed him to bear. This has been a source of trial to the brethren. At this meeting he took a good stand in laying aside this burden and taking hold according to the advice of his

---

[27]Ellen G. White to W.H. Littlejohn, Aug. 3, 1894, Ellen G. White Estate, manuscript DF588 (1894). A portion of this letter is found in Ellen White, *Counsels to Writers and Editors*, p. 155.
[28]Ellen White to Littlejohn, Aug. 3, 1894, manuscript L-49-1894, CAR, JWL, AU.

brethren. This brought great relief to the church, and we believe will prove a great blessing to himself and to the cause.[29]

Two decades after his own apostasy in 1887, however, Canright presented a darker view of Edson in his book *Seventh-day Adventism Renounced*. "Elder Hiram Edson and Elder S.W. Rhodes, noted pioneers in the work," he wrote, "died confirmed cranks, and a trial to the church."[30]

The idea that Edson, a "confirmed crank," had for a while left the church after his manuscript was rejected was first shared with Elder Herbert Kelley by Edson's daughter, Viah Ophelia Cross. Kelley then related the story to J.N. Loughborough, who, in a December 1919 letter to Kelley, added the phrase that Edson had been "out of the church" but had reunited with it before he died in 1882.[31] However, since Loughborough was abroad in England from 1879 to 1883, he could not have known firsthand how Edson ended his days. Nevertheless, this view that Edson "left the church" became the standard interpretation among Adventist authors. Jim Nix restated it in 1971 when he wrote that Edson, "old, ill, and discouraged," had simply stopped going to Adventist services, although he never worked against the church or opposed its doctrines.[32]

However, the case could be made that Hiram Edson never left the church; instead, the church left him. Edson's theological speculations from 1849 to 1857 regarding the time of the end, the Kings of the North and South, the sixth and seventh trumpets, and the seventy-weeks prophecy ending in 1850 are probably no different from his

---

[29]Dudley Canright, letter to the *Review*, Jan. 25, 1877, pp. 30-31.
[30]Dudley M. Canright, *Seventh-day Adventism Renounced* (London and Edinburgh: Fleming H. Revell, 1905), p. 63.
[31]J.N. Loughborough to H.M. Kelley, Dec. 23, 1919, p. 1, manuscript WDF3006, CAR, JWL, AU.
[32]Nix, "Edson," p. 90.

184 | Brian E. Strayer

1870s speculations regarding the role that England would play before Christ's second coming. Edson had not changed at all, but the church had changed.

Edson had matured in the 1840s and 1850s when the Sabbatarian Adventist movement was a flexible, open-minded forum in which a broad spectrum of views was permitted—indeed, encouraged. Theological speculation and vigorous debates regarding biblical theology and prophecy were the norm. But after 1872, when Uriah Smith compiled a list of Adventists' "Fundamental Principles,"[33] such speculation and debate were no longer welcome in the church. The tiny sect sometimes disparagingly called "Seventh-day Door-Shutters"[34] in the 1840s and 1850s was becoming a respectable denomination. The spectrum of prophetic interpreters that had once been numerous had by the 1870s been narrowed to only a handful—James White, Uriah Smith, and J.N. Andrews—and Hiram Edson was no longer a member of the "Apocalyptic Club."

He had not left the church; the church had left him behind. Perhaps the bitterness he felt was a reflection of his frustration at no longer being able to share his theological speculations freely and elicit reactions from *Review* readers. Issues of the *Review* in the 1870s and 1880s no longer shared the same open dialogues as they had in the 1850s. Like Washington Irving's character Rip Van Winkle, who returned home after a 20-year sleep to discover that his friends were Americans and not Britons,[35] Edson in the 1870s no longer fit the contentious theological milieu of the 1850s in which he had once flourished. Like Rip Van Winkle, Hiram doubtless felt out of place, unappreciated, and rejected.

---

[33]Gary Land, *Uriah Smith, Apologist and Biblical Commentator* (Hagerstown, MD: Review and Herald Pub. Assn., 2014), p. 107.
[34]Schwarz and Greenleaf, *Light Bearers*, p. 91.
[35]Washington Irving wrote his fictional short story "Rip Van Winkle" in 1819 when Edson was 13. The setting is the Catskill Mountains of eastern New York.

In a letter to Elder J.S. Washburn in 1950, Arthur Spalding, after acknowledging Edson's many faults, offered a somewhat more generous view of his final years. "We must be kind to our brethren. They may do us wrong, they may make some lamentable missteps; but they have also done service for God."[36]

The hymn "Calvary"

One individual who shared Spalding's positive view of Hiram Edson was Elder A.E. Place, whose ministry, centered in Rome, New York, began in 1882, the year Edson died. Born in 1856,[37] Place had been converted in the 1870s by Edson at a camp meeting in Kirkville. He always treasured Edson's visits because the aged minister never failed to pray for every member of the family. "He was the mightiest man in prayer I have ever heard pray," exclaimed Place. "I have heard him in our home when it seemed that the angels were in the home all around him, and I was always thrilled and trembled greatly. And many times I prayed that I might pray as Elder Edson prayed."[38]

Edson also loved to sing, and his "deep, sweet voice" brought tears to Place's eyes. In fact, it was Hiram's singing of "Come, O My Soul, to Calvary" that had brought Place into the Adventist Church.[39] The words of this 11-stanza hymn are as follows:

(1) Come, O my soul, to Calvary, Calvary, Calvary,
      And see the man who died for thee, Upon th'accursed tree.

---

[36]A.W. Spalding to J.S. Washburn, Aug. 24, 1950, Spalding Correspondence, Collection 10, Box 2, Folder 3, CAR, JWL, AU.

[37]*Ellen G. White Encyclopedia*, s.v., "Place, Albert E.," p. 491.

[38]A.E. Place, sermon preached in Rome, New York, 1890, quoted in Randall, "Rome, N.Y. Church," p. 29.

[39]Place, sermon preached in Rome, New York, 1890, quoted in Randall, "Rome, N.Y. Church," p. 29.

(2) Behold the Saviour's agony,
   While groaning in Gethsemane,
   Beneath the sins of men.

(3) With purple robe and thorny crown,
   And mocking soldiers bowing down,
   The Saviour bears my shame.

(4) Behold, they shed his precious blood,
   Oh! hear him cry, 'My God, my God,
   Hast thou forsaken Me?'

(5) He died—the earth was robed in gloom;
   they laid him, then, in Joseph's tomb,
   While soldiers watched around.

(6) But in the light of dawning day,
   Bright angels rolled the rock away,
   And Christ, the conq'ror, rose.

(7) Now he who died on Calvary
   Still lives to plead for you and me,
   And bids us look and live.

(8) He sits upon a throne of grace,
   And bids the helpless seek his face;
   O sinner, come to-day.

(9) Soon, he who once was scourged and bound

Shall come again, with glory crowned,

And reign forevermore.

(10) His saints shall crown him Lord of all;

Before him every foe shall fall,

And every knee shall bow.

(11) Oh! then, the Man of Calvary

Shall reign supreme from sea to sea;

All hail that glorious day!

(Chorus) How can I forget thee! How can I forget my Lord!

How can I forget thee! Dear Lord, remember me.[40]

The curtain falls

As the decade of the 1880s began, the last "bird" in the Edson family "flew the nest." On January 15, 1880, Hiram and Esther's youngest daughter, Lucy Jane,[41] 24, wed Charles Edward Pickard as friends gathered in the parlor at Palermo. Once again, Elder David Arnold, a close family friend, presided over this Adventist ceremony. Now Hiram, going on 74, and Esther, almost 64, were left to face life's challenges alone.[42]

On September 23, 1881, Hiram visited the courthouse in Oswego County to draw up his last will and testament. Describing himself simply as a retired farmer, he gave his estate and real property (after "all my just debts and funeral expenses to be paid") to his wife and executor of

---

[40]"Calvary," in James White, comp., *Hymns and Spiritual Songs for Camp-Meetings and Other Religious Gatherings* (Battle Creek, MI: Steam Press, 1872), pp. 160-161.

[41] Wurst, et al., *Archaeological-Historical Investigations*, p. 28.

[42]Nix, "Edson," p. 91.

his will, Esther Mariah Edson. He directed Esther to sell their property "as soon as she can get it's [sic] value after my decease."[43]

The will is short—only 24 lines—yet 12 of them are devoted to the one project that had consumed Edson's final years:

> I devise my work entitled *The last great trumpet of alarm or voice of warning* to be published and the expenses of such publication to be paid out of my property, and the proceeds or profits arising from the sale of my work herein named, I wish to remain in the office of the Advent Review subject to the disposal of my executrix provided that the office shall negotiate with my agent Mr. Place for the printing.... John Place of South West Oswego [is] to act as my agent in the publication of my said work.[44]

Stubborn and persistent to the end, Edson was determined that his precious manuscript be published, even from the grave.

From July to December 1881, Edson was largely confined to his bed. In the words of New York Conference President Buel Whitney, he was "almost entirely helpless and his sufferings were almost beyond endurance," yet "he bore them all with Christ-like patience and fortitude, though earnestly praying that he might sleep in Jesus."[45] In October 1881, Elder M.C. Wilcox visited Edson, who at the time was suffering from tuberculosis. Wilcox reported in the *Review*: "Although weak, feeble, and suffering great pain, his [Edson's] trust was strong

---

[43]Hiram Edson, "Last Will and Testament," quoted in Wurst, et al., *Archaeological-Historical Investigations*, p. 47.

[44]Edson, "Last Will and Testament," quoted in Wurst, et al., *Archaeological-Historical Investigations*, p. 47; italics mine.

[45]Obituary for Hiram Edson, *Review*, Feb. 21, 1882, p. 126.

in God. May God bless him in his old age."[46]

Three months later, on January 8, 1882, Hiram Edson died at the age of 75 years and nine days. Elder Whitney, who presided at his funeral, chose Revelation 14:13 to share at the beginning of his homily: "And I heard a voice from heaven saying unto me, Write, Blessed are the dead which die in the Lord from henceforth: Yea, saith the Spirit, that they may rest from their labours; and their works do follow them" (KJV). Whitney, who also wrote Edson's obituary for the *Review*, said that Hiram had enjoyed "a rich experience in connection with the movement of 1843-4" and after October 22, 1844, he "was among the first to receive the third angel's message and identify himself with the work, giving largely of his time and means for its advancement." Moreover, the cause of present truth had been "dearer to him than life," and his early devotion to that cause "fully entitles him to a place among its pioneers."[47] Interestingly, Whitney made no mention of Edson's cornfield "vision," nor did he credit him with providing new insights into the cleansing of the heavenly sanctuary in 1844.

The *Oswego Palladium* briefly reported his passing as well, stating that "Hiram Edson died at his residence Sunday morning after a long illness. He has been a resident of Palermo about 25 years [actually 22 years], leaves a wife [Esther] and one daughter [Lucy Jane Pickard, but his son and all four daughters were still alive, although not all of them lived nearby]. He was aged 75 years."[48] His body was laid to rest in the country cemetery across the road (today Highway 49) from the Roosevelt Seventh-day Adventist Church he had helped to build nearly a quarter of a century earlier.[49]

---

[46]M.C. Wilcox, letter to the *Review*, Nov. 1, 1881, p. 283.
[47]Obituary for Hiram Edson, *Review*, Feb. 21, 1882, p. 126.
[48]Obituary for Hiram Edson, *Oswego Palladium*, Jan. 10, 1882, p. 3.
[49]*Footsteps of the Pioneers* (1990), pp. 116, 122.

As mentioned above, Esther Edson dutifully followed her husband's two wishes. Shortly after his death, she submitted the lengthy manuscript to the Review and Herald Book Committee, but when the brethren rejected it again, she took it home and allegedly burned the portions devoted to theological speculation. Then on April 29, 1883, Esther sold the farm (147.55 acres) in Palermo to her daughter Lucy Jane and son-in-law Charles Pickard for $800.[50]

Following the sale of her land in Palermo, Esther moved to Oswego Falls. There, on December 1, 1891, at the age of 76, she drew up her last will and testament. After ordering all her debts paid, she bequeathed to her daughter, Viah Ophelia Cross of Gognac, Kansas, $300 toward a debt of $700. She also left one-fourth of her property to Ophelia. To her other daughter, Lucy J. Pickard, who was also her executrix, she gave $500 and "the rest and remainder of my estate."[51]

Esther outlived her husband by more than 11 years. Toward the end of her life, she battled Bright's disease, "suffering much in her last sickness," but she was "resigned to the will of God, and gave evidence of her acceptance with him." She died on May 1, 1893, at nearly 77 years of age. Elder S.M. Cobb presided at her funeral and wrote her obituary for the *Review*, in which he (or the copyeditors) misspelled her surname as "Edeson" rather than Edson. The brief obituary also mentions that she and her husband had been "engaged in giving the first and second [angels'] messages." Esther was buried beside Hiram in the little cemetery across the road from the Roosevelt Seventh-day Adventist Church.[52]

---

[50]Indenture (deed) for the sale of the Edson property, Palermo, New York, April 29, 1883; document in the author's possession.

[51]Esther Edson's last will and testament, Dec. 1, 1891, quoted in Wurst, et al., *Archaeological-Historical Investigations*, p. 48.

[52]S.M. Cobb, obituary for Esther Edson, *Review*, May 30, 1893, p. 351.

Edson's reputation

One indication that Hiram Edson was not highly regarded by his ministerial colleagues at the time of his death is the striking brevity of his obituary in the *Review*—only 22 lines. When Joseph Bates died in 1872, the *Review* summed up his life in 34 lines, 50 percent more than his contemporary, Edson, received.[53] The apostate Adventist Alonzo T. Jones, who died in 1923, received a 31-line notice in the church paper.[54] Even such relatively unknown lay Adventists as Addie Farnsworth (who died in 1881)[55] and Wallace Larkin (who died in 1882)[56] received 32- and 23-line obituaries, respectively. Thus, an argument could be made that the brevity of Edson's obituary when compared to those of other Adventists clearly indicates that at the time of his death, Hiram was not on the best of terms with his brethren.

Unfortunately, Edson passed away beneath a cloud—a cloud of disappointment, dejection, and doubt regarding his orthodoxy and his loyalty to the church. Another sign of this is the "deafening silence" of Seventh-day Adventist publications after his passing. Rarely does his name appear in any books, articles, or printed sermons dealing with Adventist history over the next 70 years (1882-1952). In truth, Hiram Edson was in danger of being relegated to the dust heap of history along with such third-ranked Adventist pioneers as Elon Everts, E.L.H. Chamberlain, Washington Morse, and Aaron Hilliard, about whom most church members today know nothing.

So how did the name of Hiram Edson become so highly esteemed among Seventh-day Adventists today? Who is responsible for burnishing his tarnished image and restoring his damaged reputation? In real-

---

[53]Obituary for Joseph Bates, *Review*, April 16, 1872, p. 143.
[54]Obituary for A.T. Jones, *Review*, June 28, 1923, p. 22.
[55]Obituary for Addie Farnsworth, *Review*, Aug. 16, 1881, p. 126.
[56]Obituary for Wallace T. Larkin, *Review*, Feb. 21, 1882, p. 126.

ity, the rehabilitation of this early pioneer is primarily due to the efforts of one Adventist church historian and a group of zealous volunteers who were determined to perpetuate the legacy of Hiram Edson and the sanctuary doctrine for generations of Adventist youth and laity to appreciate. That story is the subject of Chapter 12, "Edson's Legacy."

Chapter 12

Edson's Legacy

As Chapter 11 explains, after Hiram Edson died in 1882, a dark cloud of distrust and doubt concerning his orthodoxy and loyalty to the church tarnished his memory. Some, like Dudley Canright, considered him to be a "crank" and "a trial to the church";[1] others no doubt saw him as stubborn, willful, and uncooperative. For the next six decades, few books, articles, or sermons published by Seventh-day Adventists mentioned his contributions to the church.

On rare occasions, those who remembered him in better days mentioned his name. In 1904, Elder J.W. Hofster was preaching on "The Signs of the Times, Past and Fulfilling" in Grand Rapids, Michigan, when to his surprise, Owen Crosier, 84 years old and leaning on a cane, entered the hall and sat on the front row, listening intently with one hand cupped behind his right ear. After the service, Crosier told Hofster how it had felt to pass through the October 22, 1844, Disappointment with "its grief and its distress"; how he had joined Edson for an all-night prayer and Bible study session; how joyful they

[1] Dudley M. Canright, *Seventh-day Adventism Renounced*, p. 63.

had felt after discovering that the sanctuary was in heaven; and how he (Crosier) had ridden on horseback "to tell the good news and to cheer those [former Millerites] whom I could reach." Despite Crosier's "alienation of feeling" with some Sabbath-keeping pioneers, he had only warm memories of Hiram Edson.[2]

Elder Herbert Kelley had a similar experience in 1921 when he visited with Edson's daughter, Ophelia Cross, then 80 years old and an invalid since 1917. He reported that her "faith and courage are strong" as she recited some of her recent poems and told of her father's experiences in the early Advent movement. Although Ophelia's memories (as previous chapters show) were not always accurate, she remembered how her mother had sold some of her silver wedding spoons to finance Crosier's February 7, 1846, *Day-Star* Extra article on the sanctuary. As Kelley was leaving, Ophelia handed him one of those remaining silver spoons as a memento of their visit together.[3]

In 1926, the *General Conference Bulletin* printed a montage of ten pioneer preachers, all of them deceased. The collection included photos of J.N. Loughborough, J.O. Corliss, S.N. Haskell, Joseph Bates, Uriah Smith, H.H. Wilcox, Frederick Wheeler, J.H. Waggoner, J.G. Matteson—and Hiram Edson.[4] Nearly 60 years later, Walter Saxby, a great-grandson of Hiram Edson, donated Edson's 1838 Bible to the Department of Archives and Special Collections in the Loma Linda University Library. At a special ceremony held on that campus, Jim Nix, chair of the Department, received the Bible, noting that it contained the records of many family members.[5]

---

[2] O.R.L. Crosier, quoted in William A. Spicer, "A Meeting with O.R.L. Crosier," *Review*, March 29, 1945, p. 5.

[3] Kelley, "Spirit of 1844," *Review*, June 23, 1921, pp. 4-5.

[4] *General Conference Bulletin*, May 27, 1926 (Takoma Park, Washington, D.C.: Review and Herald Pub. Assn., 1926), p. 7.

[5] "Edson Bible," *Review*, Nov. 10, 1983, p. 22.

But with these few exceptions, the name, face, and contributions of Hiram Edson had largely disappeared from the annals of Adventist history by the mid-20th century. In 1989, the artist Elfred Lee painted a huge mural for the White Estate at the General Conference headquarters in Silver Spring, Maryland. Entitled "The Christ of the Narrow Way," it depicted Ellen Harmon's first vision in December 1844.[6] Trudging up the narrow path were 144 men and women; some of them were early Adventist pioneers, others were employees at the White Estate or at the General Conference headquarters; and still others were friends or acquaintances of Elfred Lee.[7] While the faces of several early Adventist pioneers could clearly be seen on the path, the face of Hiram Edson was absent. Instead, a heavenly beam of light shone on his peripatetic partner, Joseph Bates.[8]

John Norton Loughborough

One man who could have rehabilitated Edson's reputation was his early preaching partner, J.N. Loughborough. As described in Chapter 7, Edson took Loughborough on weeks-long evangelistic tours of New York and Pennsylvania, first in 1851, when John was only 19, and again in the winter of 1852-1853, when John turned 21. Facing numerous challenges over rough terrain for days on end, the two men bonded as friends. During their time together, Loughborough interviewed Edson concerning his experiences in the Millerite and early Sabbatarian Adventist movements, taking copious notes, which he used in writing his many books and articles.

Yet when Loughborough wrote his first history of the Adventist

---

[6]Ross Winkle, "Disappearing Act: Hiram Edson's Cornfield Experience," *Spectrum* 33, no. 1 (Winter 2005), p. 50.
[7]James Nix, email to Brian Strayer, Sept. 30, 2021.
[8]Winkle, "Disappearing Act," *Spectrum* (Winter 2005), p. 50.

movement, a 392-page volume entitled *Rise and Progress of the Seventh-day Adventists* (1892), he made only four passing remarks about his mentor. These brief sentences mentioned Edson's cornfield experience on October 23, 1844;[9] his attending the 1848 Volney, New York, conference;[10] his selling the farm in 1850;[11] and his donating funds to the Review and Herald to purchase the Washington Hand Press.[12] Thirteen years later when Loughborough wrote his greatly expanded 573-page tome, *The Great Second Advent Movement* (1905), he could have added many more details concerning Edson's contributions to the church, but he did not. Instead, he repeated exactly the same comments that he had made in his 1892 book, but condensed them onto three (instead of four) pages.[13]

One can only conjecture as to why Loughborough minimized Edson's role in the early history of the Advent movement. Was he merely reflecting the prevailing negative attitudes toward Edson among some church leaders at the time? Was he still bitter over the confrontation Edson had had with James White, Uriah Smith, J.N. Andrews, and himself two decades earlier when Edson had insisted that all of his manuscript (including the theological speculations on prophecy) be published or none of it? Or did he think that Edson had played a relatively minor role in the rise and progress of present truth?

Arthur Whitefield Spalding

One historian who would have disagreed with that assessment was Arthur W. Spalding. Spalding was only five years old when Edson died in 1882; moreover, since Spalding grew up in Michigan, he

---

[9]J.N. Loughborough, *Rise and Progress*, p. 114.
[10]Loughborough, *Rise and Progress*, p. 137.
[11]Loughborough, *Rise and Progress*, p. 160.
[12]Loughborough, *Rise and Progress*, p. 167.
[13]Loughborough, *Great Second Advent Movement*, pp. 193, 267-268, 285.

could not have met Edson, who did not visit Michigan in the 1870s or 1880s.[14]

However, Spalding became an Edsonian cheerleader, determined to rehabilitate the reputation of this early pioneer. In his books *Footsteps of the Pioneers* (1947), *Captains of the Host* (1949), and *Origin and History of Seventh-day Adventists*, volume 1 (1961), he gave Edson top billing along with James and Ellen White, Joseph Bates, J.N. Andrews, and J.N. Loughborough. He presented Edson as a key player in discovering present truth, organizing Sabbath conferences, and bringing unity to and financially supporting the fledgling Sabbatarian Adventist movement in the 1840s and 1850s.

For example, in *Origin and History*, volume 1, he mentioned Hiram Edson numerous times on 14 different pages, devoting far more coverage to him than Loughborough had. He described the roles of Edson, Crosier, and Hahn in sharing the sanctuary message in *The Day-Dawn* and the *The Day-Star* Extra;[15] frequently quoted from Hiram's autobiographical manuscript;[16] related in some detail Edson's cornfield experience[17] and his roles in the Sabbath Conferences of 1846, 1848, and 1852;[18] and told of how he sold two farms to finance the early Adventist work.[19] Furthermore, Spalding praised Edson as "the chosen instrument of God," "one of the deep-thinking students who developed the Seventh-day Adventist faith," a "self-sacrificing servant of God" who "labored in the evangelistic field with earnestness and ardor."[20] He was one of "the heralds of the message" in Can-

---

[14]*Seventh-day Adventist Encyclopedia*, s.v., "Spalding, Arthur Whitefield," p. 687.
[15]A.W. Spalding, *Origin and History*, vol. 1, pp. 110-112.
[16]Spalding, *Origin and History*, vol. 1, pp. 99, 101.
[17]Spalding, *Origin and History*, vol. 1, p. 101.
[18]Spalding, *Origin and History*, vol. 1, pp. 191, 194, 205.
[19]Spalding, *Origin and History*, vol. 1, pp. 205, 216.
[20]Spalding, *Origin and History*, vol. 1, p. 216.

ada West (Ontario) even before Joseph Bates entered that region.[21]

In addition, it is Spalding who provided the indelible images (painted by Vernon Nye and Harry Anderson) that thousands of Adventist youth who read his books for Missionary Volunteer credit or studied them as textbooks in academy and college would remember for the rest of their lives: the five men praying in Edson's granary;[22] Edson and Crosier crossing the cornfield;[23] and photos of Hiram and Esther's house and barn.[24] In subsequent years, many of those young people, now grown to adulthood, would make the pilgrimage to the Edson farm in Port Gibson to kneel in that old granary, walk down the rows of the nearby cornfield, and tour Luther Edson's 1840s barn and the visitor center. From the 1940s to the 1960s, Arthur Spalding planted the seeds that helped to rehabilitate the tarnished reputation of Hiram Edson. Many others have since watered that seed.

Adventist Historic Properties

In 1981 a group of lay members, church employees, and administrators formed Adventist Historic Properties (AHP) in Battle Creek, Michigan, to purchase and restore as many early Millerite and Sabbatarian Adventist buildings as possible. By 1987 they had acquired the homes of Deacon John White, James and Ellen White, John Daigneau, J.N. Loughborough, William Miller, and the Washington, New Hampshire, church property.[25] In January 1989, they bought the Hiram Ed-

---

[21]Spalding, *Origin and History*, vol. 1, p. 248.
[22]Spalding, *Origin and History*, vol. 1, p. 98.
[23]Spalding, *Origin and History*, vol. 1, p. 100.
[24]Spalding, *Origin and History*, vol. 1, p. 104.
[25]*Seventh-day Adventist Encyclopedia*, s.v., "Adventist Heritage Ministry," p. 19. The three chairmen of Adventist Historic Properties/Adventist Heritage Ministries have been Lawrence E. Crandall (1981-1988), Robert L. Dale (1988-1997), and James R. Nix (1997-2021). See *Adventist Historic Properties Directory* (2021), p. 40. Its five presidents have been Lawrence E. Crandall (1981-1999), James R. Nix (1991-1995), Alice R. Voorheis (1995-2001), Thomas R. Neslund (2001-2016), and Markus Kutzschbach (2016-).

son farm site, which contained an old house and 17 and a half acres of land, in Clifton Springs, New York.[26]

Although many Adventist Historic Properties board members believed that Hiram and Esther had lived in the house, a series of professional examinations between 1991 and 2005 of its wood, structure, paint, nearby artifacts, soil samples, and old maps proved that it had been built between the 1850s and 1900, so it was demolished.[27] In 1992 Adventist Historic Properties acquired Luther Edson's 1840s barn, with its hand-hewn lumber and pegged superstructure, and moved it to Hiram's farm site.[28]

Subsequently, this spacious barn became the venue for many anniversary celebrations. On October 23, 1994, the 150th anniversary of Edson's cornfield experience, over 150 Adventists and community members gathered to dedicate the barn.[29] On August 21-22, 1998, some 200 guests from across the United States and Canada celebrated the 150th anniversary of the 1848 Sabbath and Sanctuary Conference that the Edsons had hosted.[30] On October 19, 2002, Rochester, New York, Bay Knoll Seventh-day Adventist Church members held a Sanctuary Festival there.[31] On October 20-22, 2006, Ad-

---

[26]"Edson Farm News," *Adventist Heritage Ministries Bulletin*, Winter 2001, p. 6.

[27]For further details of these studies, see "Hiram Edson Farmsite [sic]: Adventist Historic Properties, Inc.: Restoration and Development Assessment" (Syracuse, NY: Crawford & Stearns, Dec. 1991), pp. 24-27; Randall W. Younker and Ralph E. Hendrix, "Team Conducts Survey of Hiram Edson Farm," Andrews University Archaeology Publication (March 1995), p. 3; Lou Ann Wurst, "Public Archaeology Facility Report: Archaeological Investigations of the Hiram Edson Farm Site," pp. 16-20; Lou Ann Wurst, "Proposal: Hiram Edson Farm Site" (Syracuse, NY: Department of Anthropology, Syracuse University, Oct. 6, 1995), pp. 1-4; Lou Ann Wurst, et al., *Archaeological-Historical Investigations,* pp. 11, 20, 21, 35; Robert W. Meyer to Jo Ellen Walton, Sept. 14, 1997; Randall T. Crawford and Carl D. Stearns, Hiram Edson Site Visit, Dec. 30, 2002; Carol Griggs, "Dendrochronology of the Hiram Edson Site, Port Gibson, Ontario County, New York" (Ithaca, NY: Cornell University, Aug. 26, 2005), pp. 1, 3; documents in the author's possession.

[28]"Hiram Edson Farm Master Plan," pp. 3-4. Adventist Historic Properties was renamed Adventist Heritage Ministries in Sept. 1993. See Adventist Heritage Ministries Board of Trustees Directory, 2021, p. 6.

[29]"Restored Barn Dedicated at Hiram Edson Farm," *Review*, Nov. 24, 1994, p. 6.

[30]"Sabbath and Sanctuary Conference to be Held at Edson Barn," *Adventist Heritage Ministries Bulletin*, July 1998, p. 7.

[31]"Coming to the Edson Farm," *Adventist Heritage Ministries Bulletin*, Fall 2002, p. 4.

ventist Heritage Ministries convened a 160th anniversary of the 1846 Sabbath Conference held at the Edson farm.[32] High school history teacher Howard Krug brought camp meeting tour groups there every summer.[33] Luxury buses transported hundreds of delegates at the General Conference sessions in Toronto, Canada (2000)[34] and St. Louis, Missouri (2005)[35] to worship, sing, pray, and hear stories about the Adventist pioneers at the site. In addition, Adventists from Rochester,[36] Geneva,[37] Elmira,[38] East Palmyra,[39] and Union Springs Academy's choir sang for Sanctuary Festivals, vesper programs, and weekend services in the barn.[40]

At the vesper program held on October 19, 2002, Edson Site Committee member Robert Allen shared a poem, entitled "Edson's Barn," that he had composed five years earlier:

Edson's barn may be a thing of the past,
That some would leave there to rot.
But because of events that it witnessed long ago,
Many there be who think not!

Though barns give dimensions to the men that they serve,

[32] Jo Ellen Walton, "Special Weekend Planned to Commemorate Adventist History," *Lake Union Herald*, Sept. 2006, pp. 34-35.

[33] Howard Krug, "Visitors to Camp Meeting Take the Fifth Annual Heritage Tour," *Atlantic Union Gleaner*, Oct. 2005, p. 19.

[34] Jo Ellen Walton, "Traffic Jam at Edson Farm," *Adventist Heritage Ministries Bulletin*, Special Issue 2000, p. 5.

[35] "4000 Visitors From Over 90 Countries," *Adventist Heritage Ministries Board*, Aug. 2005, p. 3.

[36] Robert Allen, "Sanctuary Festival 2002," *Adventist Heritage Ministries Bulletin*, Feb. 2003, pp. 12-13.

[37] Howard Krug, "Adventist Heritage Celebrated at Hiram Edson Farm," *Atlantic Union Gleaner*, Jan. 2012, p. 10.

[38] Louise Nettles, "A Busy Summer at the Hiram Edson Farm," *Adventist Heritage Ministries Bulletin*, Fall 2014, p. 2.

[39] Jo Ellen Walton and Louise Nettles, "Visitors Flock to Edson Farm, Learn Core Beliefs of Advent Message," *Adventist Heritage Ministries Bulletin*, Winter 2014, p. 2.

[40] Howard Krug, "Adventist Heritage Celebrated at Hiram Edson Farm," p. 10.

As they protect their beasts and work,
They also give storage and shelter, too,
And a place for shovel and fork.

But Edson's barn saw men wrestle with God,
And witnessed their study of His Word;
It was there God came close to His faithful few,
Revealing to them that He heard.

Where God meets with men is a holy place,
And its memory lingers and inspires
Giving hope and trust in the leading of God,
And in all that His Word requires.

May Edson's faith be renewed in each heart
Of those who linger here,
Reviving in each their trust in God,
As they feel His presence draw near.[41]

Visionary leaders such as Jim Nix (director of the Ellen G. White Estate at the General Conference), Jo Ellen Walton (Edson Site Committee chair), and Robert Allen (civil engineer and local historian), among others, saw the evangelistic potential of the Edson site. In 2001, Adventist Heritage Ministries purchased adjacent land[42] to create a parking area for buses, cars, and RVs and put in a 45-foot road to the site.[43] On this land in 2005 they erected a large-scale model of

---

[41]Robert H. Allen, "Edson's Barn," found in "Sanctuary Festival 2002," *Atlantic Union Gleaner*, Feb. 2003, p. 13.
[42]"Update From the Edson Farm," *Adventist Heritage Ministries Bulletin*, Summer 2001, p. 5.
[43]"Good News for the Hiram Edson Site," *Adventist Heritage Ministries Bulletin*, Fall 2001, p. 2.

the earthly tabernacle, complete with furnishings and actors playing the roles of Moses, Aaron, and Bezalel. This tabernacle attracted the attention of two youth groups from the Assembly of God and the Evangelical Church who were studying the biblical sanctuary in their Sunday School classes.[44] Between 2008[45] and 2010,[46] Adventist Heritage Ministries erected a visitors' center in the 1840s Greek Revival Style featuring glass display cases, Edson's handmade cherry table, copies of his publications, and wall murals explaining the sanctuary doctrine.[47] On August 20-21, 2010, about 275 people gathered to dedicate this new center.[48]

Upstairs the center had comfortable rooms to accommodate the various on-site directors. The first, Louise Nettles (2010-2015), arrived from Georgia; Rowena Rick (2012-2015) served as her co-director. Subsequent directors included Darwin Whitman (2016) and Jim and Linda Everhart (2017-2020).[49] These directors invited Adventist church school teachers to bring their pupils to the site to sing, pray, hear stories, and play games.[50] After 2011, visiting groups could also watch the short DVD "Meet Hiram Edson" with its authentic 1840s furnishings, artifacts, costumes, and music. Produced by Grooters Productions of Holland, Michigan, this film covered the second com-

---

[44]Howard Krug, "Hiram Edson Farm Hosts Sanctuary Exhibit," *Adventist Heritage Ministries Bulletin*, Aug. 2005, pp. 1, 3.

[45]Jo Ellen Walton, "Visitor Center at Edson Farm on Fast Forward," *Adventist Heritage Ministries Bulletin*, Winter 2008, p. 1.

[46]Lewis Walton, "Edson Farm Visitor Center Dedicated in Clifton Springs, N.Y.," *Review*, Oct. 28, 2010, p. 11.

[47]Lewis R. Walton, "History Preserved," *Adventist World*, July 2007, pp. 28-29.

[48]Alice Voorheis, "Hiram Edson Farm Visitor Center Dedicated," *Adventist Heritage Ministries Bulletin*, Fall 2010, pp. 4-5.

[49]*Adventist Heritage Ministries Directory* (2021), p. 41.

[50]For children's activities at the Edson farm, see Louise Nettles, "A Day to Remember," *Adventist Heritage Ministries Bulletin*, Winter 2010, p. 2; Diana Rowe, "Bay Knoll Students Visit Hiram Edson Farm," *Atlantic Union Gleaner*, Jan. 2014, p. 10; Jo Ellen Walton, "Edson Bible Prophecy Garden Ministers to Tourists," *Adventist Heritage Ministries Bulletin*, Fall 2016, p. 4; and Jim and Linda Everhart, "Teen Volunteers to the Rescue!" *Adventist Heritage Ministries Bulletin*, Summer 2019, p. 2.

ing of Jesus, the 2300-days prophecy, the heavenly sanctuary, and the investigative judgment.[51]

News of the quality programs at the Edson site soon began to attract international attention. In April 2013, a group of Brazilian Adventist youth representing the TV program "Novo Tempo" arrived to tape a program in Spanish, English, and Portuguese. Half of the visitors to the site in 2013 came from Brazil and Australia;[52] other busloads arrived from Canada and all over the United States.[53] During 2014, over 700 visitors arrived,[54] including 50 Mexican pastors and a Voice of Prophecy team from Hope Channel Brazil.[55] In addition, scores of church groups, Pathfinder clubs, and Vacation Bible School students flooded the grounds. There they learned about the "Six 'S' Doctrines" (salvation, second coming of Christ, Sabbath, sanctuary, Spirit of Prophecy, and state of the dead) that had come together at the Sabbath conferences between 1846 and 1850.[56]

Between 2013 and 2019, Adventist Heritage Ministries invested over $120,000 in developing an elaborate Bible Prophecy Trail and Garden on the grounds with 12 "stations."[57] Its 12 handicap-accessible stations, featuring God's plan of salvation, included high quality art, a professionally narrated script, and a musical soundtrack.[58] Each station had a granite bench, a waterproof picture, and a doc-

---

[51]Louise Nettles, "New Orientation DVD Filmed at the Hiram Edson Farm," *Adventist Heritage Ministries Bulletin,* Winter 2011, p. 2.

[52]Rowena Rick, "Youthful Visitors Spend Time at the Edson Farm," *Adventist Heritage Ministries Bulletin,* Summer 2013, p. 2.

[53]Jo Ellen Walton, "Crowds Visit Edson Farm Bible Prophecy Garden," *Adventist Heritage Ministries Bulletin,* Winter 2015, p. 2.

[54]Jo Ellen Walton and Nettles, "Visitors Flock to Edson Farm," p. 2.

[55]Louise Nettles, "A Busy Summer at the Hiram Edson Farm," p. 2.

[56]Jo Ellen Walton and Nettles, "Visitors Flock to Edson Farm," p. 2.

[57]Jo Ellen Walton, "Edson Farm Bible Prophecy Garden Approved," *Adventist Heritage Ministries Bulletin,* Fall 2013, p. 2. Each of the twelve stations cost $10,000.

[58]Jo Ellen Walton, "Hiram Edson Bible Prophecy Garden Still Needs Donations," *Adventist Heritage Ministries Bulletin,* Spring 2014, p. 2.

trinal message lithographed on metal, and each was surrounded by colorful flowers and budding trees provided by Adventist Heritage Ministry volunteers Dana and Sylvia Borglum of Wayside Gardens.[59] Well-known artists such as Lars Justinen[60] and Nathan Greene[61] provided the art work; Lewis Walton (for adults) and Betti Knickerbocker (for children) recorded the narrations, which participants could hear on one of 12 MP3 players available at the visitors' center.[62]

All of these projects, of course, required untold hours of labor to achieve, and most of that work was provided by volunteers. Among the many local groups to donate their time were the students of nearby Union Springs Academy. On one visit in the spring of 2019, for example, a busload of them arrived on a Sunday morning. After the Everharts provided them a breakfast of Stripples, pancakes, hash browns, and orange juice, the teens formed work bees to prepare the trail and garden for winter. After several hours of cutting brush, pulling weeds, trimming bushes, and crating the artwork for winter storage, they returned to the academy, tired but happy.[63]

In 2020, Adventist Heritage Ministries began encouraging families to take a six-day "Adventist Heritage Vacation" tour of various pioneer sites. This tour encompassed Historic Adventist Village in Battle Creek, Michigan (Day One); Niagara Falls and Rochester, New York (Day Two); the Edson Farm (Day Three); the William Miller home, chapel, and grave in Whitehall, New York (Day Four); the Washington, New Hampshire, Adventist church and Joseph Bates' boyhood home in Fairhaven, Massachusetts (Day Five); and places of interest

[59]Jo Ellen Walton, "Crowds Visit Edson Farm Bible Prophecy Garden," p. 2.
[60]Jo Ellen Walton, "Hiram Edson Bible Prophecy Garden Still Needs Donations," *Adventist Heritage Ministries Bulletin*, Spring 2014, p. 2.
[61]Jo Ellen Walton, "Edson Farm Bible Prophecy Garden Approved," p. 2.
[62]Jim and Linda Everhart, "Teen Volunteers to the Rescue!" p. 2.
[63]Jim and Linda Everhart, "Teen Volunteers to the Rescue!" p. 2, and Linda Everhart, "Volunteers: The Life Blood of Adventist Heritage Ministries," *Adventist Heritage Ministries Bulletin*, Summer 2019, p. 2.

in Boston, Plymouth Plantation, and Old Sturbridge Village, also in Massachusetts (Day Six).[64]

It had taken more than 30 years for Adventist Heritage Ministries to realize its dream and implement its plans for the Edson site. But with an army of volunteers, they had turned a barren, swampy, brush-covered sheep farm into an attractive historic site that welcomed hundreds of visitors every year and told them about the sanctuary service in heaven. If Hiram Edson could visit his property today, he would be amazed—not only by the physical changes on his old farm but also by the positive transformation of his reputation among 21st-century Adventists.

---

[64]"Plan Your Vacation!" *Adventist Heritage Ministries Bulletin*, March 2020, p. 5.

Selected Bibliography

Aamodt, Terrie, Gary Land, and Ronald Numbers, eds. *Ellen Harmon White: American Prophet* (Oxford: Oxford University Press, 2014).

"Acquisition of Hiram Edson Farm—a Possibility," *Canadian Adventist Messenger* (May 1989), p. 7.

Adventist Heritage Ministries. Board of Trustees Directory (2021).

"Adventist Heritage Sites Vacation." *Adventist Heritage Ministries Bulletin* (March 2020).

Allen, Robert H. "Remembering October 23, 1844," *Adventist Heritage Ministries Bulletin* (Holiday Issue, 1999), p. 11.

Allen, Robert H. "Sanctuary Festival 2002," *Atlantic Union Gleaner* (Feb. 2003), pp. 12-13.

Allen, Robert H. "The Washington Hand Press" (one-page typed manuscript, n.d.).

Allen, Robert H. "Heritage Sabbath at Rochester," *Adventist Heritage Ministries Bulletin* (Dec. 2003), p. 7.

Andrews, J.N. "The Antitypical Tabernacle," *Review* (July 7, 1853), pp. 25-28.

Andrews, J.N. "The Antitypical Tabernacle," *Review* (Aug. 28, 1853), pp. 60-61.

Andrews, J.N. "The Cleansing of the Sanctuary," *Review* (Feb. 21, 1856), pp. 164-165.

Andrews, J.N. Letter, *Review* (Nov. 4, 1862), p. 182.

Andrews, J.N. "Position of the *Advent Herald* on the Sanctuary Question," *Review* (May 12, 1853), pp. 204-205.

Andrews, J.N. "The Sanctuary," *Review* (Dec. 23, 1852), pp. 121-125.

Andrews, J.N. "The Sanctuary," *Review* (Jan. 6, 1853), pp. 129-133.

Andrews, J.N. "The Sanctuary," *Review* (Jan. 20, 1853), pp. 137-139.

Andrews, J.N. "The Sanctuary," *Review* (Feb. 3, 1853), pp. 145-149.

Andrews, J.N. "The Sanctuary and Its Cleansing," *Review* (Oct. 30, 1855), pp. 68-69.

Appel, Alva R. "Hiram Edson" (term paper, Seventh-day Adventist Theological Seminary, March 1954).

Bailey, Thomas A. *The American Pageant: A History of the Republic.*

3rd ed. (Boston: D.C. Heath, 1966).

Ballenger, Albion Fox. *An Examination of 40 Fatal Errors Regarding the Atonement* (Riverside, CA: Author, 192-).

Ballenger, Albion Fox. "A Letter to Mrs. White Which Was Never Answered." (Manuscript #006688. Center for Adventist Research, James White Library, Andrews University, Berrien Springs, MI).

Bartle, F.W. Letter to W.A. Spicer (Sept. 4, 1935).

Barton, Don. "The Investigative Judgment: Adventism's Life Raft," *Spectrum* 41:3 (Summer 2013), pp. 16-19.

Bates, Joseph. *An Explanation of the Typical and Anti-Typical Sanctuary* (New Bedford, MA: Benjamin Lindsey, 1850).

Bates, Joseph. Letter, Jan. 1, 1852, *Review* (Jan. 13, 1852), p. 80.

Bates, Joseph. Letter, March 25, 1852, *Review* (May 6, 1852), pp. 6-7.

Bates, Joseph. *The Opening Heavens, or a Connected View of the Testimony of the Prophets and Apostles, Concerning the Opening Heavens, Compared with Astronomical Observations, and of the Present and Future Location of the New Jerusalem, the Paradise of God* (New Bedford, MA: Benjamin Lindsey, 1846).

Bates, Joseph. *A Seal of the Living God, a Hundred Forty-four Thousand of the Servants of God Being Sealed in 1849* (New Bedford, MA: Benjamin Lindsey, 1849).

Bates, Joseph. *Second Advent Waymarks and High Heaps: Or a Connected View of the Fulfillment of Prophecy by God's Peculiar People, From the Year 1840 to 1847* (New Bedford, MA: Benjamin Lindsey, 1847).

Bates, Joseph. *The Seventh Day Sabbath, a Perpetual Sign* (New Bedford, MA: Benjamin Lindsey, 1847).

Bell, Skip. Letter to Bob Allen (Aug. 27, 1998).

Bowe, Derek C. "Night of No Return," *Guide* (May 8, 2004), pp. 2-15.

Bull, Malcolm, and Keith Lockhart. *Seeking a Sanctuary: Seventh-day Adventism and the American Dream* (New York: Harper and Row, 1989).

Burt, Merlin D. *Adventist Pioneer Places: New York and New England* (Hagerstown, MD: Review and Herald Pub. Assn., 2011).

Burt, Merlin D. CHIS674: Development of Seventh-day Adventist Theology Syllabus (Seventh-day Adventist Theological Seminary, Andrews University, 2019).

Burt, Merlin D. "Remembering the Mighty Acts of God," *Adventist World* (July 2017), pp. 30-31.

Byington, John. "Conference At Buck's Bridge, N.Y.," *Review* (Nov. 27, 1856).

Cabose, Rachel W. "Light in a Cornfield," *Guide* (Oct. 13, 2018), pp. 14-19.

Calhoun, Everett Allen. "Hiram Edson" (handwritten manuscript, May 12, 1980).

Campbell, Michael W. *The Pocket Dictionary for Understanding Adventism* (Nampa, ID: Pacific Press Pub. Assn., 2020.)

Campbell, Michael and Jud Lake, eds. *The Pocket Ellen G. White Dictionary* (Nampa, ID: Pacific Press Pub. Assn., 2018).

Canright, Dudley M. Letter, Jan. 10, 1877, *Review* (Jan. 25, 1877), pp. 30-31.

Canright, Dudley M. *Seventh-day Adventism Renounced* (London & Edinburgh: Fleming H. Revell Company, 1905).

Casebolt, Donald E. *Father Miller's Daughter: Ellen Harmon White* (Eugene, OR: Wipf & Stock, 2022).

Child, L. Maria. *Letters from New York* (New York: C.S. Francis, 1846).

Clark, Jerome L. *1844*. 3 vols. (Nashville: Southern Pub. Assn., 1968).

Clemons, Emily. *Hope within the Veil* (1845).

Coit, Margaret L., and Henry F. Graff, eds. *The Life History of the United States,* vol. 3: *The Growing Years, 1789-1829* (New York: Time-Life Books, 1963).

Coit, Margaret L., and Henry F. Graff, eds. *The Life History of the United States*, vol. 4: *The Sweep Westward, 1829-1849* (New York: Time-Life Books, 1963).

Collins, Norma J. *Heartwarming Stories of Adventist Pioneers,* Book 1 (Hagerstown, MD: Review and Herald Pub. Assn., 2005).

"Come, O My Soul, to Calvary," in James White, comp., *Hymns and Spiritual Songs for Camp-Meetings and Other Religious Gatherings* (Battle Creek, MI: Steam Press, 1872).

"Coming to the Edson Farm," *Adventist Heritage Ministries Bulletin* (Fall 2002), p. 4.

"Conference," *Present Truth*, no. 7 (March 1850).

Conover, George S., ed., and Lewis C. Aldrich, comp. *History of On-*

tario County, New York with Illustrations and Family Sketches of Some of the Prominent Men and Families (Syracuse, NY: D. Mason and Company, 1893).

Conradi, Louis R. *The Founders of the Seventh-day Adventist Denomination* (Plainfield, NJ: The American Sabbath Tract Society, 1939).

Cooper, Emma H. *The Great Advent Movement* (Washington, DC: Review and Herald Pub. Assn., 1947).

Cramer, Carl. *Listen for a Lonesome Drum: A York State Chronicle* (New York: D. McKay, 1950; New York: Farrar & Rinehart, 1936).

Crawford, Randall T. and Carl D. Stearns. "Hiram Edson Site Visit Report" (Dec. 30, 2002).

Crosier, O.R.L. Autobiographical article in *The Daily Messenger* (Nov. 22, 1923), pp. 17, 22-23.

Crosier, O.R.L. "The Law of Moses," *The Day-Star* Extra (Feb. 7, 1846).

Crosier, O.R.L. "The Sanctuary," *Review* Extra (Sept. 1850), pp. 42-47, 57-63.

Crosier, O.R.L. "The Sanctuary," *Review* (May 5, 1851), pp. 78-80.

Crosier, O.R.L. "The Sanctuary," *Review* (Sept. 2, 1852), pp. 68-69.

Crosier, O.R.L. "The Sanctuary," *Review* (Sept. 16, 1852), pp. 76-77.

Crosier, O.R.L. "The Sanctuary," *Review* (Sept. 30, 1852), pp. 84-85.

Crosier, O.R.L. "The Sanctuary," *Review* (Oct. 16, 1852), pp. 90-91.

Crosier, O.R.L. "To All Who Are Waiting for Redemption, the Following Is Addressed," *The Day-Dawn* 1:1, reprinted in *The Ontario Messenger* (March 26, 1845), back page.

Cross, Ophelia. Letter to O.A. Olsen (Sept. 14, 1913).

Cross, Viah. "Hiram Edson's Experience" (affidavit to P.Z. Kinne regarding the Hiram Edson Autobiographical Manuscript, n.d.).

Cross, Viah. Letter to L.E. Froom (Aug. 23, 1944).

Cross, Viah. "Recollections of the Message," *Review* (April 1, 1920), pp. 22-23.

Cross, Whitney R. *The Burned-Over District: The Social and Intellectual History of Enthusiastic Religion in Western New York, 1800-1850* (New York: Cornell University Press, 1950).

Crozier, O.R.L. *The Daily Messenger* (Canandaigua, NY, Nov. 22, 1923), pp. 17, 22-23.

Damsteegt, P. Gerard. *Foundations of the Seventh-day Adventist Mes-*

sage and Mission (Grand Rapids, MI: William B. Eerdmans, 1977).

Deed for Hiram and Esther's purchase of property in Palermo, New York. Jan. 6, 1860. (Hannibal, NY: Deeds Book 85), pp. 276-277.

Deed for the sale of Hiram Edson's property (Palermo, New York, April 29, 1883).

Department of Education, General Conference of Seventh-day Adventists. *The Story of Our Church* (Mountain View, CA: Pacific Press Pub. Assn., 1956).

Dudley, Roger, and Edwin Hernandez. *Citizens of Two Worlds: Religion and Politics among Seventh-day Adventists* (Berrien Springs, MI: Andrews University Press, 1992).

Dudley, Roger, and V. Bailey Gillespie. *Valuegenesis: Faith in the Balance* (La Sierra, CA: La Sierra University, 1992).

"Edson Bible Donated to Loma Linda," *Review* (Nov. 10, 1983), p. 22.

Edson, Esther. Obituary. *Review* (May 30, 1893), p. 351.

Edson, Hiram. "An Appeal to the Laodicean Church," *Review* Extra (Sept. 1850), pp. 1-16.

Edson, Hiram. "Beloved Brethren, Scattered Abroad," *Present Truth* (Dec. 1849), pp. 34-36.

Edson, Hiram. "The Commandments of God and the Mark of the Beast Brought to View by the Third Angel of Chap. VII, Having the Seal of the Living God," *Review* (Sept. 2, 1852), pp. 65-67.

Edson, Hiram. "The Commandments of God and the Mark of the Beast Brought to View by the Third Angel of Chap. VII, Having the Seal of the Living God," *Review* (Sept. 16, 1852), pp. 73-75.

Edson, Hiram. "The Commandments of God and the Mark of the Beast Brought to View by the Third Angel of Chap. VII, Having the Seal of the Living God," *Review* (Sept. 30, 1852), pp. 81-84.

Edson, Hiram. "Daniel Standing in His Lot," *Review* (July 30, 1857), p. 101.

Edson, Hiram. "Description of Hiram Edson's Experience in the Cornfield on Oct. 23, 1844 Plus Some Other Experiences in His Life Around that Same Time" (undated handwritten manuscript, c. 1850s).

Edson, Hiram. "Experience in the Advent Movement." In George Knight, *1844 and the Rise of Sabbatarian Adventism: Reproduc-*

tion of Original Historical Documents (Hagerstown, MD: Review and Herald Pub. Assn., 1994).

Edson, Hiram. *An Exposition of Scripture Prophecy: Showing the Final Return of the Jews in 1856* (Canandaigua, NY: n.p., 1849).

Edson, Hiram. "The Holy Covenant," *Review* (May 5, 1851), p. 80.

Edson, Hiram. Letter to S.S. Snow, *The Jubilee Standard* (May 29, 1845), pp. 90-91.

Edson, Hiram. Letter of March 1, 1847, *The Day-Dawn* (April 2, 1847), pp. 7-8.

Edson, Hiram. Letter of Feb. 13, 1851, *Review* (Feb. 1851), p. 48.

Edson, Hiram. Letter, *Review* (March 1851), p. 51.

Edson, Hiram. Letter of Aug. 20, 1851, *Review* (Sept. 2, 1851), p. 24.

Edson, Hiram. Letter of Oct. 28, 1853, *Review* (Nov. 8, 1853), p. 143.

Edson, Hiram. Letter of March 10, 1854, *Review* (March 21, 1854), p. 71.

Edson, Hiram. Letter of Nov. 20, 1854, *Review* (Dec. 5, 1854), p. 127.

Edson, Hiram. Letter of June 15, 1856, *Review* (June 26, 1856), p. 71.

Edson, Hiram. Letter of March 21, 1857, *Review* (April 9, 1857), p. 182.

Edson, Hiram. Letter of March 1858, *Review* (April 1, 1858), p. 159.

Edson, Hiram. Letter, *Review* (June 16, 1859), p. 32.

Edson, Hiram. Letter, *Review* (June 11, 1861), p. 23.

Edson, Hiram. Letter, *Review* (Oct. 22, 1861), p. 167.

Edson, Hiram. Letter of Jan. 30, 1866, *Review* (Feb. 13, 1866), p. 87.

Edson, Hiram. List of Births, Marriages, and Deaths in Hiram Edson's Family Bible (Adventist Heritage Room, Loma Linda University Library, Loma Linda, CA).

Edson, Hiram. Notebook/Scrapbook/Diary (Advent Source Collection, Center for Adventist Research, James White Library, Andrews University, Berrien Springs, MI).

Edson, Hiram. Obituary. *Oswego Palladium* (Jan. 10, 1882), p. 3.

Edson, Hiram. "The Shortening of the Days, And Typical Bearing of the Forty Years Sojourn of Israel in the Wilderness," *Review* (July 30, 1867), pp. 102-103.

Edson, Hiram. "The Shortening of the Days, And Typical Bearing of the Forty Years Sojourn of Israel in the Wilderness," *Review* (Aug. 6, 1867), p. 118.

Edson, Hiram. "The 69 Weeks and 2300 Days." *Review* (March 1851), pp. 49-50.

Edson, Hiram. *The Time of the End: Its Beginning, Progressive Events, and Final Termination* (Auburn, NY: Henry Oliphant, 1849).

Edson, Hiram. "The Times of the Gentiles and the Deliverance and Restoration of the Remnant of Israel from the Seven Times, or 2520 Years of Assyrian or Pagan and Papal Captivity Considered," *Review* (Jan. 3, 1856), pp. 105-107.

Edson, Hiram. "The Times of the Gentiles and the Deliverance and Restoration of the Remnant of Israel from the Seven Times, or 2520 Years of Assyrian or Pagan and Papal Captivity Considered," *Review* (Jan. 10, 1856), pp. 113-115.

Edson, Hiram. "The Times of the Gentiles and the Deliverance and Restoration of the Remnant of Israel from the Seven Times, or 2520 Years of Assyrian or Pagan and Papal Captivity Considered," *Review* (Jan. 17, 1856), pp. 121-123.

Edson, Hiram. "The Times of the Gentiles and the Deliverance and Restoration of the Remnant of Israel from the Seven Times, or 2520 Years of Assyrian or Pagan and Papal Captivity Considered," *Review* (Jan. 24, 1856), pp. 129-131.

Edson, Hiram. "The Times of the Gentiles and the Deliverance and Restoration of the Remnant of Israel from the Seven Times, or 2520 Years of Assyrian or Pagan and Papal Captivity Considered," *Review* (Feb. 14, 1856), pp. 153-155.

Edson, Hiram. "The Times of the Gentiles and the Deliverance and Restoration of the Remnantof Israel from the Seven Times, or 2520 Years of Assyrian or Pagan and Papal Captivity Considered," *Review* (Feb. 21, 1856), pp. 162-163.

Edson, Hiram. "The Times of the Gentiles and the Deliverance and Restoration of the Remnant of Israel from the Seven Times, or 2520 Years of Assyrian or Pagan and Papal Captivity Considered," *Review* (Feb. 28, 1856), pp. 169-170.

Edson, Hiram. "The Two Laws," *Review* (Oct. 7, 1851), pp. 36-40.

Edson, Hiram. "We Wept, and Wept, Till the Day Dawn," *Spectrum* 24:2 (Oct. 1994), pp. 21-23.

Edson, Hiram, and C.B. Preston. "Certification of the Roosevelt [Seventh-day Adventist] Church" (Jan. 15, 1861).

Edson, Hiram, David Arnold, George Holt, Samuel Rhodes, and James White, eds., "Shut Door," *Review*, Sept. 1850, p. 27.

Edson, Hiram, and Frederick Wheeler. Report, *Review* (Feb. 11, 1858), pp. 110-111.

Edson, Hiram, and Frederick Wheeler. Report, *Review* (Jan. 21, 1858), p. 88.

Edson, Hiram, and Frederick Wheeler. Report, *Review* (March 11, 1858), p. 133.

Edson, Hiram, and Horace W. Lawrence. Report, *Review*, Nov. 8, 1853, p. 143.

Edson, Hiram, and John Lindsey. Letter of May 31, 1852, *Review* (June 10, 1852), pp. 22-23.

Edson, James. Revolutionary War Pension Claim #S.45369 (Syracuse, NY: Onondaga Public Library).

Edwards, Calvin W. and Gary Land. *Seeker After Light: A.F. Ballenger, Adventism, and American Christianity* (Berrien Springs, MI: Andrews University Press, 2000).

Ellen G. White Estate. *A Critique of Prophetess of Health* (Washington, DC: General Conference of Seventh-day Adventists, 1976).

Emmons, Henry. Letter, *The Day-Star* (Oct. 25, 1845).

Everhart, Linda. "Still Waiting and Watching," *Adventist Heritage Ministries Bulletin* (Feb. and March 2021).

Everhart, Linda. "Volunteers: The Life Blood of Adventist Heritage Ministries," *Adventist Heritage Ministries Bulletin* (Fall 2019), pp. 7-8.

Everhart, Linda, and Jim Everhart. "Teen Volunteers to the Rescue!" *Adventist Heritage Ministries Bulletin* (Summer 2019), p. 2.

Everts, Elon. "Communication from Bro. Everts," *Review* (Jan. 1, 1857), p. 72.

Everts, Elon. "A Few Thoughts on the Cleansing of the Sanctuary," *Review* (June 11, 1857), p. 45.

Fagal, William, and Lewis and Richard Walton. "What Hath God Wrought?" (CD set) (Harrisburg, PA: American Cassette Ministries, c. 2006).

Ferris, Roger H. "History of the Seventh-day Adventists in Oswego County (NY)," *Bulletin of the Oswego County Historical Society*

(Nov. 17, 1959), pp. 55-63.

Ferris, Roger H. "Roosevelt Seventh-day Adventist Church History" (typed manuscript, April 15, 1959).

Fisel, Fernand. "Edson's Cornfield 'Vision': Frisson or Fiction?" (Indiana, PA: Indiana University of Pennsylvania, 198-).

Fisel, Fernand. "Edson's Cornfield 'Vision': Frisson or Figment?" *Adventist Currents*, 1:1 (July 1983), pp. 25-27.

Fisel, Fernand. "Three Early Visions of E.G. White Copied by Hiram Edson: An Evaluation." (Manuscript #011528, Center for Adventist Research, James White Library, Andrews University, Berrien Springs, MI).

Fisher, Ann. "Nothing to Fear," *Lake Union Herald* (April 2005), pp. 34-35.

Fitch, Charles. "A Chronological Chart of the Visions of Daniel & John" (Boston: Joshua V. Himes, 1843).

Fitch, Charles. *The Glory of God in the Earth* (Boston: Joshua V. Himes, 1842).

Fitch, Charles. *A Wonderful and Horrible Thing* (Boston: Joshua V. Himes, 1842).

Floyd, Clark A. "Who Was Cleopas?" *Our Firm Foundation* (Sept. 2013), pp. 4-6.

Ford, Desmond. *Daniel 8:14, the Day of Atonement, and the Investigative Judgment* (Casselberry, FL: Euangelion Press, 1980).

Fortin, Denis, and Jerry Moon, eds. *The Ellen G. White Encyclopedia* (Hagerstown, MD: Review and Herald Pub. Assn., 2013).

Froom, LeRoy E. *Finding the Lost Prophetic Witness* (Washington, DC: Review and Herald Pub. Assn., 1946).

Froom, LeRoy E. "How the Full Light of the Sanctuary Came to Us." *Review* (Sept. 9, 1948), pp. 8-9.

Froom, LeRoy E. *Movement of Destiny* (Washington, DC: Review and Herald Pub. Assn., 1971).

Froom, LeRoy E. *The Prophetic Faith of Our Fathers*, vol. 4: *The Historical Development of Prophetic Interpretation* (1954, Reprint, Hagerstown, MD: Review and Herald Pub. Assn., 1982).

Gale, Robert. *The Urgent Voice: The Story of William Miller* (Washington, DC: Review and Herald Pub. Assn., 1975).

Gaustad, Edwin S., ed. *The Rise of Adventism: A Commentary on the Social and Religious Ferment of Mid-Nineteenth Century America* (New York: Harper and Row, 1974).

General Conference of Seventh-day Adventists. "Statement of Conradi Hearing" (Omaha, NE: General Conference Committee Report, Oct. 13-16, 1931).

General Conference of Seventh-day Adventists Bulletin. May 27, 1926 (Takoma Park, Washington, DC: Advent Review and Sabbath Herald, 1926).

Gilbert, Don F. Letter to James L. Sapienza (June 4, 2001).

Gillespie, V. Bailey, Michael J. Donahue, Ed Boyatt, and Barry Gane. *Valuegenesis Ten Years Later: A Study of Two Generations* (Riverside, CA: Hancock Center Publication, 2004).

Goldstein, Clifford. *1844 Made Simple* (Boise, ID: Pacific Press Pub. Assn., 1988).

"Good News for the Hiram Edson Site," *Adventist Heritage Ministries Bulletin* (Fall 2001), p. 2.

Graybill, Ronald. "Mrs. Temple: A Millennial Utopian," *Spectrum*, 47:4 (2019), pp. 73-77.

"The Great Appointment," *Guide* (Oct. 15, 2016), pp. 26-29.

Greenwalt, Glen. "The Sanctuary: God in Our Midst," *Spectrum* 24:2 (Oct. 1994), pp. 42-49.

Griggs, Carol. "Dendrochronology of the Hiram Edson Site, Port Gibson, Ontario County, New York" (Ithaca, NY: Cornell University, Aug. 26, 2005).

Guy, Fritz. "Good News from the Sanctuary in Heaven: God's Continuing Initiative," *Spectrum* 14:1 (Aug. 1983), pp. 39-46.

Guy, Fritz. "The Journey of an Idea," *Adventist Heritage* 16:3 (Spring 1995), pp. 9-13.

Hale, Appollos. *The Advent Herald* (Feb./March 1845).

Hamilton, John. Letter of Aug. 11, 1852, *Review* (Sept. 2, 1852), p. 70.

Hewitt, Clyde E. *Midnight and Morning* (Charlotte, NC: Venture Books, 1983).

Himes, Joshua V. *Views of the Prophecies and Prophetic Chronology, Selected from Manuscripts of William Miller, with a Memoir of His Life* (Boston: Moses A. Dow, 1841).

"Hiram Edson." *Southern Asia Tidings* (Oct. 1994), pp. 10-13.

Hiram Edson Farm Master Plan (typed manuscript, n.d.).

"Hiram Edson Farm Site: Adventist Historic Properties, Inc.: Restoration and Development Assessment" (typed manuscript, Syracuse, NY: Crawford & Stearns, Dec. 1991).

Holifield, E. Brooks. *Theology in America: Christian Thought from the Age of the Puritans to the Civil War* (New Haven, CT: Yale University Press, 2003).

Holt, George W. Letter, *Review* (Feb. 1851), p. 48.

Holt, George W. Letter of June 15, 1852, *Review* (June 24, 1852), p. 32.

Holt, George W. Letter of June 21, 1852, *Review* (July 8, 1852), p. 39.

Hosmer, Howard C. *Monroe Country, 1821-1971* (Rochester, NY: Rochester Museum and Science Center, 1971).

Howell, Emma E. *The Great Advent Movement* (Washington, DC: Review and Herald Pub. Assn., 1935).

"In the Footsteps of a Pioneer," *Review* (Oct. 24, 2002), p. 11.

In the Footsteps of the Pioneers (Washington, DC: E.G. White Estate, 1981).

In the Footsteps of the Pioneers (Silver Spring, MD: E.G. White Estate, 1990).

"Inspired by Our Theology." *Youth Ministry Accent* (April-June 2001), pp. 43-45.

Jacobs, Enoch. *The Day-Star* (Nov. 29, 1844).

Jemison, T. Housel. *A Prophet Among You* (Mountain View, CA: Pacific Press Pub. Assn., 1955).

Jenkins, Philip. *Climate, Catastrophe, and Faith: How Changes in Climate Drive Religious Upheaval* (New York: Oxford University Press, 2021).

Johnson, Doug R. *Adventism on the Northwestern Frontier* (Berrien Springs, MI: Oronoko Books, 1996).

Joiner, James. "These Were the Courageous: Hiram Edson," *Guide* (Oct. 24, 1979), pp. 20-22, 31.

Kelley, Herbert M. (affidavit regarding his ownership of the Edson manuscript, n.d., Center for Adventist Research, James White Library, Andrews University, Berrien Springs, MI).

Kelley, Herbert M. Letter to L.E. Froom (July 1, 1936) (Center for Adventist Research, James White Library, Andrews University, Berrien Springs, MI).

Kelley, Herbert M. "The Spirit of 1844," *Review* (June 23, 1921), pp. 4-5.

Kinne, P.Z. "Hiram Edson's Experience" (typed manuscript, Nov. 11, 2002).

Knight, George R. *Anticipating the Advent: A Brief History of Seventh-day Adventists* (Boise, ID: Pacific Press Pub. Assn., 1993).

Knight, George R. *1844 and the Rise of Sabbatarian Adventism: Reproductions of Original Historical Documents* (Hagerstown, MD: Review and Herald Pub. Assn., 1994).

Knight, George. *Joseph Bates: The Real Founder of Seventh-day Adventism* (Hagerstown, MD: Review and Herald Pub. Assn., 2004).

Knight, George. *Millennial Fever and the End of the World* (Boise, ID: Pacific Press Pub. Assn., 1993).

Knight, George. *A Search for Identity: The Development of Seventh-day Adventist Beliefs* (Hagerstown, MD: Review and Herald Pub. Assn., 2000).

Knight, George. *William Miller and the Rise of Adventism* (Nampa, ID: Pacific Press Pub. Assn., 2010).

Koeppel, Gerard. *Bond of Union: Building the Erie Canal and the American Empire* (Philadelphia: Da Capo Press, 2009).

Krug, Howard. "Adventist Heritage Celebrated at Hiram Edson Farm," *Atlantic Union Gleaner* (Jan. 2012), p. 10.

Krug, Howard. "Hiram Edson Farm Hosts Sanctuary Exhibit," *Adventist Heritage Ministries Bulletin* (Aug. 2005), pp. 1, 3.

Krug, Howard. "October Morn," *Review* (Oct. 24, 2002), pp. 8-12.

Krug, Howard. "Phase One of Visitor's Center Dedicated," *Atlantic Union Gleaner* (Nov. 2008), p. 7.

Krug, Howard. "Visitors to Camp Meeting Take the Fifth Annual Heritage Tour," *Atlantic Union Gleaner* (Oct. 2005), p. 19.

Kuykendall, Richard E. *The Dreamer and the Two Men She Loved* (n.p.: Trufford Publishing, 2021).

Lake, Jud. "The Heart of Adventist Theology," *Review* (Oct. 2018), pp. 34-36.

Land, Gary, ed. *Adventism in America* (Grand Rapids, MI: William B.

Eerdmans, 1986).

Land, Gary, ed. *Historical Dictionary of Seventh-day Adventists* (Lanham, MD: The Scarecrow Press, 2005).

Lindsey, John. Report, *Review* (May 27, 1852), p. 16.

Litch, Josiah. *The Probability of the Second Coming of Christ about A.D. 1844* (Boston: J. Litch, 1838).

Loughborough, J.N. *The Great Second Advent Movement, Its Rise and Progress* (Nashville: Southern Pub. Assn., 1905).

Loughborough, J.N. Letter to R.M. Kelley (Dec. 13, 1910).

Loughborough, J.N. Letter of March 10, 1853, *Review* (March 17, 1853), p. 176.

Loughborough, J.N. Report, *Review* (Dec. 27, 1855), p. 101.

Loughborough, J.N. *Review Anniversary Issue* 101:38 (1924).

Loughborough, J.N. *Rise and Progress of the Seventh-day Adventists* (Battle Creek, MI: General Conference Association, 1892).

Loughborough, J.N. "The Second Advent Movement—No. 8." *Review* (Sept. 15, 1921), p. 5.

Marsh, Joseph. *The Bible Doctrine: or True Gospel Faith Concerning the Gathering of Israel, the Millennium, Personal Coming of Christ, Resurrection, Renovation of the Earth, Kingdom of God, and Time of the Second Advent of Christ* (Rochester, NY: Advent Harbinger and Bible Advocate Office, 1849).

Marsh, Joseph. *The Voice of Truth and Glad Tidings* (Feb. 24, 1847).

Marsh, Joseph. "The World's End in 1843" (Portland, ME: n.p., 1843).

Maxwell, C. Mervyn. "Cornfield Cleopas," *Adventist World* (Oct. 2006), pp. 34-35.

Maxwell, C. Mervyn. *Magnificent Disappointment* (Boise, ID: Pacific Press Pub. Assn., 1994).

Maxwell, C. Mervyn. *Tell It to the World: The Story of Seventh-day Adventists* (Mountain View, CA: Pacific Press Pub. Assn., 1976).

"Meet Hiram Edson" (DVD) (Silver Spring, MD: Adventist Heritage Ministry, 2012).

Melone, Harry R. *History of Central New York Embracing Cayuga, Seneca, Wayne, Ontario, Tompkins, Cortland, Schuyler, Yates, Chemung, Steuben, and Tioga Counties,* vol. 1 (Indianapolis: Historical Publishing Company, 1932).

Meyer, Robert W. Letter to Jo Ellen Walton (Sept. 14, 1997).

Miller, Perry. *The New England Mind: From Colony to Province* (Boston: Beacon Paperback, 1961).

Miller, William. *Dissertations on the True Inheritance of the Saints, and the 1260 Days of Daniel and John* (Boston: Joshua V. Himes, 1842).

Miller, William. *Evidence from Scripture and History of the Second Coming of Christ about the Year 1843* (Boston: Joshua V. Himes, 1842).

Miller, William. *A Lecture on the Typical Sabbaths and Great Jubilee* (Boston: Joshua V. Himes, 1842).

Miller, William. *Remarks on Revelations Thirteenth, Seventeenth, and Eighteenth* (Boston: Joshua V. Himes, 1844).

Miller, William. "Synopsis of Miller's Views," *Signs of the Times* (Jan. 25, 1843), p. 147.

Milliken, Charles F. *A History of Ontario County, New York and Its People.* 2 vols. (New York: Lewis Historical Publishing Company, 1911).

Mitzewich, Pauline. Letter to Robert Allen (Nov. 17, 1997).

Morgan, Douglas. *Adventism and the American Republic: The Public Involvement of a Major Apocalyptic Movement* (Knoxville: University of Tennessee Press, 2001).

Morse, Washington. "Remembrance of Former Days," *Review* (May 7, 1901), p. 291.

Mustard, Andrew G. *James White and Seventh-day Adventist Organization: Historical Development, 1844-1881* (Berrien Springs, MI: Andrews University Press, 1987).

Nettles, Louise. "A Busy Summer at the Hiram Edson Farm," *Adventist Heritage Ministries Bulletin* (Fall 2014), p. 2.

Nettles, Louise. "A Day to Remember," *Adventist Heritage Ministries Bulletin* (Winter 2010), p. 2.

Nettles, Louise. "New Orientation DVD Filmed at the Hiram Edson Farm," *Adventist Heritage Ministries Bulletin* (Winter 2011), p. 2.

Neufeld, Donald F. "Anniversary of an Important Event in Sacred History," *Review* (Oct. 22, 1970), pp. 2-4.

Neufeld, Donald F. "Aftermath of Autumn Disappointment," *Review* (Jan. 10, 1980), pp. 15-16.

Neufeld, Donald F. "The Disappointment According to Hiram Edson," *Review* (Oct. 22, 1970), pp. 1, 30.

Neufeld, Donald F. "Edson's October 23 Experience," *Review* (Jan. 17, 1980), pp. 18-19.

New York-Pennsylvania Conference Session (1866). *Review* (Oct. 16, 1866), p. 158.

New York-Pennsylvania Conference Session (1867). *Review* (Oct. 29, 1867), p. 308.

New York-Pennsylvania Conference Session (1868). *Review* (Nov. 17, 1868), p. 246.

New York-Pennsylvania Conference Session (1870). *Review* (Aug. 23, 1870), p. 78.

New York-Pennsylvania Conference Session (1871). *Review* (Sept. 12, 1871), p. 102.

New York-Pennsylvania Conference Session (1872). *Review* (Sept. 10, 1872), p. 102.

New York-Pennsylvania Conference Session (1873). *Review* (Aug. 26, 1873), p. 86.

New York-Pennsylvania Conference Session (1874). *Review* (Oct. 13, 1874), p. 127.

New York-Pennsylvania Conference Session (1875). *Review* (Sept. 30, 1875), p. 103.

Nichol, Francis D. Correspondence (1943-1945) (Collection 264, Box 6a, Folder 1, Center for Adventist Research, James White Library, Andrews University, Berrien Springs, MI.

Nichol, Francis D. *The Midnight Cry* (Takoma Park, MD: Review and Herald Pub. Assn., 1944).

Nix, James R. "The Life and Work of Hiram Edson" (term paper for Church History 600—Problems in Church History, Seventh-day Adventist Theological Seminary, Andrews University, 1971).

Noll, Mark. *America's God: From Jonathan Edwards to Abraham Lincoln* (New York: Oxford University Press, 2002).

Numbers, Ronald L. *Prophetess of Health: A Study of Ellen G. White* (New York: Harper and Row, 1976).

Numbers, Ronald L., and Jonathan M. Butler, eds. *The Disappointed: Millerism and Millenarianism in the Nineteenth Century* (Bloomington, IN: Indiana University Press, 1987).

Obituary for Byron Tefft. *Review* (July 4, 1929), p. 29.

Odom, Robert L. "Philadelphians or Laodiceans?" *Review* (Jan. 5, 1956), pp. 4-5.

Olsen, M. Ellsworth. *A History of the Origin and Progress of Seventh-day Adventists* (Takoma Park, MD: Review and Herald Pub. Assn., 1925).

Palmer, Richard F. *The "Old Line Mail": Stagecoach Days in Upstate New York* (Lakemont, NY: North Country Books, 1977).

Patrick, Arthur N. "Charles Fitch, Hiram Edson and the Raison d'Etre of the Seventh-day Adventist Church" (term paper for CH570, CH597, CH600 History of the Seventh-day Adventist Church, Seventh-day Adventist Theological Seminary, Andrews University, 1971).

Paulien, Jon. *What the Bible Says About the End-Time* (Hagerstown, MD: Review and Herald Pub. Assn., 1994).

Peavey, G.W. *Jubilee Standard* (April 1845).

"Plan Your Vacation." *Adventist Heritage Ministries Bulletin* (March 2020), p. 5.

Prior, Terrance M., and Natalie J. Siembor. *Images of America Around Oswego* (Charleston, SC: Arcadia Publishing, 1996).

Randall, Robert N. "The Rome, NY [Seventh-day Adventist] Church, 1875-1890" (term paper for CH600, Seventh-day Adventist Theological Seminary, Andrews University, 1975).

Ratzlaff, Dale. *The Cultic Doctrine of Seventh-day Adventists* (Sedona, AZ: Life Assurance Ministries, 1996).

Ravage, Jessie. "Hiram Edson Site Report" (typewritten manuscript, July 1, 2005).

"Receipts," *Gospel Standard* (Aug. 1, 1844), p. 19.

"Restored Barn Dedicated at Hiram Edson Farm," *Review* (Nov. 24, 1994), p. 6.

Rhodes, Samuel W. Letter, *Review* (Aug. 5, 1851), p. 7.

Rhodes, Samuel W. Letter of Sept. 23, 1851, *Review* (Oct. 7, 1851), p. 40.

Rhodes, Samuel W., and R.F. Cottrell. Report, *Review* (March 10, 1857), p. 157.

Rice, Richard. "The Relevance of the Investigative Judgment," *Spec-*

trum 14:1 (Aug. 1983), pp. 32-38.

Rick, Rowena. "October Updates from the Hiram Edson Farm," *Adventist Heritage Ministries Bulletin* (Winter 2013), pp. 2-3.

Rick, Rowena. "Youthful Visitors Spend Time at the Edson Farm," *Adventist Heritage Ministries Bulletin* (Summer 2013), p. 2.

Robinson, D.E. "The Gift of Tongues in Early Advent History" (typed manuscript, Center for Adventist Research, James White Library, Andrews University, Berrien Springs, MI, n.d.).

Roosevelt Seventh-day Adventist Church. "Historical Tour: Seventh-day Adventist Church in Oswego County" (typed manuscript, Sept. 1,1990).

Rowe, Diana. "Bay Knoll Students Visit Hiram Edson Farm," *Atlantic Union Gleaner* (Jan. 2014), p. 10.

"Sabbath and Sanctuary Conference to be Held at Edson Barn," *Adventist Heritage Ministries Bulletin* (July 1998), p. 7.

Sapienza, James L. Letter to Don F. Gilbert (April 5, 2001).

Schwarz, Richard W. and Floyd Greenleaf. *Light Bearers: A History of the Seventh-day Adventist Church* (Silver Spring, MD: Department of Education, General Conference of Seventh-day Adventists, 2000).

Shoemaker, Ron. "The Hand of God on Hiram Edson's Ancestors" (typed manuscript, April 2010).

Smith, Uriah. "The Cleansing of the Sanctuary," *Review* (Oct. 2, 1855), pp. 52-54.

Smith, Uriah. "A Comprehensive View of the Sanctuary," *Review* (Jan. 24, 1856), p. 132.

Smith, Uriah. "History of the Worldly Sanctuary," *Review* (Aug. 21, 1856), p. 124.

Smith, Uriah. "History of the Worldly Sanctuary," *Review* (Aug. 28, 1856), p. 132.

Smith, Uriah. "History of the Worldly Sanctuary," *Review* (Sept. 4, 1856), pp. 140-141.

Smith, Uriah. "History of the Worldly Sanctuary," *Review* (Sept. 11, 1856), p. 148.

Smith, Uriah. "History of the Worldly Sanctuary," *Review* (Sept. 18, 1856), p. 156.

Smith, Uriah. "History of the Worldly Sanctuary," *Review* (Oct. 2, 1856), pp. 172-173.

Smith, Uriah. "Is the Silence in Heaven During the Cleansing of the Sanctuary?" *Review* (Dec. 18, 1856), p. 52.

Smith, Uriah. "The Sanctuary," *Review* (March 21, 1854), pp. 69-70.

Smith, Uriah. "The Sanctuary," *Review* (March 28, 1854), pp. 77-78.

Smith, Uriah. "The Sanctuary," *Review* (April 4, 1854), pp. 84-86.

Smith, Uriah. "The Sanctuary: A Novel Argument," *Review* (Jan. 9, 1855), pp. 156-157.

Smith, Uriah. "The Scape-goat," *Review* (Nov. 27, 1856), pp. 28-29.

Smith, Uriah. "Synopsis of the Present Truth, No. 14," *Review* (Feb. 11, 1858), pp. 108-109.

Smith, Uriah. "Synopsis of the Present Truth, No. 14," *Review* (Feb. 18, 1858), pp. 116-117.

Smith, Uriah. "Synopsis of the Present Truth, No. 14," *Review* (Feb. 25, 1858), pp. 124-125.

Smith, Uriah. "Synopsis of the Present Truth, No. 14," *Review* (March 11, 1858), p. 132.

Smith, Uriah. "Synopsis of the Present Truth, No. 14," *Review* (March 18, 1858), pp. 140-141.

Smith, Uriah. "Synopsis of the Present Truth, No. 14," *Review* (March 25, 1858), p. 148.

Spalding, Arthur W. *Captains of the Host* (Washington, DC: Review and Herald Pub. Assn., 1949).

Spalding, Arthur W. Correspondence (1908-1953) (Collection 010, Boxes 1-3, Center for Adventist Research, James White Library, Andrews University, Berrien Springs, MI).

Spalding, Arthur W. *Footprints of the Pioneers* (Washington, DC: Review and Herald Pub. Assn., 1947).

Spalding, Arthur W. "The House of Refuge," *Review* (March 9, 1950), p. 11.

Spalding, Arthur W. "Light on the Sanctuary: Adapted from the Manuscript of Hiram Edson," *Youth's Instructor* (March 8, 1910), pp. 4-6.

Spalding, Arthur W. *Origin and History of Seventh-day Adventists*, vol. 1 (Washington, DC: Review and Herald Pub. Assn., 1961).

Spalding, Arthur W. *Origin and History of Seventh-day Adventists*, vol. 3 (Washington, DC: Review and Herald Pub. Assn., 1962).

Spalding, Arthur W. "A Western Ally," *Review* (Jan. 19, 1950), p. 11.

Sperry, C.W. "The Sanctuary," *Review* (Feb. 7, 1856), p. 148.

Spicer, William A. *Certainties of the Advent Movement* (Washington, DC: Review and Herald Pub. Assn., 1929).

Spicer, William A. "A Meeting with O.R.L. Crosier," *Review* (March 29, 1945), p. 5.

Spicer, William A. *Pioneer Days of the Advent Movement with Notes on Pioneer Workers and Early Experiences* (Washington, DC: Review and Herald Pub. Assn., 1941).

Stearns, Carlo. "Proposal for Services" (Syracuse, NY: Crawford and Stearns, Sept. 1, 2004).

Strayer, Brian E. "The Cause Is Onward: The History of Seventh-day Adventism in Indiana, 1849-1900" (typed manuscript, Center for Adventist Research, James White Library, Andrews University, Berrien Springs, MI, 2022).

Strayer, Brian E. "Charts Analyzing the Number of Articles on the Sanctuary in the *Review* for Volumes 1-15 (1850-1876)" (typed manuscript, 1974-1975).

Strayer, Brian E. "The Hand That Still Guides" (typed manuscript, 1990).

Strayer, Brian E. *J.N. Loughborough: The Last of the Adventist Pioneers* (Hagerstown, MD: Review and Herald Pub. Assn., 2014).

Strayer, Brian E. *John Byington: First General Conference President, Circuit-Riding Preacher, and Radical Reformer* (Nampa, ID: Pacific Press Pub. Assn., 2017).

Strayer, Brian E. "Joseph Bates: Captain of the Blessed Hope" (typed manuscript, n.d.).

Strayer, Brian E. "Presentation at the Hiram Edson Farm" (typed manuscript, Oct. 2019).

Strayer, Brian E. *Where the Pine Trees Softly Whisper: The History of Union Springs Academy* (Union Springs, NY: Union Springs Academy Alumni Association, 1993).

Taylor, C.O. Letter of Feb. 1868, *Review* (March 3, 1868), pp. 182-183.

Thompson, Alden. *Inspiration: Hard Questions, Honest Answers*, 2nd ed. (Gonzalez, FL: Energion Publications, 2016).

Timm, Alberto and Dwain Esmond, eds. *The Gift of Prophecy in Scripture and History* (Silver Spring, MD: Review and Herald Pub. Assn., 2015).

Turner, Joseph. *The Advent Mirror* (Jan. 1845).

Turner, Joseph. *The Hope of Israel* (Jan. 1845).

Uhl, Henry. "Church and State—A Dual Celebration," *Atlantic Union Gleaner* (Aug. 27, 1974), pp. 2-4.

"Update from the Edson Farm," *Adventist Heritage Ministries Bulletin* (Summer 2001), p. 5.

Valentine, Gilbert M. *J.N. Andrews: Mission Pioneer, Evangelist, and Thought Leader* (Nampa, ID: Pacific Press Pub. Assn., 2019).

Vance, Laura L. *Seventh-day Adventism in Crisis: Gender and Sectarian Change in an Emerging Religion* (Urbana and Chicago: University of Chicago Press, 1999).

Vick, Edward W. "Must We Keep the Sanctuary Doctrine?" *Spectrum* 14:3 (Dec. 1983), pp. 52-55.

Voorheis, Alice R. "Hiram Edson Farm Visitor Center Dedicated," *Adventist Heritage Ministries Bulletin* (Fall 2010), pp. 4-5.

Voorheis, Alice R. "Looking for the Waymarks," *Review* (May 4, 2000), pp. 33-34.

Voorheis, Alice R. "Sanctuary Message Memorial," *Adventist Heritage Ministries Bulletin* (Spring 1999), p. 14.

Walton, Jo Ellen. "Crowds Visit Edson Farm Bible Prophecy Garden," *Adventist Heritage Ministries Bulletin* (Winter 2015), p. 2.

Walton, Jo Ellen. "Edson Bible Prophecy Garden Ministers to Tourists," *Adventist Heritage Ministries Bulletin* (Fall 2016), p. 4.

Walton, Jo Ellen. "Edson Farm Bible Prophecy Garden Approved," *Adventist Heritage Ministries Bulletin* (Fall 2013), p. 2.

Walton, Jo Ellen. "Finally, After 18 Years of Waiting, Another Evangelistic Outreach," *Adventist Heritage Ministries Bulletin* (Spring 2007), p. 4.

Walton, Jo Ellen. "Funds Urgently Needed for Completion of Edson Farm Bible Prophecy Garden Trail," *Adventist Heritage Ministries Bulletin* (Spring 2016), p. 3.

Walton, Jo Ellen. "Hiram Edson Bible Prophecy Garden Still Needs

Donations," *Adventist Heritage Ministries Bulletin* (Spring 2014), p. 2.

Walton, Jo Ellen. "Hiram Edson Needs Your Help!" *Adventist Heritage Ministries Bulletin* (Summer 2007), p. 1.

Walton, Jo Ellen. "Installation Begins on Edson Farm Prophecy Garden Trail," *Adventist Heritage Ministries Bulletin* (Fall 2015), p. 4.

Walton, Jo Ellen. Letter to Robert Allen (Aug. 17, 1998).

Walton, Jo Ellen. "The Lord Continues to Bless the Hiram Edson Farm," *Adventist Heritage Ministries Bulletin* (Spring 2013), p. 2.

Walton, Jo Ellen. "Sacrificial Pioneer Spirit Alive at the Hiram Edson Farm," *Adventist Heritage Ministries Bulletin* (Fall 2008), p. 1.

Walton, Jo Ellen. "Traffic Jam at Edson Farm," *Adventist Heritage Ministries Bulletin* (Special Issue, 2000), p. 5.

Walton, Jo Ellen. "Visitor Center at Edson Farm on Fast Forward," *Adventist Heritage Ministries Bulletin* (Winter 2008), p. 1.

Walton, Jo Ellen, and Louise Nettles. "Visitors Flock to Edson Farm, Learn Core Beliefs of Advent Message," *Adventist Heritage Ministries Bulletin* (Winter 2014), p. 2.

Walton, Lewis. "History Preserved," *Adventist World* (July 2007), pp. 27-29.

Weisberger, Bernard A., and Henry F. Graff, eds. *The Life History of the United States*, vol. 7: *Steel and Steam, 1877-1890* (New York: Time-Life Books, 1963).

Wellcome, Isaac C. *History of the Second Advent Message and Mission, Doctrine and People* (Yarmouth, ME: I.C. Wellcome, 1874).

Wells, Ronald A. *History Through the Eyes of Faith* (San Francisco: HarperCollins, 1989).

Wheeler, Frederick. Letter of April 11, 1859, *Review* (April 28, 1859), p. 182.

Wheeler, Frederick. Report, *Review* (June 30, 1859), p. 48.

Wheeler, Gerald. *James White: Innovator and Overcomer* (Hagerstown, MD: Review and Herald Pub. Assn., 2003).

White, Arthur L. *Ellen G. White: The Early Years*, vol. 1: *1827-1862* (Hagerstown, MD: Review and Herald Pub. Assn., 1985).

White, Ellen G. "Article," *Present Truth* (Dec. 1849), pp. 34-35.

White, Ellen G. *Christ's Object Lessons* (Mountain View, CA: Pacific

Press Pub. Assn., 1941).

White, Ellen G. *Counsels to Writers and Editors* (Nashville: Southern Pub. Assn., 1996).

White, Ellen G. *Early Writings*, 1852 (Washington, DC: Review and Herald Pub. Assn., 1945).

White, Ellen G. *Evangelism* (Washington, DC: Review and Herald Pub. Assn., 1996).

White, Ellen G. Letter to W.H. Littlejohn (Aug. 3, 1894) (Document File 588, Center for Adventist Research, James White Library, Andrews University, Berrien Springs, MI).

White, Ellen G. *Life Sketches of Ellen G. White* (Mountain View, CA: Pacific Press Pub. Assn., 1943 [1915]).

White, Ellen G. *Manuscript Releases*, vol. 6, no. 7 (Aug. 24, 1850).

White, Ellen G. *Manuscript Releases*, vol. 3, no. 7 (1852).

White, Ellen G. *Manuscript Releases*, vol. 3, no. 207 (1903).

White, Ellen G. *Spirit of Prophecy*, vol. 4 (1884).

White, Ellen G. *Spiritual Gifts* (Battle Creek, MI: Published by James White, 1860).

White, Ellen G. *Testimonies for the Church*, vol. 1 (Mountain View, CA: Pacific Press Pub. Assn., 1948).

White, James S. *An Appeal to the Working Men and Women in the Ranks of Seventh-day Adventists* (Battle Creek, MI: Steam Press, 1873).

White, James S., comp. *Hymns and Spiritual Songs for Camp-Meetings and Other Religious Gatherings* (Battle Creek, MI: Steam Press of the Seventh-day Adventist Pub. Assn., 1872).

White, James S., comp. *Hymns for God's Peculiar People, that Keep the Commandments of God and the Faith of Jesus* (Oswego, NY: Richard Oliphant, 1849).

White, James S. "The Judgment," *Review* (Jan. 29, 1857), pp. 100-101.

White, James S. Letter, *Review* (Aug. 30, 1861), p. 72.

White, James S. Letter, *Review* (July 26, 1864), p. 77.

White, James S. Letter to "My Dear Brother" (July 2, 1848) (typed manuscript, Center for Adventist Research, James White Library, Andrews University, Berrien Springs, MI).

White, James S. *Life Incidents, in Connection with the Great Advent Movement, as Illustrated by the Three Angels of Revelation XIV*

(Battle Creek, MI: Steam Press of the Seventh-day Adventist Pub. Assn., 1868).

White, James S. "Our Present Position," *Review* (Jan. 1851), pp. 27-30.

White, James S. "Remarks on This Work," *Review* (Special Edition, Sept. 1850), pp. 1-48.

White, James S. Report, *Review* (Sept. 20, 1853), pp. 84-85.

White, James S. "The Sanctuary," *Review* (Jan. 13, 1859), p. 60.

White, James S. "The Sanctuary and 2300 Days," *Review* (March 17, 1853), pp. 172-173.

White, James S. "The Sanctuary and 2300 Days," *Review* (March 31, 1853), p. 18.

White, James S. "To Ira Fancher," *Review* (March 1851), pp. 52-53.

White, James S., Ellen G. White, Joseph Bates. *A Word to the Little Flock* (Brunswick, ME: n.p., 1847).

White, William C. "Sketches and Memories of James and Ellen G. White, V: Laying a Sure Foundation," *Review* (March 28, 1935), pp. 8-10.

Whitley, Raymond O. "Ellen White, a Cornfield and Hiram Edson," *North Pacific Union Gleaner* (Jan. 5, 1981), pp. 6-7.

Whitney, Buel L. Obituary for Hiram Edson, *Review* (Feb. 21, 1882), p. 126.

Wilcox, M.C. Letter, *Review* (Nov. 1, 1881), p. 283.

Williams, T. Harry, and Henry F. Graff, eds. *The Life History of the United States*, vol. 5: *The Union Sundered, 1849-1865* (New York: Time-Life Books, 1963).

Williams, T. Harry, and Henry F. Graff, eds. *The Life History of the United States*, vol. 6: *The Union Restored, 1861-1876* (New York: Time-Life Books, 1963).

Wilson, Brian C. *Dr. John Harvey Kellogg and the Religion of Biologic Living* (Bloomington and Indianapolis: Indiana University Press, 2014).

Winkle, Ross E. "Disappearing Act: Hiram Edson's Cornfield Experience," *Spectrum* 33:1 (Winter 2005), pp. 46-51.

Wurst, Lou Ann. "Proposal: Hiram Edson Farm Site" (Syracuse, NY: Department of Anthropology, Syracuse University, Oct. 6, 1995).

Wurst, Lou Ann. "Public Archaeology Facility Report: Archaeological

Investigations of the Hiram Edson Farm Site" (Binghamton, NY: State University of New York, Nov. 15, 1994).

Wurst, Lou Ann, Jason Reimers, and Nicole Bourque. *Archaeological-Historical Investigations: The Hiram Edson Farm Site and Millerites in Upstate New York* (typed manuscript, Syracuse, NY: Department of Anthropology, Syracuse University, Aug. 27, 1996).

Younker, Randall W., and Ralph E. Hendrix. "Team Conducts Survey of Hiram Edson Farm," *Andrews University Archaeology Publication* (March 1995), p. 3.

Index

Made in the USA
Las Vegas, NV
17 May 2024

90055800R00163